What's Wrong With

The Chosen?

Updated Through Season 5

Timothy J. Mulder

This book may be ordered through booksellers or by contacting:

Timothy J. Mulder
www.timothymulder.com
www.armchairtheology.org

Because of the dynamic nature of the Internet, any web addresses or links contained in this book may have changed since publication and may no longer be valid. The views expressed in this book are solely those of the author and do not necessarily reflect the views of the publisher, and the publisher hereby disclaims any responsibility for them.

Unless otherwise indicated, Scripture quotations are from the ESV Bible ® (The Holy Bible, English Standard Version ®), copyright © 2001 by Crossway Bibles, a publishing ministry of Good News Publishers. Used by permission. All rights reserved.

ISBN: 979-8-9901934-4-4 (sc)
ISBN: 979-8-9901934-5-1 (e)

Revision date: 08/15/2025

Table of Contents

A

A Word from the Author

AS AN ITINERANT PREACHER, I preach in a few small-town churches in South Texas. Several of those churches used the Bible Study accompanying *The Chosen* for Adult Sunday School. Many of my Reformed friends on the Facebook group, the Reformed Pub, have spoken out against the show, so I decided to watch it and judge for myself. After watching the first season of *The Chosen*, it has become very clear to me that almost none of it is based on the Bible. Most of the show's plot is not found in Scripture, so, perhaps it would be better labeled as a first century fictional drama loosely based on Jesus and His followers and containing the occasional Scripture.

This book is designed to allow you to quickly read the first five chapters and understand the four primary issues with *The Chosen*. The later chapters serve as a scene-by-scene, analysis of the show. It provides greater detail on discrepancies between the show and Scripture. The last chapters are designed for you to read as a companion to the show. However, I cannot recommend anyone watch the show as it contains so much fiction and information that contradicts the Bible that there is a danger to forever confuse believers and non-believers alike. I suspect that Christian teachers in the future will be required to help believers sort the wheat from the chaff of *The Chosen* for many years to come.

1

Introduction

⌐⌐

THE CHOSEN IS ARGUABLY THE most well-received religious television series ever created. The series has received rave reviews, with thousands of professing Christians loving it and a 90%+ rating on major review sites.[1] It is the first-ever multi-season television show about the life of Jesus Christ. *The Chosen* claims to help its viewers see Jesus through the eyes of those who knew Him. According to a study by the show's producers[2], 108 million people worldwide have watched at least part of one episode as of December 2022.[3]

The show aims to spread the Word[4] to a billion people worldwide.[5] *The Chosen* has been translated into over 50 languages and can be streamed on at least 15 different platforms. The first four seasons of *The Chosen* are available for free on YouTube. In addition to the show, there are at least a dozen Bible

---

[1] It has a 9.8 out of 10 rating on IMDB and a 99% average score on Rotten Tomatoes. Secular shows hardly rate this high!

[2] Ruth Graham, "Jesus Christ, Streaming Star," *The New York Times*, November 25, 2022. Retrieved April 16, 2024.

[3] Interestingly, the study was published one month before the end date of the study, December 2022. This leads the author to question the validity of the data.

[4] It is unclear what is meant by "the Word." Is it the Word about the show? Is it the Bible? Or is it something else? If the producers meant the Bible, they should have said, "God's Word."

[5] https://www.youtube.com/watch?v=9LI484mywHU 11:00. Accessed May 8, 2024.

studies to accompany *The Chosen*.[6] DVDs, coloring books, t-shirts, baseball caps, posters, journals, and other swag from *The Chosen* are available at nearly every Christian bookstore. Christian Book Distributors, one of the largest Christian book and supply houses, features *The Chosen* in virtually all of their catalogs. *The Chosen* won the K-Love Fan Film and Television Impact Award in 2023. The show has the unwavering support of millions of believers.

The Chosen was originally produced by Angel Studios, the same studio that produced *Sound of Freedom*, a film based on the true story of a government agent who seeks to save hundreds of children from traffickers. *Sound of Freedom*, starring Jim Caviezel, has grossed $250.6 million as of December 2023. This made it the tenth highest-grossing film of 2023 in the United States and Canada.[7]

In 2024, *The Chosen* changed production companies to 5&2 Studios, an independent production company that is distributed by Lionsgate. The problem with 5&2 Studios is the same as Angel Studios. Both companies are run by Mormons.

Positive Aspects of *The Chosen*

The actors in *The Chosen* do an excellent job in portraying their characters. Many viewers relate to them, and that is a good thing. *The Chosen* is not your typically cheesy Christian show, as previous religious productions have been. Angel Studios has produced a believable screen adaptation of Jesus's life. The show is well-produced. The actors in *The Chosen* do a fantastic job of portraying their relatable characters.

Five positive aspects of *The Chosen* make it seem like an excellent show to binge.

- Believable Characters—While most religious television shows and movies are poorly produced and often inferior to their secular counterparts, *The Chosen* is not. The complexity of the characters extends far beyond simple support roles. They each have backstories, personalities, strengths, and faults. The appearance of the characters is accurate to first-century Palestine—they are not the pale white people used in most religious movies. These characters are relatable to their viewers, and that is one of the show's main draws.

---

[6] These Bible studies include Spanish translations and children's versions.
[7] https://www.boxofficemojo.com/release/rl4254237441/ Accessed April 16, 2024

- Real Emotion – Again, the characters in *The Chosen* display real emotion. They are not the lifeless, bland characters typically used in religious movies in years gone by. These are real people with real emotions. For example, Simon Peter is called a fool[8], while Matthew is portrayed as being on the autism spectrum. The show has believable anger, sorrow, and humor. According to Brett McCracken at the Gospel Coalition, *"The Chosen's* inability to 'go big' with flashy set pieces and special effects means the scale is necessarily more intimate and restrained, with the focus squarely on good characters and good storytelling."[9]

- Individual Encounters – Another of the main draws for *The Chosen* is the focus on individual encounters with Jesus. The believable portrayal of Jesus, especially in His interactions with other characters, gives Him a personal, knowable feeling. At its essence, Jesus, as portrayed by *The Chosen*, is compassionate, and that is much needed in today's cold and unfeeling world.

- Production Quality—*The Chosen's* production quality is modern, as opposed to the outdated production methods of many religious dramas. The show utilizes flashbacks to the Old Testament to explain the Hebrew Scriptures. By using handheld cameras, it has a more realistic feel. *The Chosen* frequently bypasses the need for a narrator by letting the on-screen action tell the story. Since the show is light on Scripture, it tends to focus more on individual stories.

- The entire production of *The Chosen* was made without Hollywood's influence. According to director Dallas Jenkins, the show was financed, distributed, and produced outside Hollywood. As such, it has been filmed in Texas and Utah.

What's the Problem?

On the surface, *The Chosen* seems like an excellent tool for studying the life of Jesus Christ. With such widespread evangelical Christian support, what could be wrong with it? Here is a brief overview of the four main problems with the show. Each is presented briefly but will be examined in detail in the following chapters.

---

[8] In the words of Andrew, his brother, in Season 1, Episode 1 at approximately 44:21.
[9] https://www.thegospelcoalition.org/article/four-reasons-chosen-works/

The show's first and most apparent issue is violating the Second Commandment. The Second Commandment instructs God's people not to make images of God or false gods and worship those images. It also shows us that how we think about God is important to Him. This is one of God's commands, and we are to take it seriously. Sadly, many evangelical Christians have no problem breaking this commandment.

Another problem with *The Chosen* is that almost all of its content is not Scriptural. Dallas Jenkins, the writer and producer of the show, has admitted that 95% of the material in *The Chosen* is not Biblical.[10] Where does the material come from? This extra-Biblical content comes from historical documents, the gnostic gospels, the *Book of Mormon*, and the writers' imaginations. Yet, millions of viewers will believe everything presented in the show is Biblical. That cannot be further from the truth.

The third issue is that 5&2 Studios, a Mormon-based production company, produces *The Chosen*. As such, the show promotes Mormon[11] theology. A television show about Jesus must be accurate, and *The Chosen* is not. Dallas Jenkins has unequally yoked himself with Mormon leadership to produce the show. Since the Jesus that the Mormons worship is an entirely different Jesus than Christians worship, there will be conflict. Jenkins has compromised his beliefs and claims that Mormons and Christians worship the same Jesus.[12]

The fourth issue with *The Chosen* is that it is unnecessary. We already have a 100% accurately written history of Jesus. There is no need to add to that, especially when what we have is sufficient for salvation. A show written by man will contain errors, but a book inspired by God will not. Therefore, watching *The Chosen* instead of reading the Bible is a grave mistake.

---

[10] https://www.youtube.com/watch?v=-eBo2ofl7XE Accessed May 14, 2024.

[11] Mormonism is the same as LDS or the Church of Jesus Christ of Latter-Day Saints. These terms will be used interchangeably throughout the book.

[12] This will be discussed in greater detail in chapter 4, but at a minimum, Mormons believe that Jesus was born a man and ascended to godhood, and as such, believe that this is the basis for their doctrine that this is possible for all men. In other words, because Jesus became a god, all of mankind can also become gods. The LDS Jesus is not the same as the Christian Jesus.

2

The Second Commandment

MANY CHRISTIANS' MOST SIGNIFICANT ISSUE with *The Chosen* is that it violates the Second Commandment in its use of images of Jesus. What's the big deal if Jonathan Roumie plays Jesus? It can't be any worse than Jim Caviezel playing Jesus in *The Passion of the Christ*. Images of Jesus are everywhere today. The Church has used images of Jesus since the late fourth century. We see images of Jesus everywhere: Christian bookstores, Sunday school classrooms, nativity scenes, and even on the walls in the sanctuaries of churches. With images of Christ so rampant, what's the big deal if we have one on a TV series? Especially when it reaches millions of people with the story of Jesus. The intent of *The Chosen* is good, but it is a violation of God's law. Regardless of whether or not it brings people closer to God, it is offensive to Him. Therefore, we should consider *The Chosen* a second commandment violation. The second commandment in Exodus 20:4-6, states,

You shall not make for yourself a carved image,[13] or any likeness of anything that is in heaven above, or that is in the earth beneath, or that is in the water under the earth. You shall not bow down to them or serve them, for I the LORD your God am a jealous God, visiting the iniquity of the fathers on the children to the third and the fourth generation of those who hate me, but showing steadfast love to thousands of those who love me and keep my commandments.

Deuteronomy 4:15-24 elaborates on the second commandment:

Therefore, watch yourselves very carefully. Since you saw no form on the day that the LORD spoke to you at Horeb out of the midst of the fire, beware lest you act corruptly by making a carved image for yourselves, in the form of any figure, the likeness of male or female, the likeness of any animal that is on the earth, the likeness of any winged bird that flies in the air, the likeness of anything that creeps on the ground, the likeness of any fish that is in the water under the earth. And beware lest you raise your eyes to heaven, and when you see the sun and the moon and the stars, all the host of heaven, you be drawn away and bow down to them and serve them, things that the LORD your God has allotted to all the peoples under the whole heaven. But the LORD has taken you and brought you out of the iron furnace, out of Egypt, to be a people of His own inheritance, as you are this day. Furthermore, the LORD was angry with me because of you, and He swore that I should not cross the Jordan, and that I should not enter the good land that the LORD your God is giving you for an inheritance. For I must die in this land; I must not go over the Jordan. But you shall go over and take possession of that good land. *Take care, lest you forget the covenant of the LORD your God, which He made with you, and make a carved image, the form of anything that the LORD your God has forbidden you.* For the LORD your God is a consuming fire, a jealous God. (Italics added.)

The Second Commandment teaches us three things.[14]

1. According to verse 4, we should not make images of God or false gods. The problem with making images of God is that we don't know what He looks like. God told Moses in Exodus 33:20, "Man shall not

---

[13] "Carved image" can also be translated as "idol." The same is true with "graven image."

[14] https://ligonduncan.com/the-second-commandment-no-idols-48/ Accessed May 10, 2024.

see me and live." Outside of the person of Jesus Christ,[15] man has not seen God. Therefore, we are not to make images of Him. Puritan scholar Thomas Vincent said, "It is not lawful to have pictures of Jesus Christ, because His divine nature cannot be pictured at all, and because His body, as it is now glorified, cannot be pictured as it is, and because, if it does not stir up devotion, it is in vain; if it does stir up devotion, it is a worshipping by an image or picture, and so a palpable breach of the second commandment."[16] There is no benefit in creating images of God. Although many of us long to see Jesus face-to-face, we don't have to see Him to improve our relationship with Him. We are to think about God only as He describes Himself in the Bible.

2. When referring to idols, verse 5 says that we "shall not bow down to them or serve them." Not only are we not to make images of either God or false gods, but we are also not to worship those images. Ligon Duncan says, "There is a tendency today to seek to serve the God we want, not the God who is."[17] Instead of worshiping God the way He wants, we worship Him in the fashion we want. And when we do so, we are not worshiping the same God. *We must worship God as He commands*. His Word tells us how we are to worship Him. And the use of images is not the way to do so. You may argue that no one actually worships Jonathan Roumie's portrayal of Jesus, so the second part of the second commandment has not been violated. However, looking through *The Chosen* Fan Club's Facebook page, we see evidence that people do, in fact, worship the image of Jesus as portrayed in *The Chosen*. One fan commented, "Sometimes when I pray to Jesus, I imagine Jonathan's face. I've told the Lord I hope that

---

[15] In Exodus 20:18-23, "Moses said, "Please show me your glory." **19** And he said, "I will make all my goodness pass before you and will proclaim before you my name 'The LORD.' And I will be gracious to whom I will be gracious and will show mercy on whom I will show mercy. **20** But," he said, "you cannot see my face, for man shall not see me and live." **21** And the LORD said, "Behold, there is a place by me where you shall stand on the rock, **22** and while my glory passes by, I will put you in a cleft of the rock, and I will cover you with my hand until I have passed by. **23** Then I will take away my hand, and you shall see my back, but my face shall not be seen."

[16] Thomas Vincent, *Pictures of Christ*. https://www.all-of-grace.org/pub/others/images.html Accessed May 11, 2024.

[17] Ligon Duncan, *The Second Commandment: No Idols*. https://ligonduncan.com/the-second-commandment-no-idols-48/ Accessed May 11, 2024.

is okay." It is not only not okay, but it also openly violates the second commandment.

3.   The second commandment teaches us that how we think about God and how we worship Him is important to Him. Even though it is freely violated in evangelical Christianity and Roman Catholicism today, the second commandment is just as important as the sixth commandment, "You shall not murder." We are to obey all of God's moral law as commanded in Exodus 20.

Here is what the show's producer / writer says about the 2ⁿᵈ Commandment:

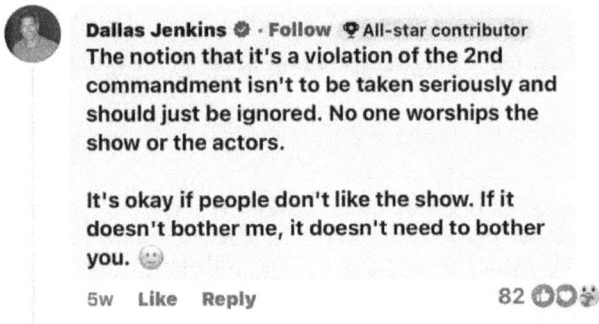

The second commandment does not, however, forbid all visual arts. Man is still allowed to create works of art. Religious themed paintings, such as Rembrandt's *The Return of the Prodigal Son*, are permissible. Charlton Heston's rendition of Moses is permissible under the second commandment.

After all, God, in the instructions for the construction of the tabernacle, commanded the Israelites to carve images of pomegranates, bells, and winged cherubim. The only thing not permitted under the second commandment is the image of God, whether the Father, the Son, or the Holy Spirit. Therefore, Michelangelo's *Creation of Adam* violates the Second Commandment, while His sculpture of *David* does not. Mel Gibson's *Passion of the Christ* is a second commandment violation, while *Braveheart* is not. Angel Studio's *The Chosen* violates the second commandment, while *Sound of Freedom* does not. Scripture tells us images of God are strictly forbidden, regardless of their beauty or popularity. The images of Christ contained in *The Chosen* violate the Second Commandment.

Most people watching *The Chosen* do not intentionally violate God's Word, however their actions are still a violation of God's law. We must be careful to know and obey God's Word in every area of our lives. What about using pictures of Jesus when teaching about Him? What about in children's coloring books and posters on Sunday School walls? Don't we need images to teach others about God? J.M. Kik wrote, "The apostle Peter did not need pictures of Christ to instruct the young or bring the Gospel to adults. The apostle John did not need pictures of Christ to convert pagans and instruct the Church. The apostle Paul did not need pictures of Christ to convert Barbarians and Greeks. The early church did not need pictures of Christ to conquer paganism. They accomplished it by preaching the Word in the power of the Holy Spirit."[18] Everything needed to teach others about Jesus is contained in the Bible.

What about the historic use of images of God? When this Israelites grew impatient waiting for Moses to return from Mt. Sinai, they made the golden calf, a visual image of the one true God, to worship. This was how the Egyptians and Canaanites worshiped. Aaron and the Israelites had decided they needed to worship God how Ra and Baal were worshiped. However, God is holy; that is, He is set apart. He does not want to be worshiped how false gods are worshiped. God's punishment for worshiping the golden calf was that only two of the Israelites were allowed to enter the Promised Land.

What about the church? Hasn't the church always used images of Jesus? The Synod of Elvira (306 AD - 312 AD), in Canon 36, "prohibited the exhibition of images in churches. "The use of images of Christ didn't start until later in the 4th century. Before that, Christians used only symbols, not

---

[18] J. Marcellus Kik, *Images of Christ a Violation of the Second Commandment*. https://www.all-of-grace.org/pub/others/images.html Accessed May 11, 2024.

images.[19] Images of saints, Mary, and Jesus became more prominent in the Middle Ages, specifically during the Byzantine and Romanesque eras. The dangers of using these images becomes apparent if you look at the practices in those religions of venerating the crucifix or kissing relics. The debate on whether or not to use images in the church became a source of fierce disagreement during the Protestant Reformation. The Westminster Larger Catechism 109, which was written in 1643, goes into greater detail about what is forbidden in the second commandment:

> WLC 109: **Q**. What are the sins forbidden in the second command-ment? **A**. The sins forbidden in the Second Commandment are, all devising, counseling, commanding, using, and anywise approving, any religious worship not instituted by God himself; the making any representation of God, of all or of any of the three persons, either inwardly in our mind, or outwardly in any kind of image or likeness of any creature whatsoever; all worshiping of it, or God in it or by it; the making of any representation of feigned deities, and all worship of them, or service belonging to them; all superstitious devices, corrupting the worship of God, adding to it, or taking from it, whether invented and taken up of ourselves, or received by tradition from others, though under the title of antiquity, custom, devotion, good intent, or any other pretense whatsoever; simony; sacrilege; all neglect, contempt, hindering, and opposing the worship and ordinances which God hath appointed.

Christians who want to worship God are to do so in the manner in which God commanded. This applies to any image of God but should also direct what type of shows we watch, what books we read, how we teach our children, and which visual arts to which we expose ourselves to. Images of Christ are everywhere. Individuals who follow the Second Commandment are in the minority. When we violate the Second Commandment and use images, whether we worship them or not, we mock God's holiness. Scripture tells us everything we need to know about God. We don't need images to learn about Him. "Images of Jesus fall short in communicating God's glory and communicating His character."[20] Additionally, images of Christ are incomplete – they don't display His godliness. They only show His humanity.

---

[19] The first four centuries is when the Church experienced astonishing growth. This was when the Christians conquered pagan Rome.

[20] The Chorus in the Chaos. Podcast. 43:28-43:42. Accessed May 10, 2024.

And that is but one part of Jesus Christ. We are missing out on His divinity. As T.A. McMahon says of the film-making process, "Character descriptions are limited, at best, and must be added in order for a casting director to select the actors. Along that line, how does one cast the sinless God/Man, Jesus Christ? The perfect attributes and righteous characteristics of the Son of God could never be displayed by an actor on the screen. When such an idea is incorporated into the script, the end result is a counterfeit Christ, at best. In fact, such an attempt fits the very definition of blasphemy as one strives to apply human characteristics to Jesus that undermine His divine character."[21] Therefore, it is important that as God-fearing Christians that we do not partake of or support entertainment such as *The Chosen* because it violates God's command.

---

[21] https://www.thebereancall.org/content/chosen-fiction Accessed May 14, 2024.

3

Extra-Biblical Content

ANOTHER ISSUE WITH *THE CHOSEN* is that the writers and producers freely add fictional stories and dialogue to the storyline.[1] To be fair, before the first episode of season 1, the producers of *The Chosen* placed a disclaimer that reads:

> *The Chosen* is based on the true stories of the gospels of Jesus Christ. Some locations and timelines have been combined or condensed. Backstories and some characters or dialogue have been added. However, all Biblical and historical context and any artistic imagination are designed to support the truth and intention of the Scriptures. Viewers are encouraged to read the gospels. The original names, locations, and phrases have been transliterated into English for anything spoken.

However, this disclaimer does not appear before any other episode, thus giving the impression that the fictional content of each episode is based on the Bible. Viewers have been conditioned to accept the storyline regardless

---

[1] An in-depth look at extra-Biblical content is contained in chapters 6-9.

of Biblical accuracy. The average viewer is not a Biblical scholar, so when fictional information is presented, they take it as truth, even if it's not in the Bible. *The Chosen* contains miracles and statements not performed or said by the Biblical Jesus. For example, writer and producer Dallas Jenkins posted on his Facebook page, "In this world . . . bones will still break. Hearts will still break. But in the end, light will overcome the darkness." Jenkins attributes the quote to Jesus. Even more disturbing is that over 500 people shared that fictional quote! It's very concerning that so many Christians watch the show and are not bothered by such additions. Most of the extra-Biblical content does not contradict Scripture. However, the writers place a large amount of emphasis on the main characters, which distracts from Christ Himself.

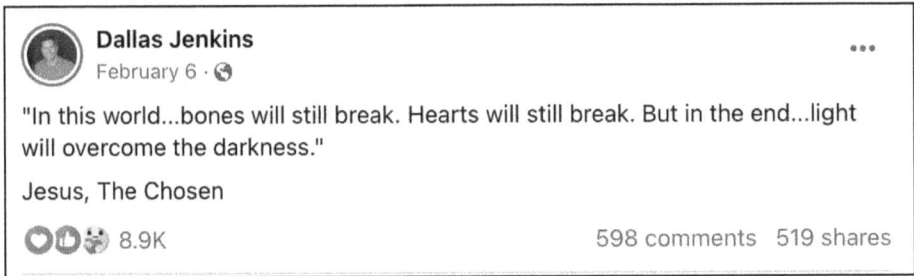

Dallas Jenkins
February 6 · 🌐   ●●●

"In this world...bones will still break. Hearts will still break. But in the end...light will overcome the darkness."

Jesus, The Chosen

👍❤️😊 8.9K   598 comments   519 shares

Additionally, most of the show's time is spent on Jesus' love and compassion rather than the serious topic of man's sin and need for salvation. The Jesus presented in *The Chosen* is a kind, compassionate Jesus, rather than one who hates sin and encourages sinners to repent and have faith in Him for salvation. This seems to be what modern evangelicalism wants in a Savior: love and compassion only. On *The Chosen* fan sites, the top comment of those who watch the show is, "I like the human qualities displayed by *The Chosen's* Jesus. It's so easy to relate to him."[2] The problem with this is that the Jesus portrayed is not the true Jesus. They are presenting a modern evangelical version Jesus. One fan of the show referred to viewing the show as "like having a date with Jesus . . ." In essence, the show waters down the Biblical sacrosanctity of Jesus Christ.

---

[2] https://www.thebereancall.org/content/chosen-fiction Accessed May 14, 2024.

Things That Did Not Happen

Dallas Jenkins said, "95% of the content for *The Chosen* is not from the Bible."[3] Almost all of *The Chosen* is made up! And people use it for Bible Studies? That would be akin to doing a Bible study on *The Red Tent*[4] by Anita Diamant. A Bible study based on *The Chosen* is not a Bible study. It's the study of a work of fiction. Since that seems like a big claim, here are a few extra-Biblical sub-plots from *The Chosen.*

- In season 1, brothers Peter and Andrew have a significant tax debt to settle with the Romans. There is no indication from Scripture that they had any tax debt or that they dealt with Matthew to address those issues. The writers added the tax debt to increase the emotional response[5] to the miracle of the fishes, which is featured in season 1, episode 4.

- In season 2, episode 5, Mary Magdalene, a recovering alcoholic, relapses. Like Peter's tax debt, this sub-plot has no Scriptural support. Statistically, many people with mental illness self-medicate with alcohol. Mary Magdalene did not suffer from a mental illness, but she was demon-possessed and might have self-medicated as a result.

- In season 2, episode 8, Jesus and Matthew rehearse the Sermon on the Mount while the disciples build a stage for Jesus to preach. There is no indication that any of this occurred. It is difficult to believe that the Son of God would rehearse a sermon. The fact that He does so emphasizes His humanity over His divinity, which fits well with the Mormon doctrine of Christ being only human during His time on earth. The subplot that Jesus' disciples handed out invitations and built Him a stage contradicts Scripture. Matthew 5:1[6] says that Jesus *sat down* with His disciples,[7] indicating that a stage was not used to deliver the Sermon on the Mount.

- In season 3, episode 4, Zebedee (James and John's father) sells his fishing boat and prepares to buy an olive grove. This is neither

---

[3] https://www.youtube.com/watch?v=-eBo2ofl7XE Accessed May 14, 2024.

[4] The Red Tent is a fictional account of the relationship between Jacob and his wives. The story is fictional, but the historical figures are real.

[5] The key to a successful television show or film is the emotional response of the audience. The more emotional the audience, the higher the ratings. The miracle of the fish was very emotional.

[6] Matthew 5:1, "Seeing the crowds, He went up on the mountain, and when *He sat down*, His disciples came to Him." (Italics added.)

[7] When Matthew states that Jesus sat down with His disciples, there were likely more than twelve people sitting with them. While crowds followed Jesus, only twelve of them were considered His disciples.

Scriptural nor likely. Typically, in the time of Christ, families kept the same occupation for multiple generations. Additionally, according to John 21:1-3,[8] after Jesus' crucifixion, seven disciples, including James and John, went fishing on a boat. Since James and John were business partners with Peter and Andrew, the boat likely belonged to the four of them. Therefore, it is unlikely that Zebedee sold the boat.

- In season 3, episode 5, Simon's wife Eden miscarries their baby. Nothing in Scripture indicates that Simon had any children. The only thing we know about Simon's family is that he was married and had a mother-in-law, whom Jesus healed.[9]
- In season 4, episode 3, Thomas' fiancé, Ramah, is killed by a Roman officer. Thomas begs Jesus to heal her, but Jesus refuses to do so. There is no biblical indication that Thomas was engaged or married. Nor is there any indication that his fiancé, wife, or girlfriend was murdered. Nor is there any indication that Jesus refused to heal anyone who came to Him for healing.

While some of these stories contradict Scripture, others do not. Those that do not contradict Scripture may have happened; they may not have happened. But that's not the point. The point is that the writers have added fictional material to Biblical stories. Millions of people, many unfamiliar with the Bible, believe all of this – the truth and the fiction – to exist in the Bible. And that's a major problem. Revelation 22:18-19[10] commands us not to do that. One can argue that the writers are not adding to Scripture but are telling a story that aligns with Scripture. However, many people watch the show and believe that all of it is Biblical. So, in essence, the writers and producers are adding to Scripture. The Jesus presented in the sub-plots and character

---

[8] John 21:1-3, "After this Jesus revealed himself again to the disciples by the Sea of Tiberias, and he revealed himself in this way. ² Simon Peter, Thomas (called the Twin), Nathanael of Cana in Galilee, the sons of Zebedee, and two others of his disciples were together. ³ Simon Peter said to them, "I am going fishing." They said to him, "We will go with you." They went out and got into the boat, but that night they caught nothing."

[9] Matthew 8:14-15, "And when Jesus entered Peter's house, He saw his mother-in-law lying sick with a fever. ¹⁵ He touched her hand, and the fever left her, and she rose and began to serve him."

[10] Revelation 22:18-19, "I warn everyone who hears the words of the prophecy of this book: if anyone adds to them, God will add to him the plagues described in this book, ¹⁹ and if anyone takes away from the words of the book of this prophecy, God will take away his share in the tree of life and in the holy city, which are described in this book."

developments are one thing, but the writers have added to things that Jesus said, which is an even more significant problem. If the Jesus presented in Scripture is not the same Jesus as presented in *The Chosen*, the Jesus from *The Chosen* is a false Christ. Matthew 24:3-5[11] warns against false Christs coming in the final days. Granted, Jonathan Roumie has not said he is Christ, but how he is presented in the show can lead viewers to believe he is playing the Biblical Christ. People are then led astray by worshiping a false Christ.

Things Jesus Did Not Say

Throughout the show, the writers of *The Chosen* have added to the Biblical dialogue of Jesus. Granted, most of the fictitious lines from Jesus are harmless. However, a line was added several times that contradicted Scripture or presented Mormon theology. According to *The Chosen*, Jesus said things not in the Bible but found in Mormon writings. Jesus endorsed Mormon theology in *The Chosen*. That should cause great concern for most Bible-believing Christians. The following examples are not all-inclusive. There are other heretical statements that Jesus of *The Chosen* has made that are not included on this list.

In season 1, episode 5, Simon tells Jesus that he will follow Jesus to the ends of the earth. Jesus replies, "I hope so." While this seems like a flippant comment, it is important. Since Jesus was fully God, He would have known whether or not Simon would follow Him to the ends of the earth. Jesus would never have said, "I hope so," for He knows beyond the shadow of a doubt that Simon would deny Him three times. Jesus also knew that Simon would be influential in the spread of the gospel to the early church. However, Mormon doctrine maintains that Jesus, during His time on earth, was merely a man. He was not God during His earthly life. Mormons hold that after Jesus' death, He became a god. This is an excellent example of the writers slipping Mormon theology into the show's dialogue.

In season 1, episode 7, Nicodemus meets in secret with Jesus. The readers are exposed to a good amount of Scripture during their dialogue. Throughout

---

[11] Matthew 24:3-5, "As He sat on the Mount of Olives, the disciples came to Him privately, saying, "Tell us, when will these things be, and what will be the sign of your coming and of the end of the age?" [4] And Jesus answered them, "See that no one leads you astray. [5] For many will come in my name, saying, 'I am the Christ,' and they will lead many astray."

the conversation, Nicodemus and Jesus quote John 3:5-6,[12] 3:10,[13] 3:12,[14] 3:14-15,[15] and 3:16-17.[16] At one point in the conversation, Nicodemus asked Jesus, "Is the Kingdom of God coming?"[17] Jesus replied, "What does your heart say?" Then Jesus said, "I hope you do come, Nicodemus."[18] There are three issues with this conversation. The first concern is that the scene contains so much Scripture before it strays into Mormon theology. This would cause those viewers who are vaguely familiar with the Bible to believe that everything said was Biblical. This issue is significant because viewers can easily confuse Biblical and Mormon doctrines.

Additionally, the second statement made by *The Chosen's* Jesus after the Scripture quotations is also problematic. Just like in season 1, episode 5, Jesus again said, "I hope..." Jesus, the omniscient (all-knowing) God of the universe, would know that Nicodemus would not follow him at that moment. He would never say, "I hope you do come." Again, this emphasizes the Mormon belief that Jesus was only a man during His time on earth.

The introduction to the Book of Mormon contains the line, "We invite all men everywhere to read the Book of Mormon, to *ponder in their hearts* the message it contains, and then to ask God, the Eternal Father, in the name of Christ if the book is true." (Italics added.) Mormon missionaries use this same tact when meeting with non-Mormons. They explain Mormon doctrine, then ask the listener, "What does your heart tell you?" They encourage their listeners to use their emotions to decide. Jesus, in season 1, episode 7, says the same thing, "What does your heart tell you?" Both the Old and New

---

[12] John 3:5-6, "Jesus answered, "Truly, truly, I say to you, unless one is born of water and the Spirit, he cannot enter the kingdom of God. ⁶ That which is born of the flesh is flesh, and that which is born of the Spirit is spirit."

[13] John 3:10, "Jesus answered him, "Are you the teacher of Israel and yet you do not understand these things?"

[14] John 3:12, "If I have told you earthly things and you do not believe, how can you believe if I tell you heavenly things?"

[15] John 3:14-15, "And as Moses lifted up the serpent in the wilderness, so must the Son of Man be lifted up, ¹⁵ that whoever believes in Him may have eternal life."

[16] John 3:16-17, "For God so loved the world, that He gave His only Son, that whoever believes in Him should not perish but have eternal life. ¹⁷ For God did not send His Son into the world to condemn the world, but in order that the world might be saved through Him."

[17] This is not recorded as being part of their conversation.

[18] Again, this is something that is not Scriptural. Jesus would know if Nicodemus would join Him or not. He wouldn't hope. Jesus is omniscient (all-knowing). 1 John 3:20 says, "For whenever our heart condemns us, God is greater than our heart, and he knows everything." See also Psalm 147:5, Hebrews 4:13, and Proverbs 15:3. So, to say that Jesus hopes something will happen violates this omniscience of God. This promotes the Mormon doctrine that states that Jesus was not God during His time on earth.

Testaments warn readers about the evil in everyone's heart. Jeremiah 17:9 tells us, "The heart is deceitful above all things, and desperately sick; who can understand it?" Jesus would never tell someone to listen to their hearts because He knows the depravity contained within.

Season 3, episode 3 has Jesus quoting directly from The Book of Mormon. In the scene beginning at 24:02, Jesus argues with Rabbi Benjamin, who states that he will invoke the law of Moses. Jesus responded with the statement, "I am the law of Moses!" Nowhere in Scripture does Jesus call Himself the law of Moses. "I am the law," comes from 3 Nephi 15:9 in the *Book of Mormon*, which reads, "Behold, *I am the law*, and the light. Look unto me, and endure to the end, and ye shall live; for unto him that endureth to the end will I give eternal life." (Italics added.) As an evangelical Christian and a writer for a "Biblical" television show, Dallas Jenkins should be more careful with the words that he puts in Jesus' mouth. However, he is not. Rather than apologize for Jesus making a Mormon statement, Jenkins doubled down and posted it on his Facebook page as a quotation from *The Chosen's* Jesus.

Dallas Jenkins, when interviewed about the line, said, "Around 99% of people "went crazy and loved" the "I am the law of Moses" line while only a tiny percentage made a fuss . . . It's not a direct quote," Jenkins said. "It wasn't referring to the law of Moses in that quote . . . And I have never read the Book of Mormon, to be honest with you. I've read some of it. People will share with me. I read it when someone told me, 'Hey, that's from the Book of Mormon.' I was like, 'OK,' and I went and looked it up . . . It's a cool line. So, either way, it's in the show because I believe it's a really great line and I believe that it's also theologically plausible . . . The point is God is over these things. Jesus is over these things. He is these things. He owns these things. They came from him. Jesus makes many 'I am' statements and is called the 'Great I Am.' So no, I didn't pull this quote from anywhere else . . . It's a theologically plausible line and, I believe, a cool, Jesus-as-king moment, and that's it." This type of disregard for following Scripture is one of the primary issues with *The Chosen*.

Another issue with the show's disclaimer is that it tells its viewers to read the gospels. However, it does not state which gospels should be read. Does the producer of the show mean "Matthew, Mark, Luke, and John?" If he did, he should have stated that because false gospels abound. *The Book of Mormon*, a fictional account of Jesus[19] is not considered another gospel but

---

[19] For a deeper examination of *The Book of Mormon*, see Appendix B.

another testament. However, many people believe *The Book of Mormon* to be another gospel. Additionally, the show's producers could be referring to the Gnostic Gospels.

The Gnostic Gospels are ancient religious writings that falsely claim to be written by famous Biblical figures such as Peter, Mary, and Thomas. Most of the Gnostic Gospels that have survived were found in 13 books from the third and fourth centuries AD. The books contain a total of 52 Gnostic texts, not all of which are "gospels" or even claim to be Christian. These were found buried in a jar near an Egyptian town called Nag Hammadi in 1945. (This is why the collection is also known as the Nag Hammadi Library.) Unlike the Biblical gospels, which have thousands of copies that date back to the second and third centuries, the Gnostic texts are the only surviving copies of many Gnostic writings.

4

Mormon Influence

~

THE CHOSEN IS DIRECTED BY Dallas Jenkins, whose father is Jerry Jenkins, author of the *Left Behind* series. Jenkins has a degree in Biblical Studies from the University of Northwestern-St. Paul. He describes his role as the producer as being a Bible-believing evangelical who has zero desire to mess with Scripture or make some sort of new theological point. He has said that *The Chosen* is about telling these stories in a way that makes the moments in Scripture even more impactful. He is an evangelical Christian. He attends Harvest Bible Chapel. However, initially, he worked with Angel Studios, a Mormon-founded movie studio.

In 2024, Dallas Jenkins started 5&2 Studios, an independent production company that is distributed by Lionsgate. *The Chosen* is now produced by 5&2 Studios. It seems as though Jenkins attempted to distance himself from the Mormon based Angel Studios. However, Jenkins has brought several Mormon bishops into company leadership at 5&2.

Therefore, several questions arise: Are there any issues with 5&2 Studios since several members of company leadership are practicing Mormons? What problem should evangelical Christians have with Mormon influence on a show about Jesus? Don't Mormons claim to be Christian? Does *The Chosen* contain any explicitly Mormon theology? Is Mormon doctrine presented in the show?

Company leadership of 5&2 Studios consists of: Dallas Jenkins, Derral Eves, Brad Pelo, J.D. Larsen, Kyle Young, and David Stidham. Jenkins' position at 5&2 is Chief Creative Officer. Derral Eves serves as the Chief Strategy Officer for 5&2 and is the CEO of *The Chosen*, a publicly traded company. Derral Eves is a Mormon bishop.[1] The CEO of *The Chosen* is a Mormon bishop. Brad Pelo, the President of 5&2 is also a Mormon bishop. One third of the leadership of 5&2 Studios are Mormon Bishops. Additionally, the show's credits state that Darral Eves and Brad Pelo are executive producers. To claim that there is no Mormon influence on the show is ludicrous.

In interviews with Dallas Jenkins, he refers to himself and the production studio as us, thus indicating that they are a team[2] – Christians and Mormons working as one.[3] However, 2 Corinthians 6:14 says, "Do not be unequally yoked with unbelievers. For what partnership has righteousness with lawlessness? Or what fellowship has light with darkness?" But Mormons are believers. Or are they? This chapter may not be popular, as many consider Mormons to be just another Christian denomination. *Make no mistake: they are not Christians.* Dallas Jenkins, however, says that Mormons and Christians worship the same God.[4] Jenkins, in several interviews, has stated that the LDS church is just another Christian denomination.[5]

Season 2 was filmed at a Mormon movie set in Utah. Therefore, at the end of each episode, the credits say, "The Producers wish to thank The Church of Jesus Christ of Latter-day Saints for the use of their New Testament period sets, costumes, and props." The LDS church very much influences the content of *The Chosen*.

Additionally, Jenkins is not above employing deceitful marketing ideas to promote the show. In April 2022, Jenkins apologized to fans for not

[1] https://leadingsaints.org/2-latter-day-saint-bishops-executive-produce-the-chosen-an-interview-with-derral-eves-and-brad-pelo/ Accessed February 27, 2025.
[2] This is to be expected. They are working on a project together.
[3] https://www.youtube.com/watch?v=0DPzq53O4DI 117:17 Accessed on April 18, 2024.
[4] https://www.puritanboard.com/threads/the-chosen.111903/
[5] https://www.youtube.com/watch?v=9LI484mywHU 24:40-25:03. Accessed May 8, 2024. Additionally, conversion from Evangelical Christianity is the number one area of growth in the LDS church.

informing them about a gag marketing campaign involving defacing their own billboards promoting *The Chosen*.[6]

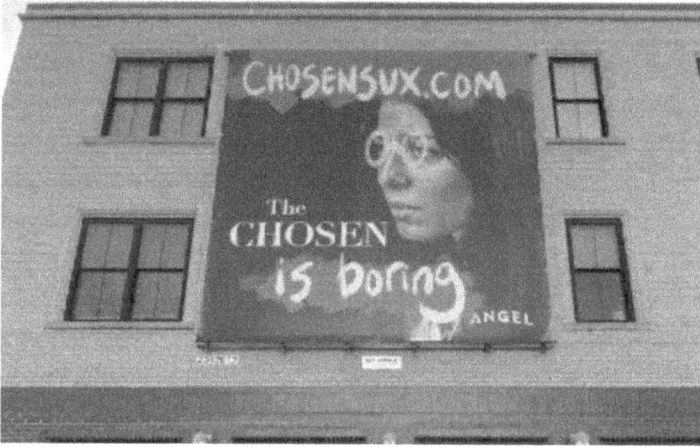

What do Mormons Believe?

Since one of the primary concerns with *The Chosen* and 5&2 Studios is their relationship with Mormonism, it follows that we should look at Mormon theology. We will look at the Mormon scriptures,[7] Mormon viewpoints on each member of the Trinity, humanity, salvation, and the church. Mormons like to say that they are Christians, too. After all, they have the name of Christ on the side of their buildings,[8] so they must worship Christ. However, the Christ that the Mormon church worships is not the same one worshiped by countless Christians across the world.

The Church of Jesus Christ of Latter-Day Saints, LDS or the Mormon church, as commonly known, relies on five different sources of authority, four written and one human. Most importantly, Mormonism accepts *the Bible* as divine revelation. However, they prefer the King James Version. Interestingly, and heretically, Joseph Smith has translated the Bible and has written himself into Genesis 50:33, "And that seer. . . I will bless, and his name shall be called Joseph, and it shall be after the name of his father." The second source of authority is the *Book of Mormon*. Written in 1830, the *Book of Mormon* has undergone several revisions, even though Joseph Smith called

---

[6]https://www.deseret.com/entertainment/2022/4/14/23025270/defaced-billboards-part-of-strategic-ad-campaign-by-the-chosen-to-grow-audience/ Accessed April 16, 2024.
[7] See Appendix B for an in-depth look at the Book of Mormon.
[8] Many Mormons claim that because their buildings have a sign that says, "The Church of Jesus Christ of Latter-Day Saints," they are Christians. After all, the sign has Jesus' name on it.

it "the most correct of any book on earth."[9] The current text is the 1981 version. The third source of authority in the LDS church is *Doctrines and Covenants*, published in 1833. Like the *Book of Mormon*, this volume was also claimed to be the perfect word of God, even though it has undergone numerous changes and additions since it was written. The fourth source of authority is *The Pearl of Great Price*, published in 1851. Interestingly, the Mormon god felt it necessary to reveal two additional works after publishing the "perfect" *Book of Mormon*. While it may have been "perfect," apparently, it was incomplete. Finally, like the Roman Catholic Church, the head prophet of the Mormon church speaks for God, and his word carries as much weight as God's Word.

Mormons believe that God the Father is an exalted man. They twist Genesis 1:27[10] to "prove" God is a man. The logic in this goes like this: since man was created in God's image, and we know what man looks like, God must look the same. Therefore, God is a man. They also twist Genesis 32:30[11] to prove God is a man. Again, the logic goes something like this: since Jacob saw God face to face, God must have a face, and if God has a face, he must be a man. From there, the Mormon view of God the Father goes off the rails. They believe God the Father lived among men, married, died, and was resurrected to be God the Father. God and His goddess wife, Mother God, had millions of spirit children in heaven. The place where those spirits dwell is called the "pre-existence." According to Joseph Smith, even though he had no training in Biblical Hebrew, the word *Elohim* is plural, which proves that there are many gods.[12]

Regarding the Trinity, Mormons believe that God the Father, God the Son, and God the Spirit were initially men and became gods at some point. They claim to believe in the Trinity like other Christians, but their view of the Trinity is that the Father, the Son, and the Holy Ghost are distinct Gods, not one God in three persons. Mormons twist Genesis 1:26[13] to support their tri-

---

[9] For a deeper look at the "perfection" of the Book of Mormon, see Appendix B.

[10] Genesis 1:27, "So, God created human beings in His own image. In the image of God, He created them; male and female He created them."

[11] Genesis 32:30, "So Jacob called the name of the place Peniel, saying, "For I have seen God face to face, and yet my life has been delivered."

[12] We can refute Mormons' beliefs that God is a man by showing Him to be a spirit. John 4:24 says, "God is spirit, and those who worship Him must worship in spirit and truth." 2 Corinthians 3:17 says, "Now the Lord is the Spirit, and where the Spirit of the Lord is, there is freedom."

[13] Genesis 1:26, "Then God said, "Let us make man in our image, after our likeness. And let them have dominion over the fish of the sea and over the birds of the heavens and over the livestock and over all the earth and over every creeping thing that creeps on the earth."

theistic view of the Trinity. They claim that because God used the words "us" and "our" that Moses must have meant that there are three gods. Mormons also twist Matthew 28:19[14] to support their tri-theistic view of the Trinity. Because there are three names mentioned, each name indicates a different god. Apparently, Christians have it all wrong.

What about the Mormon view of the main character of *The Chosen*, Jesus Christ? They must get this theology correct, as Jesus is the focus of their biggest show. Mormons believe that Jesus Christ was the natural Son of God the Father and Mary. Not the Holy Spirit and Mary. They also maintain that God the Father, being a man, sired Jesus as any man would through sexual intercourse with Mary.[15] This flies in the face of the virginity of Mary. They believe that Jesus was only a man during His time on earth. (This becomes an issue beginning in season 2.) They also state that Jesus had at least three wives before his crucifixion[16] and that Jesus fathered children through those wives.[17] Finally, they believe that Jesus became God only after his resurrection.

Is the Mormon Jesus the same as the Biblical Jesus? This is a critical question because it impacts tens of millions of viewers. 2 Corinthians 11:4 addresses the acceptance of a Mormon Jesus by Christians, "For if someone comes and proclaims another Jesus than the one we proclaimed, or if you receive a different spirit from the one you received, or if you accept a different gospel from the one you accepted, you put up with it readily enough." Dallas Jenkins has gone on record stating that he believes that the Mormon Jesus and the Biblical Jesus are the same. Says Jenkins:

> I can honestly say . . . one of the top three most fascinating and beautiful things about this project has been my growing brotherhood and sisterhood with people of the LDS community that I never would have known otherwise and learning so much about

---

[14] Matthew 28:19, "Go therefore and make disciples of all nations, baptizing them in the name of the Father and of the Son and of the Holy Spirit."

[15] John 1:14 says, "So the Word became human and made his home among us. He was full of unfailing love and faithfulness. And we have seen his glory, the glory of the Father's one and only Son." They claim the phrase "Father's one and only Son" indicates that Jesus was the begotten Son of God the Father, not the Holy Spirit.

[16] John 2:1-11, the story of the Wedding at Cana is the Scriptural basis for this heresy. Mormons claim that the wedding at Cana is one of the weddings where Jesus took a Jewish bride. (Even though the text says nothing to indicate that.)

[17] Isaiah 53:10 says, "But it was the LORD's good plan to crush him and cause him grief. Yet when his life is made an offering for sin, he will have many descendants. He will enjoy a long life, and the LORD's good plan will prosper in his hands." Since this verse refers to Jesus, Mormons take it to mean he will have literal descendants, not spiritual descendants.

your faith tradition and realizing, gosh, for all the stuff that maybe we don't see eye to eye on, that all happened, that's all based on stuff that happened after Jesus was here. The stories of Jesus, we do agree on, and we love the same Jesus. That's not something you often hear . . . I mean, I'll sink or swim on that statement, and it's controversial, and I don't mind getting criticized at all for the show, and I don't mind being called a blasphemer . . . I've made it very clear that if I go down, I'm going down swinging protecting my friends and my brothers and sisters . . . I don't deny we have a lot of theological differences, but we love the same Jesus.[18]

Mormon theology also differentiates between the Holy Spirit and the Holy Ghost. The Holy Ghost is one of the three gods in the Godhead but can only be in one location at a time.[19] The Holy Spirit is a divine influence[20] that is felt by all Mormons. The Holy Spirit bears witness to the truths of Mormonism.

Mormons believe that human beings are gods in an embryonic state. They also believe the process of becoming gods includes a probationary period on earth. According to Mormons, Adam transgressed but did not sin.[21] Adam's transgression was not passed on to the human race. Therefore, they do not believe in original sin[22] or total depravity.[23] Each person is responsible for their own sins.[24] The ultimate goal of humanity is not to worship God but to become god.[25]

---

[18] https://www.youtube.com/watch?v=9LI484mywHU. 10:29-11:00 Accessed May 7, 2024.

[19] Luke 3:22 (KJV) says, "And the Holy Ghost descended in a bodily shape like a dove upon him, and a voice came from heaven, which said, Thou art my beloved Son; in thee I am well pleased." Note that the ESV says, "and the Holy Spirit descended." Mormons conclude that since the Holy Ghost descended as a dove, it cannot be omnipresent.

[20] John 15:26, "But when the Comforter is come, whom I will send unto you from the Father, even the Spirit of truth, which proceedeth from the Father, He shall testify of me." Mormons reason that since the Spirit comes from the Father, it must be an influence, not a person.

[21] This does not make sense since sin and transgressions are, in terms of salvation, the same thing.

[22] Original sin is the sin that has been passed down from Adam to all humanity, resulting in every person since Adam (except for Jesus Christ) being sinful from the womb. (Psalm 51:5).

[23] Total depravity is the theological concept that every aspect of our lives is tainted by sin. (Titus 1:15-16).

[24] This line of thinking is salvation by works, not salvation by the blood of Jesus Christ.

[25] Exodus 7:1 – "And the Lord said to Moses, "See, I have made you like God to Pharaoh, and your brother Aaron shall be your prophet." Mormons interpret this verse as meaning that since Moses was made "a god," all men are made to be gods. Another verse in support of this heresy is John 10:34, "Jesus answered them, 'Is it not written in your Law, I said, you are gods?'"

Regarding the Atonement of Christ and Salvation, Mormonism maintains that individual salvation begins with Christ's atonement but is completed only through human works.[26] One of the initial requirements to be saved is acceptance of Joseph Smith as a prophet of God.[27] Additionally, Mormons teach that there are three degrees of heaven (or three heavens): Telestial, Terrestrial, and Celestial. In other words, people go to one level or another based on their works[28].

As far as the Christian Church goes, they believe that the original church fell away from the truth after three centuries, and as such, there is no true Christian church. Thus, they believe that the Mormon church is the restoration of the original church. Mormons claim that Matthew 16:18[29] refers to a universal apostasy of the church, thus leaving the Mormon church to be the only true remaining church.[30] Additionally, Mormons believe that the church is to be led by apostles and prophets, not elders, priests, or pastors.[31]

Based on what the Mormon church believes, we can conclude that they are indeed not a Christian denomination. Christians believe that each member of the Trinity is fully God and has been so from eternity past to eternity future. Christians specifically believe this about the person of Jesus Christ. To not believe this is to not believe in the Biblical Christ. And if one does not believe in the Biblical Christ, they cannot label themselves as a *Christ*-ian.

Additionally, since the Mormon church promotes salvation by works, they do not believe that Christ's atonement saves them. Therefore, there is no

---

[26] Philippians 2:12, "Wherefore, my beloved, as ye have always obeyed, not as in my presence only, but now much more in my absence, *work out your own salvation* with fear and trembling." (Italics added.) Mormons emphasize the "work out your own salvation" and take this to mean that you must achieve works to be saved.

[27] Doctrines of Salvation, vol. 1, page 188.

[28] The verse that they twist into support for this doctrine is 1 Corinthians 15:40-41, "There are also celestial bodies, and bodies terrestrial: but the glory of the celestial is one, and the glory of the terrestrial is another. [41] There is one glory of the sun, and another glory of the moon, and another glory of the stars: for one star differs from another star in glory." Mormons understand this verse to mean various levels of heaven.

[29] Mormons twist Scripture to support this idea, citing Matthew 16:18: "And I say also unto thee, That thou art Peter, and upon this rock I will build my church; and the gates of hell shall not prevail against it." Mormons claim that the rock upon which the church will be built is a continued revelation, not Peter's testimony about who Jesus is.

[30] Mormons use 2 Thessalonians 2:3 to support this heresy, "Let no man deceive you by any means: for that day shall not come, except there comes a falling away first, and that man of sin be revealed, the son of perdition."

[31] The text used to support this concept is 1 Corinthians 12:28, "And God hath set some in the church, first apostles, secondarily prophets, thirdly teachers, after that miracles, then gifts of healings, helps, governments, diversities of tongues." Mormons claim that this shows that apostles and prophets are to lead the church, not pastors and priests.

need for Christ's life, death, and resurrection. It then should cause us to pause and wonder whether or not we should trust a Mormon-linked studio to produce a Biblically and historically accurate summary of the life of Christ.

Remember that one bad apple can spoil the bushel. A little yeast impacts the entire loaf.[32] A single heresy should force us to stop watching and supporting the entire show. The involvement and production of Derral Eves and Brad Pelo should concern us deeply.

> Says Kenny Thomas, "my parents have been sucked into *The Chosen*, and Second Commandment violations and whatnot notwithstanding, it has led to them legitimizing Mormons in a way they never would have ten years ago."

Good Thing or Good Work?

Should we consider *The Chosen* a good thing, perhaps even a good work? The theological term, common grace, explains this. Common grace is the theological concept when God's sovereign grace is bestowed upon all of mankind regardless of whether or not they are saved. Common grace says that rain falls on the good and the evil person alike. Common grace also means that non-Christians can do good things. Take, for example, Muslims and Buddhists in Kampala, Uganda. They serve Uganda's poor by offering food and shelter. These are good things that desperately need to be done. However, since they are not being done for God's glory, they are not technically "good works" as Scripture mandates.[33]

Good Works

Six requirements must be met for a work to be considered good.

1. It must be performed by someone whom Christ has justified.

---

[32] Galatians 5:9, "A little leaven leavens the whole lump."

[33] James 2:14-17, "What good is it, my brothers, if someone says he has faith but does not have works? Can that faith save him? [15] If a brother or sister is poorly clothed and lacking in daily food, [16] and one of you says to them, "Go in peace, be warmed and filled," without giving them the things needed for the body, what good is that? [17] So also faith by itself, if it does not have works, is dead."

2. God must directly or implicitly command it. Actions not commanded by God are not good works.
3. Good works must sincerely spring from faith and love in the heart.[34]
4. Good works must be directed solely to the glory of God.
5. Good works must not be invented by man.
6. Good works must not be offered where obedience is required.

Let us look at whether or not *The Chosen* is a good work as it is directed by an evangelical Christian and produced by a Mormon production company. How does it match up against the six requirements?

1. Is it performed by someone Christ has justified? The director is an evangelical Christian, so it meets this requirement. However, concerning the production company, the answer is no. As we have seen, Mormons are not Christians. Therefore, *The Chosen* does not count as a good work.

2. Has God directly or implicitly commanded it? Since one of the purposes of *The Chosen* is to inspire people to study the Bible, we can understand it to be implicitly commanded. Jesus, in the final verses of Matthew 28,[35] tells us to teach people from all nations to observe all that He has commanded us. *The Chosen* might be considered a tool to teach people about Christ, which qualifies it as a good work in this requirement.

3. Does *The Chosen* spring from faith and love in the heart? While we don't know the motivation behind the director or producer's work on *The Chosen*, it is fair to assume, based on their religious beliefs, that they are doing so from a place of faith and love. *The Chosen* meets this requirement.

4. Is *The Chosen* directed only to the glory of God? Is this its primary purpose? Again, this is a difficult requirement to answer. Colossians 3:16[36] admonishes us to "do everything in the name of the Lord Jesus, giving thanks to God the Father through him." Is *The*

---

[34] 1 John 5:3, "For this is the love of God, that we keep His commandments. And His commandments are not burdensome."

[35] Matthew 28:18-20, "And Jesus came and said to them, "All authority in heaven and on earth has been given to me. [19] Go therefore and make disciples of all nations, baptizing them in the name of the Father and of the Son and of the Holy Spirit, [20] teaching them to observe all that I have commanded you. And behold, I am with you always, to the end of the age."

[36] Colossians 3:16, "Let the word of Christ dwell in you richly, teaching and admonishing one another in all wisdom, singing psalms and hymns and spiritual songs, with thankfulness in your hearts to God. And whatever you do, in word or deed, do everything in the name of the Lord Jesus, giving thanks to God the Father through Him."

Chosen being produced in the name of the Lord Jesus? We don't know the hearts of those directing and producing the show, so this requirement remains unanswered.

5. Is *The Chosen* a good work that man has invented? Or is it something that we are commanded to do? If we look at *The Chosen* as merely entertainment, it implies that it is a good work. "Finally, brothers, whatever is true, whatever is honorable, whatever is just, whatever is pure, whatever is lovely, whatever is commendable, if there is any excellence, if there is anything worthy of praise, think about these things."[37] If we look at this requirement with good and necessary consequences of Philippians 4:8, we may consider it as something we are commanded to do. Does *The Chosen* help man think about commendable things and things worthy of praise? The answer to this requirement will depend on your presuppositions. If you consider *The Chosen* commendable and worthy of praise, it meets this requirement. However, if you consider it a gross Second Commandment violation, then it does not meet this requirement.

6. Does *The Chosen* follow God's law as commanded in Scripture? The answer to this requirement is a resounding no. The show blatantly violates the second commandment,[38] which tells us that we shall not "make any likeness of anything that is in heaven above, or that is in the earth beneath, or that is in the water under the earth." Since Jesus sits at the right hand of God the Father, in heaven, this final requirement as a good work is negative.

Since all six requirements for something to be a good work have yet to be met, *The Chosen* cannot be considered a good work. Is it a good thing? Yes and no. It may strengthen people's faith; however, that comes at the cost of exposure to LDS beliefs. Poor theology will trip up and ultimately destroy someone's faith. And no amount of good that comes out of a show can justify that.

---

[37] Philippians 4:8.

[38] Exodus 20:4-6, "You shall not make for yourself a carved image, or any likeness of anything that is in heaven above, or that is in the earth beneath, or that is in the water under the earth. 5 You shall not bow down to them or serve them, for I the LORD your God am a jealous God, visiting the iniquity of the fathers on the children to the third and the fourth generation of those who hate me, 6 but showing steadfast love to thousands of those who love me and keep my commandments."

5

Something Better

ONE OF THE DRAWS OF visual media is that it requires less mental engagement than reading. Watching Jesus preach the Sermon on the Mount is easier than reading it. This displays the danger of exchanging reading God's Word for watching *The Chosen*. To the credit of the show's producers, they encourage viewers to read the gospels. Indeed, testimonials for the show are filled with statements that the show has given viewers a desire to read their Bibles, share the gospel with others, and even consider following Jesus in their lives. However, if the producers truly encouraged people to know their Bibles, they would not include extra-Biblical materials.

On May 7, 2024, British comedian Russell Brand posed a question asking people to guide him in selecting a Bible translation to read. Rather than referring Brand to Scripture, Dallas Jenkins told Brand to watch *The Chosen* instead. This shows that Jenkins feels his show is an acceptable substitute for God's Word. However, since God's Word contains everything we need to know about Jesus and salvation, Brand should read the Bible rather than watch a fictional television show.

The problem, though, as *The Chosen* has shown us, is that, in our hearts, Scripture is not enough for us. We want more. Now, there is nothing wrong with wanting more. After all, many of us have read religious books to learn more about God and understand our Bibles better. However, the danger comes when we read extra-Biblical material that conflicts with Scripture. History has shown us that even the most trusted Christian authors can stray from Biblical theology.[39] Therefore, it is imperative that all extra-Biblical material be compared to Scripture. To compare Christian and secular media to Scripture, we must have the Scriptures engrained in our hearts and minds.[40] The issue with watching *The Chosen* is that viewers will confuse God's perfect Word with the largely fictionalized version presented in the show.[41]

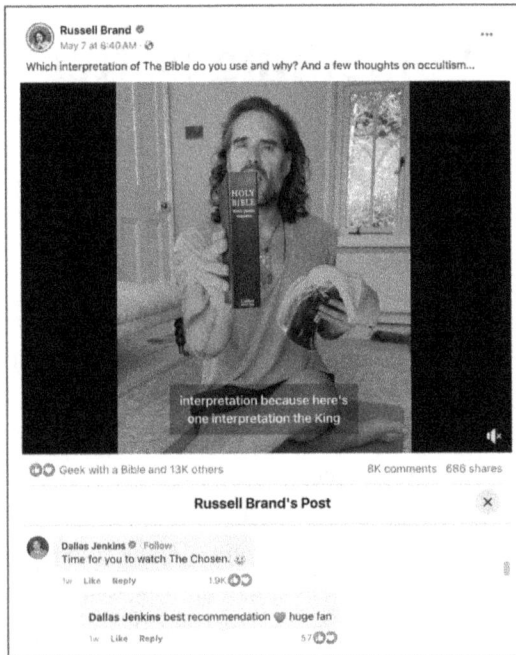

---

[39] Sometimes, sadly, those authors leave the faith and produce materials opposite to faith in Christ.

[40] Proverbs 6:20-22, "My son, keep your father's commandment and forsake not your mother's teaching. [21] Bind them on your heart always; tie them around your neck. [22] When you walk, they will lead you; when you lie down, they will watch over you; and when you awake, they will talk with you."

[41] Perhaps, in the future, people will hear questions in Sunday School such as, "Wasn't Mary Magdalene an alcoholic?" or "Wasn't Matthew on the spectrum?" These are non-Biblical depictions of Mary and Matthew being confused with those presented in Scripture.

John 21:25 tells us, "There are also many other things that Jesus did. Were every one of them to be written, I suppose that the world itself could not contain the books that would be written." Modern man can only speculate about the "other things" that Jesus did. Those events occurred two thousand years ago. We cannot know what Matthew or Philip's personalities were like. We have no idea about all of the things Jesus said and did. By speculating on those things, *The Chosen* presents fiction as truth.

There are several benefits to reading and studying the Bible instead of watching a television show, such as *The Chosen*. 2 Timothy 3:16-17 provides us with those benefits: "All Scripture is breathed out by God and profitable for teaching, for reproof, for correction, and for training in righteousness, that the man of God may be complete, equipped for every good work." Scripture tells us everything we need to know about Jesus and salvation. We do not need to rely on other sources to fill in the gaps Scripture leaves out. Scripture, being breathed out by God, is inerrant - in its original languages, it contains no errors. Because God breathed out Scripture, it is unable to have errors. God is perfect, and all that He says is perfect.

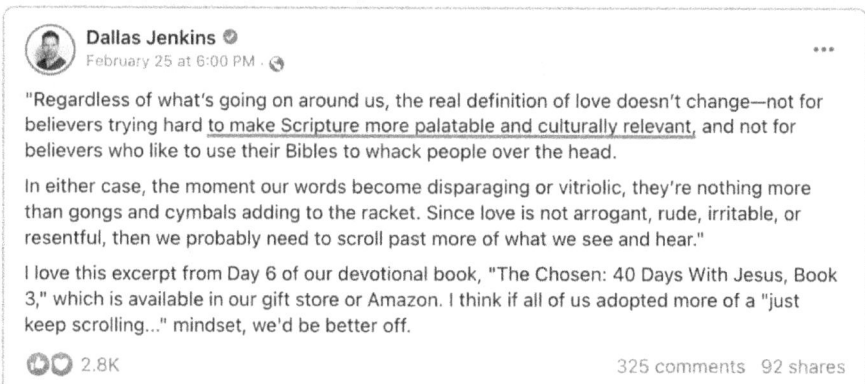

Dallas Jenkins ✓
February 25 at 6:00 PM · 🌐   •••

"Regardless of what's going on around us, the real definition of love doesn't change—not for believers trying hard to make Scripture more palatable and culturally relevant, and not for believers who like to use their Bibles to whack people over the head.

In either case, the moment our words become disparaging or vitriolic, they're nothing more than gongs and cymbals adding to the racket. Since love is not arrogant, rude, irritable, or resentful, then we probably need to scroll past more of what we see and hear."

I love this excerpt from Day 6 of our devotional book, "The Chosen: 40 Days With Jesus, Book 3," which is available in our gift store or Amazon. I think if all of us adopted more of a "just keep scrolling..." mindset, we'd be better off.

👍❤️ 2.8K   325 comments   92 shares

Dallas Jenkins feels that the Bible is neither palatable or culturally relevant. This explains his willingness to add to and change God's holy Word.

The Bible is Sufficient

2 Timothy 3:17 tells us that the purpose of the Bible is that "the man of God may be complete, equipped for every good work." Scripture is all one needs to do the Lord's work. No other instruction is necessary. Since the Bible explains what Jesus was like, we need no further revelation. In the gospels, the true words and actions of Jesus and the Holy Spirit open our hearts and minds to understand them. There is no need to add to Scripture. This is what fictional materials, such as *The Book of Mormon*[42] and *The Chosen,* do – they add to what God has already given us. The Bible is sufficient for all we need to know about Jesus Christ and our salvation. One fan of the show says, "I've learned more from *The Chosen* than I have from my Bible."

As believers, we know that God speaks to us through His Word, not by any other form of revelation. In John 20:29, Jesus says to Thomas, "Have you believed because you have seen me? Blessed are those who have not seen and yet have believed." By telling Thomas that those who have not seen Him yet believe in Him are blessed, Jesus tells us that His Word is enough. We do not need anything more. Jesus says that those who hear and believe are truly blessed. Not only do we not have to see Jesus to believe, but we will also be blessed when we don't see Him and believe.

The Chosen accurately presents Peter as an impulsive hothead, spouting off whatever thoughts come into his mind. What does Scripture tell us about Peter? Mark 9:5-6[43] shows us that he often puts his foot in his mouth. Mark 8:33[44] shows us that he got in trouble for what he said. He was impulsive, as Mark 14:47[45] shows. Mark 14:66-72[46] tells us that he sinned and felt guilty.

---

[42] For more on *The Book of Mormon*, see Appendix B.

[43] Mark 9:5-6, "And Peter said to Jesus, "Rabbi, it is good that we are here. Let us make three tents, one for you and one for Moses and one for Elijah." [6] For he did not know what to say, for they were terrified."

[44] Mark 8:33, "But turning and seeing His disciples, He rebuked Peter and said, "Get behind me, Satan! For you are not setting your mind on the things of God, but on the things of man.""

[45] Mark 14:47, "But one of those who stood by drew his sword and struck the servant of the high priest and cut off his ear."

[46] Mark 14:66-72, "And as Peter was below in the courtyard, one of the servant girls of the high priest came, [67] and seeing Peter warming himself, she looked at him and said, "You also were with the Nazarene, Jesus." [68] But he denied it, saying, "I neither know nor understand what you mean." And he went out into the gateway and the rooster crowed. [69] And the servant girl saw him and began again to say to the bystanders, "This man is one of them." [70] But again he denied it. And after a little while the bystanders again said to Peter, "Certainly you are one of them, for you are a Galilean." [71] But he began to invoke a curse on himself and to swear, "I do not know this man of whom you speak." [72] And immediately the rooster crowed a second time. And Peter remembered how Jesus had said to him, "Before the rooster crows twice, you will deny me three times." And he broke down and wept."

The Chosen presents Peter's personality in a Biblical light. What about those were not presented accurately? What about Matthew?

Matthew, in *The Chosen*, is an interesting character. He is on the autism spectrum and, as such, lacks many of the social skills necessary to interact with others. He is a math genius, often calculating odds when talking to the other disciples. Simon Peter cannot stand Matthew because of his history as a tax collector. What does Scripture tell us about Matthew? Matthew 9:9[47] tells us he was a tax collector before following Jesus. Luke 5:7-8[48] says that he was also known as Levi. Mark 2:14[49] states that Matthew was the son of Alpheus. Matthew is included in every list of the disciples. Outside of that, there is little Scripture about Matthew's personal life. Because Scripture does not tell us much about Matthew, the writers of *The Chosen* decided to augment Scripture. Matthew of *The Chosen* has been largely fictionalized.

What about salvation? Does *The Chosen* provide the viewer with any insight into salvation? *The Chosen* has Jesus speak about repentance in season 1, episode 6; season 2, episode 1; and season 3, episode 8. However, none of these gives the specifics about what one must do to be saved. This is a topic not covered in depth.[50] Acts 2:37-38, which takes place 40 days after Christ's ascension into heaven, quotes Peter as saying, "Now when they heard this they were cut to the heart, and said to Peter and the rest of the apostles, "Brothers, what shall we do?" And Peter said to them, "Repent and be baptized every one of you in the name of Jesus Christ for the forgiveness of your sins, and you will receive the gift of the Holy Spirit." As an effective evangelism tool, *The Chosen* should discuss what is required to be saved. It does not. As such, it is not an effective evangelism tool, as claimed by the show's producers.

The Bible is Without Error
Scripture is incapable of error. *The Chosen*, being written by man, is capable of error. We know this because, in Scripture, there are no errors. However, as

---

[47] Matthew 9:9, "As Jesus passed on from there, He saw a man called Matthew sitting at the tax booth, and He said to him, "Follow me." And he rose and followed him."
[48] Luke 5:7-8, "After this He went out and saw a tax collector named Levi, sitting at the tax booth. And He said to him, "Follow me." [28] And leaving everything, he rose and followed him."
[49] Mark 2:14, "And as He passed by, He saw Levi the son of Alphaeus sitting at the tax booth, and He said to him, "Follow me." And he rose and followed Him."
[50] Granted, it may be discussed in later episodes, but the topic of salvation has not been addressed at the time of writing.

we shall see in the following three chapters, *The Chosen* contains intentional and unintentional errors.

Just as the sinfulness in our lives comes out in what we write or say, when God writes or says something, His perfection shows through. God's attributes and character are reflected in His Word. According to Titus 1:2,[51] God does not lie. Since He doesn't lie, neither does His Word. Therefore, we can trust the Bible to be free from errors.

Theologians often use two words when describing Scripture: inerrancy and infallibility. *Inerrancy* means that the Bible cannot contain any errors, nor does it affirm anything untrue. This means that when the Bible gives a historical record, that record is true. All scientific principles discussed in the Bible are true. Scripture does not contain or affirm anything untrue. When we say that Scripture is *infallible*, we are saying that because God is the ultimate author, it is incapable of falsehoods. Anything produced by man has the possibility of error. We all make mistakes. Sometimes, those errors or mistakes are intentional; other times, they are not. Joe Cristman, in the Aquila Report, says,

> "When I meet Christians enamored with productions like *The Chosen*, I'm left scratching my head. Why would we settle for something which goes against God's law, alters the events of Jesus' life, and takes us away from the Word of God? Surely it is far greater to regularly commune with God through His Word, sitting daily under its instruction, that our affections would be shaped by God and stoked into a greater zeal by the true Christ! For Christians who have been caught up with shows like *The Chosen*, my simple desire would be to point you back to the Word of God, and to discover something far greater for your soul. "[52]

The Chosen is far less than what we already have in God's Word.

---

[51] Titus 1:2, "In hope of eternal life, which God, who never lies, promised before the ages began."

[52] Joe Cristman, "Why Christians Shouldn't Watch The Chosen." https://theaquilareport.com/why-christians-shouldnt-watch-the-chosen/ Accessed May 20, 2024

6

Season 1

~

THE FIRST SEASON OF *THE Chosen* tells the story of Jesus Christ's early ministry, while he is relatively unknown to the religious and civil authorities. We are introduced to many of the show's main characters in the first season. We are introduced to Mary Magdalene, known as Lilith when she is demon-possessed. We meet Simon and Andrew, two fishermen in terrible debt to the Romans. Their fishing partners, James and John, and their father, Zebedee, are featured in the first season. We are introduced to Matthew, the autistic tax collector. We meet Nicodemus, a member of the Jewish ruling council, the Sanhedrin, who has his faith challenged by Jesus. Finally, we are introduced to Thomas and Ramah, two vintners[53] employed by a wine producer.

Disclaimer

Please be advised that the content of this chapter will contain spoilers. If you don't want the plot revealed to you, do not read further. Instead of reading the chapter before watching each episode, read the chapter as you watch the

---

[53] A vintner is a wine merchant or producer of wine.

episode. That will allow you to critique each episode from a Biblical standpoint. For your convenience, most Bible references are included in the footnotes. In this chapter, the plot summaries will use different symbols to assist the reader in understanding the source for each scene.

● means that the scene is not found in Scripture but doesn't specifically conflict with it.

👍 means that the scene is Scriptural or is grounded in Scripture.

👎 means that the scene runs contrary to Scripture.

Ⓜ means that the scene presents Mormon theology.

Episode 1 – "I Have Called You By Name"

In this episode, we are introduced to a Jewish rabbi, a demon-possessed woman, two brothers behind on their taxes, and a social outcast. The episode seamlessly flows between their four stories.

1:1 Plot Summary		
0:01		Disclaimer
0:20	👍	A father comforts his daughter with the words from Isaiah 43:1.[54]
1:59	●	Twenty-eight years later, a woman wakes with blood on her hands.
4:09	●	Roman guards stop Nicodemus' carriage.
6:18	●	Matthew, the tax collector, prepares to collect Jewish taxes.
8:17	●	Nicodemus lectures a crowd of listeners[55]
10:00	●	Nicodemus enters the local synagogue's Torah room.[56] While there, Nicodemus is summoned by Roman guards to assist them in the Red Quarter (slums).[57]

---

[54] Isaiah 43:1, "But now, this is what the Lord says—He who created you, Jacob, He who formed you, Israel: "Fear not, for I have redeemed you; I have summoned you by name; you are mine."

[55] Nicodemus says, "The Messiah will not come until this wickedness (fishing on the Sabbath) is purged from our midst." This phrase appears nowhere in Scripture, although it is consistent with Old Testament law.

[56] In ancient Israel, synagogues did not have a "Torah Room." Instead, they had a Torah ark, an ornate cabinet that held the sacred Torah scrolls used for public worship.

[57] There is no record of any of these actions in Scripture. They are purely extra-Biblical.

12:47	✚	Matthew is dropped off at the market and is looked upon with disdain by the townspeople.[58]
15:23	✚	Nicodemus arrives in the Red Quarter to perform an exorcism on Lilith, a demon-possessed woman.
18:30	✚	Men are gambling while Simon and his brother-in-law fight.
19:49	✚	Simon and Andrew worry about losing their boat due to back taxes.
21:43	Ⓜ	Nicodemus attempts to exorcise Lilith's demons. In the process, he names five angels, three of which are not Scriptural: Raphael,[59] Julio, and Russia.[60]
23:30	✚	Lilith's demons claim that they are many. Nicodemus becomes frightened and leaves.
24:53	✚	Simon returns home from fishing and speaks to his wife, Eden.[61]
27:46	✚	Flashback to Lilith's father quoting Isaiah 43:1 to her. This time, the flashback shows her father dying and being covered by a blanket.
30:49	✚	Lilith rips up her tiny scroll of Isaiah 43:1 and heads to a tavern. In the tavern, Lilith declares that she is in hell with her demonic possession.
34:36	✚	Nicodemus and his wife talk. He questions his faith in light of the failed exorcism.
38:54	✚	Nicodemus speaks to a group of listeners explaining what occurred during the failed exorcism.
40:04	✚	Lilith throws her torn-up paper containing Isaiah 43:1 into the sea. A dove flies overhead.
41:17	✚	Simon and Andrew meet with Matthew to discuss their tax debt, which threatens their livelihood. There is no Biblical evidence that Simon and Andrew were behind on their taxes. Simon tells Matthew that Quintus has forgiven their debt.[62]

---

[58] This displays how much the Jews hated the tax collectors.
[59] Raphael is a Mormon angel. (Doctrines and Covenants, 128).
[60] Scripture only names two angels: Michael and Gabriel.
[61] We know Simon was married because Jesus healed his mother-in-law in Matthew 18:14-15.
[62] In the show, Quintus is the praetor in charge of the Roman forces in Capernaum.

47:46	Ⓜ	The dove leads Lilith back to the tavern. The scene implies that she is an alcoholic. The tavern proprietor pours her some wine, but as she is about to drink it, Jesus lays his hand over hers and stops her from drinking. He says, "That is not for you."[63]
50:39	➊	Outside the tavern, Jesus calls Lilith by her real name, Mary of Magdalene. He then quotes Isaiah 43:1[64] to her. He then holds her head as she breaks down and cries. Jesus has healed her.

Episode 1 is an excellent introduction to the series. The characters are believable, the music is well done, and the production is far beyond that of most Christian films and television shows. The final scene between Jesus and Mary Magdalene is a tearjerker. It was very well done.

However, when Nicodemus names the five angels, two are Scriptural, two are not found anywhere in Christian or Mormon documents, and one, Raphael, is a Mormon angel who allegedly appeared to Joseph Smith.[65] When we look at the Scriptural support for this episode, it is non-existent. Not a single scene is found in Scripture. That is quite a bit of artistic license to take for a series based on the life of Jesus. Except for Isaiah 43:1, none of this episode is from the Bible, which is a problem.

~~~

Episode 2 – "Shabbat"
In this episode, we are shown the importance of Shabbat (the Sabbath) and get a closer look at the characters who will follow Jesus.

---

[63] This scene is an excellent example of Mormon theology influencing the story. It infers that Jesus was against the consumption of alcohol when, in fact, He was not. Jesus turned water into wine at the wedding in Cana. See John 2:1-12.

[64] Isaiah 43:1, "Thus says the Lord who created you - He who formed you, "Fear not, for I have redeemed you, I have called you by name and you are mine."

[65] Doctrines and Covenants, 128:21, "And the voice of Michael, the archangel; the voice of Gabriel, and of *Raphael*, and of divers angels, from Michael or Adam down to the present time, all declaring their dispensation, their rights, their keys, their honors, their majesty and glory, and the power of their priesthood; giving line upon line, precept upon precept; here a little, and there a little; giving us consolation by holding forth that which is to come, confirming our hope!" (Italics added.)

1:2 Plot Summary		
0:01	➕	Episode 2 opens with a flashback to 948 BC, where a mother explains the Shabbat (Sabbath) to her young son.
3:15	➕	Capernaum, AD 26 - Matthew meets with Quintus to verify Simon's story about taxes.
10:08	➕	Simon gambles with the merchant fisherman.
12:16	➕	Nicodemus hears about Lilith's healing and agrees to investigate this miracle.
16:04	➕	Simon and Andrew spy on the merchant fishermen and their fleet.[66]
17:46	➕	Nicodemus and his wife discuss guests coming and Lilith's miracle.
18:36	➕	In the market, two Jews are fighting, and the fight is ended with violence from a Roman soldier.
19:34	➕	Matthew and Gaius discuss Matthew's father, who has disowned him for being a tax collector.
20:08	➕	Mary in the hair salon talking about hosting the Shabbat meal.
20:54	➕	Nicodemus confronts Lilith about her healing. Lilith tells him her name is Mary Magdalene.
24:30	➕	Peter and his wife argue about him working on Shabbat.
26:40	➕	Matthew goes to attend the Shabbat meal but turns away at the last minute, presumably because he is worried about not being accepted.
27:50	➕	Nicodemus hosts the Shabbat meal.
30:17	➕	Mary Magdalene's Shabbat meal. Jesus shows up unannounced and joins them for dinner. Mary quotes Genesis 2:1-3 before the meal.
36:15	➕	The episode ends with soldiers approaching Simon.

Episode 2, again, is very well done. The episode emphasizes two details about Jewish culture. The main detail emphasized is the hatred between the Jews and the tax collectors. Matthew is hated by those he comes in contact with. He is fearful of what his fellow Jews might do to him were they given the

---

[66] This scene emphasizes Andrew's sense of ethics and Simon's lack of scruples.

chance. However, like episode 1, Scriptural support for this episode is virtually nonexistent. However, everything that happens does not conflict with Scripture. It is simply not based on Scripture. Except for the use of Genesis 2:1-3, which is read before the Shabbat meal, none of this episode is Biblically based, which is a problem.

⌒

Episode 3 – "Jesus Loves the Little Children"
In this episode, children from Capernaum discover Jesus' camp. They visit him multiple times and interact with Him. He encourages their faith and obedience to the law.

1:3 Plot Summary		
0:05	➕	Outskirts of Capernaum, AD 26. The episode opens with Jesus at camp.
3:39	➕	A girl, Abigail, comes across Jesus' camp. She plays there.
7:34	➕	Abigail and her family have dinner.
8:56	➕	Jesus prays and goes to bed.
10:02	➕	Abigail brings her friend, Joshua, to camp. They talk to Jesus.
13:36	➕	Jesus is at camp. He makes a lock. When He is finished, He says, "It is good."[67]
14:34	👍	Children visit Jesus at His camp. He asks them to recite the Shema,[68] which they do perfectly.
27:46	➕	Jesus packs up His camp and leaves.
28:23	➕	Abigail returns to Jesus' camp alone, only to find Him gone. However, Jesus left a toy stable and horses for her.

Episode 3 is also well done. It is considerably shorter than the previous episodes but specifically focuses on Jesus' relationship with the children of

[67] This was an attempt at humor – Jesus created something and declared it "good," as in Genesis 1 and 2.
[68] The Shema can be found in Deuteronomy 6:4-9, 11:13-21 and Numbers 15:37-41.

Capernaum. Once again, though, none of the story is grounded in Scripture. However, the Shema is recited in its entirety.

Episode 4 – "The Rock on Which it is Built"

In this episode, Matthew is instructed to spy on Simon, John the Baptist is arrested and thrown into prison, the miracle of the large catch of fish by Simon, Andrew, James, and John, and we see the calling of the first disciples.

1:4 Plot Summary		
0:07	✚	Soldiers are rowing a boat, and Simon tells them where to go.
4:18	✚	Simon meets with the merchant fisherman and tells them what he is doing with the Romans.
8:14	✚	Quintus and Matthew talk. Quintus tells him to spy on Simon.
11:14	✚	Pharisees discuss John the Baptist with Nicodemus. They are upset that John called them snakes.[69]
13:09	✚	Simon returns home and argues with his wife and brothers-in-law. He refuses to allow his sick mother-in-law to live with him and his wife. Eden, his wife, asks him, "Where is your faith?"[70]
19:12	✚	Andrew tells Simon about seeing Jesus' baptism by John the Baptist. Simon catches Matthew spying on him and confronts him.
23:50	✚	Nicodemus and his wife eat a meal together. They are interrupted by news of John the Baptist's arrest.
25:21	✚	Simon attempts to fish at night. Zebedee, James, and John show up to help.
34:04	✚	Jesus is teaching on the shore of the lake. Simon and Zebedee's boats row to shore, empty. Jesus asks if he can use their boat to teach from. Jesus converses with Simon

---

[69] Matthew 3:7, "But when he saw many of the Pharisees and Sadducees coming to his baptism, he said to them, 'You brood of vipers! Who warned you to flee from the wrath to come?'"
[70] There is no indication from Scripture that Simon lost his faith before meeting Jesus.

		and then states that "angels will come and separate the good from the righteous."[71]
39:28	👎	Jesus tells Simon to cast his net at the shore.[72] Simon reluctantly obeys. The nets are so full of fish that Zebedee, James, and John have to come help pull them in. Matthew observes from a distance.
42:24	➕	Simon kneels before Jesus and asks if He is the Lamb of God. Jesus says, "I am."[73] Simon confesses to Jesus that he is a sinner, to which Jesus tells Simon to follow Him. Jesus says, "From now on I will make you fishers of men."[74]
45:02	➕	Matthew approaches Zebedee and asks him the value of the catch.
45:29	➕	Nicodemus visits John the Baptist in prison.

Again, the episode is well done. The characters are believable and display depth. The miracle of the fish is the highlight of episode 4. The back story of Simon and Andrew's debt draws out the miraculous nature of the catch. Again, the bulk of the episode is extra-Biblical – it has no basis in Scripture. The scene of the miraculous catch of fish contradicts Scripture in that Simon casts his nets out at the shore, whereas in Luke 5:4, Jesus told Simon to go out to the deep part of the lake and do so. While this is not a principal contradiction, it raises concern that more of the plot will deviate from Scripture.

~~~

Episode 5 – "The Wedding Gift"
This episode contains Jesus' first miracle – turning water into wine at the wedding at Cana.

---

[71] Matthew 13:49, "So it will be at the end of the age. The angels will come out and separate the evil from the righteous."

[72] This directly contradicts Luke 5:4, which reads, "And when he had finished speaking, he said to Simon, "Put out into *the deep* and let down your nets for a catch." (Italics added.) In episode 4, Simon casts his nets at the shore."

[73] This is not recorded in Scripture, but there are other places where Jesus refers to Himself as "I Am" (God's name in the Old Testament.) In the gospel of John, Jesus refers to Himself as "I Am" seven times: John 6:35, 8:12, 10:9, 10:11, 11:25-26, 14:6, and 15:5.

[74] Matthew 4:19, "And He said to them, "Follow me, and I will make you fishers of men.""

1:5 Plot Summary		
0:11	👍	AD 8 – Jerusalem. Mary and Joseph are searching for 12-year-old Jesus. When they find Him, He says, "Didn't you know I must be in my Father's house?"[75] (view of the temple)
3:53	⊕	AD 26 – Cana. Mary and the mother of the groom (Dinah) converse.
4:46	⊕	John the Baptist and Nicodemus discuss the miracle of Mary Magdalene and John's ministry.
7:57	👍 ⊕	Simon and his wife, Eden, smash grapes and discuss Jesus and the miracle of the fish. Simon calls Jesus "the Lamb of God who takes away the sins of the world." Later in the conversation, Eden tells Simon, "Everyone is a sinner."
14:10	⊕	Thomas and Ramah, two vintners, discuss not having enough wine for the wedding.
15:36	⊕	Wedding preparation.
16:46	⊕	Simon and Andrew meet up with Jesus and the other disciples and head to the wedding.
18:53	⊕	Mary and Dina discuss wedding preparation.
21:00	⊕	Jesus and Simon discuss what will happen at Cana.
22:24	⊕	Mary and Dina discuss Jesus while Thomas and Ramah, his co-worker, arrive with the wine. Dinah says to Mary, "Wish me luck."
25:50	⊕	Jesus and His disciples arrive.
26:06	⊕	Nicodemus and John the Baptist discuss Mary's healing. John tells Nicodemus to finish the oracle of Agoura.[76] John then rejoices at the news of the Messiah's arrival.

---

[75] Luke 2:49, "And He said to them, "Why were you looking for me? Did you not know that I must be in my Father's house?"

[76] The Oracle of Agoura is a non-existent book. While this would usually not be an issue, it plants a seed in the viewer's mind that there can be other canonical books outside the Bible. This fits in neatly with Mormonism, which holds that there are three additional books to the Bible: *The Book of Mormon*, *The Pearl of Great Price*, and *Doctrines and Covenants*.

28:17	➕	Wedding preparation – the guest count was 80 when it was supposed to be only 40. Before tasting the wine, Dinah says one of her daily prayers, "Blessed are you, Lord our God, king of the universe who brings forth the fruit of the vine."[77] This is said every time wine is consumed. The vintners are very concerned about the lack of wine. A short clip of Jesus playing sleight-of-hand games with the children was shown.[78]
26:22	➕	The disciples discuss Jesus building a handicap-accessible ramp for a privy.[79]
37:47	👍	The host discovers that there is no more wine. Mary intervenes and speaks with Jesus, who says, "What does this have to do with me? My time has not yet come."[80] Mary pleads with Jesus and then tells the vintners to "do whatever He tells you."[81]
39:52	Ⓜ	In the back room at the wedding, Jesus tells the vintners to fill the purification jars with water. He then invites Thomas to follow Him. Jesus then prays and turns the water into wine. Simon tells Jesus that he will follow Jesus to the ends of the earth. Jesus replies, "I hope so."[82]
51:07	Ⓜ	Jesus, when talking about how bad of a dancer Andrew is, jokes, "there are some things even I cannot do."[83]

---

[77] While this statement is extra-Biblical, it is one of a group of daily prayers that Jews have said for thousands of years. In that, the producers are accurate to the culture of Israel at the time of Christ. (See Appendix A.)

[78] Again, this is extra-Biblical. While it seems harmless, it seems to trivialize Jesus' other miracles.

[79] While this is possible, it is improbable. Handicap ramps have existed for over 2300 years but were typically only used for very important buildings – temples and other holy sites.

[80] John 2:4, "And Jesus said to her, "Woman, what does this have to do with me? My hour has not yet come."

[81] John 2:5, "His mother said to the servants, "Do whatever He tells you."

[82] Since Jesus is fully God, He knows whether or not Simon will follow Him to the ends of the earth. He would not say, "I hope so," for He knows beyond the shadow of a doubt that Simon will deny Him three times. This statement emphasizes the Mormon belief that, while on earth, Jesus was only a man.

[83] It is doubtful that Jesus would ever joke about this. It makes it seem as though Jesus is more concerned about having fun than about teaching those around Him to trust Him unwaveringly. Again, this emphasizes the Mormon doctrine that Jesus was only a man during his time on earth.

While there is still a considerable amount of extra-Biblical content in Episode 5, the writers are beginning to get into Biblical support. The Scriptures quoted are accurate. The writers emphasize the problem of running out of wine at a wedding feast. They state that there are 80 guests when they only planned on 40. They show what a social faux pas it is to run out of wine at a wedding. Showing the vintners and family of the groom worried about it emphasizes the miraculous nature of turning water into wine.

Additionally, several quotes are taken verbatim from Scripture: Luke 2:49 and John 2:4-5, to be specific. *The Chosen* has been accurate in quoting Scripture so far. Considering that the show's studio has Mormon connections, the inclusion of wine, which goes against Mormon doctrine, is shown and is true to Scripture.

Episode 6 – "Indescribable Passion"

This episode focuses on Jesus' teaching and the healing of two individuals. Jesus quotes various Scriptures on prayer and heals a leper and a paralytic. Scripture is quoted frequently in this episode.

1:6 Plot Summary		
0:03	⊕	The episode opens with a scene from a market where a leper is trying to sell his tools to a pawnbroker.
3:27	⊕	Matthew and Gaius are guarding a box containing all of Simon and Andrew's taxes.
5:18	⊕	Nicodemus reports to the Pharisees on John the Baptist.
6:02	⊕	Jesus and His disciples are packing up camp. Jesus tells Simon to tend to matters at home.
10:30	⊕	Matthew is in front of Quintus, telling him about the miracle of the fish.
14:43	👍	When a leper approaches, Jesus and His disciples are on their way to Capernaum. The leper tells Him, "Lord if you are willing, you can make me clean. Jesus replied, "I am willing." Jesus then healed him.
19:42	⊕	Zebedee and Salome (James and John's parents) meet Jesus.

21:44	⊕	Simon takes care of his sick mother-in-law.
23:08	⊕	Simon and Andrew come across Matthew and speak with him.
24:45	⊕	Nicodemus meets with Shmuel, the Pharisee who turned John the Baptist into the authorities.
25:18	⊕	Dinner at Zebedee and Salome's house. When they ask about His father, Jesus says that He is in heaven.[84] Neighbors show up, and Jesus begins a story loosely based on the ten bridesmaids.[85]
29:00	👍	Nicodemus and Shmuel read Isaiah[86] and relate it to John the Baptist. They quote John the Baptist as saying, "After me comes He who is mightier than I, the strap of whose sandals I am not worthy to stoop down and untie."[87]
33:02	👍 ⊕	A crowd gathers outside Zebedee and Salome's house. Jesus talks about the Tower of Siloam, which fell, killing 28 people. He was then asked if the people who died were worse sinners. Jesus replied, "All must repent or perish."[88] Later in the scene, Jesus says, "Pray to your Father who sees you in secret."[89] When you give to the needy, do not let your left hand know what your right hand is doing."[90]
34:59	⊕	The market is empty. The soldiers wonder what is happening.

[84] Jesus' statement here was ambiguous, as His heavenly Father and His early father were both in heaven.
[85] The bridesmaids are not mentioned, but the point of Jesus's story is the same – no one knows when Judgment Day is, so we must all be ready.
[86] Isaiah 40:3, "A voice cries: "In the wilderness prepare the way of the LORD; make straight in the desert a highway for our God."
[87] Mark 1:7, "And he preached, saying, "After me comes He who is mightier than I, the strap of whose sandals I am not worthy to stoop down and untie."
[88] Luke 13:4-5, "Or those eighteen on whom the tower in Siloam fell and killed them: do you think that they were worse offenders than all the others who lived in Jerusalem? [5] No, I tell you; but unless you repent, you will all likewise perish."
[89] Matthew 6:5-6, "And when you pray, you must not be like the hypocrites. For they love to stand and pray in the synagogues and at the street corners, that they may be seen by others. Truly, I say to you, they have received their reward. [6] But when you pray, go into your room and shut the door and pray to your Father who is in secret. And your Father who sees in secret will reward you."
[90] Matthew 6:3-4, "But when you give to the needy, do not let your left hand know what your right hand is doing, [4] so that your giving may be in secret. And your Father who sees in secret will reward you."

36:08	👍	At Zebedee and Salome's house, Jesus is still teaching on prayer.[91] A large crowd gathers outside. While He is teaching, people carry a paralytic to the roof. Jesus continues his teaching on prayer.[92]
40:07	👍	Nicodemus and the Pharisees arrive at Zebedee and Salome's house. Jesus tells the paralytic that his sins are forgiven. Jesus turns to the Pharisees and asks, "Which is easier to say, "your sins are forgive" or "rise and walk?"[93] He then heals the paralytic. A few moments later, Nicodemus asks to speak to Jesus in private.
49:02	⊕	Matthew and Jesus make eye contact, but only for a moment.

Five scenes stand out in episode 6 for their Biblical accuracy. The healing of the leper follows Scripture well. The interaction between Nicodemus and Shmuel was very Scriptural as far as quoting Isaiah 40:3 and Mark 1:7 verbatim. The scene where Jesus teaches at Zebedee and Salome's house quotes Scripture very closely. Jesus' teaching on prayer combines several different verses, but those that he quotes are spot on with Scripture. The healing of the paralytic and subsequent conversation with the Pharisees is also accurate. However, the episode still contains plenty of extra-Biblical content. That content may fit with Scripture but is not expressly found in the Bible.

Episode 7 – "Invitations"
In this episode, Matthew struggles to reconcile the miracles he has witnessed with reality. Jesus and Nicodemus meet at night.

---

[91] Luke 18:1-14. Jesus, while teaching on prayer, summarizes the two stories contained in these pericopes.
[92] Matthew 6:30, "But if God so clothes the grass of the field, which today is alive and tomorrow is thrown into the oven, will He not much more clothe you, O you of little faith?"
[93] Matthew 9:5-6, "For which is easier, to say, 'Your sins are forgiven,' or to say, 'Rise and walk'? [6] But that you may know that the Son of Man has authority on earth to forgive sins"— He then said to the paralytic— "Rise, pick up your bed and go home."

1:7 Plot Summary		
0:07	➕	Sinai Peninsula 13th century BC. Joshua and Moses discuss the serpents killing the Israelites.[94] Moses is making a serpent out of bronze to hang on a cross. Moses refers to God as Adonai.[95]
4:05	➕	Matthew is at home preparing for his day. He arrives at his tax booth and speaks with Gaius. During their conversation, Matthew says, "There is no such thing as luck."[96]
6:03	➕	Nicodemus and his wife discuss his investigation of Jesus and her wanting to return to Jerusalem. Quintus bursts in and tells Nicodemus to investigate Jesus.
10:44	➕	Jesus and His disciples are in camp. Mary Magdalene speaks to Jesus about Nicodemus. Jesus agrees to meet with Him.
14:48	➕	Matthew visits his parents. He asks his mother if she thinks miracles are possible.
18:30	➕	Simon and Jesus discuss Jesus' meeting with Nicodemus.
20:34	Ⓜ	Nicodemus meets with Jesus.[97] Nicodemus loosely quotes John 1:2-3. Throughout the rest of the conversation, they quote John 3:5-6,[98] 3:10,[99] 3:12,[100]

---

[94] Numbers 21:6-9, "Then the LORD sent fiery serpents among the people, and they bit the people, so that many people of Israel died. 7 And the people came to Moses and said, "We have sinned, for we have spoken against the LORD and against you. Pray to the LORD, that he take away the serpents from us." So, Moses prayed for the people. 8 And the LORD said to Moses, "Make a fiery serpent and set it on a pole, and everyone who is bitten, when he sees it, shall live." 9 So Moses made a bronze serpent and set it on a pole. And if a serpent bit anyone, he would look at the bronze serpent and live."

[95] Jews, out of respect for God's name, "Yahweh" said "Adonai" instead.

[96] John Calvin agreed with Matthew when he said, "Fortune and chance are heathen terms… and there is no place in human affairs for fortune and chance." *Institutes of the Christian Religion,* Book 1, Chapter 16, Section 8 (Grand Rapids: Eerdmans, 1981), 169.

[97] This scene had so much potential. There was so much Scripture being quoted. It was wonderful. However, any good that was done by quoting Scripture was undone by saying things that contradicted Scripture or attributes of God.

[98] John 3:5-6, "Jesus answered, "Truly, truly, I say to you, unless one is born of water and the Spirit, he cannot enter the kingdom of God. 6 That which is born of the flesh is flesh, and that which is born of the Spirit is spirit."

[99] John 3:10, "Jesus answered him, "Are you the teacher of Israel and yet you do not understand these things?"

[100] John 3:12, "If I have told you earthly things and you do not believe, how can you believe if I tell you heavenly things?"

		3:14-15,[101] and 3:16-17.[102] Jesus invites Nicodemus to follow Him. Nicodemus then asked Jesus, "Is the Kingdom of God coming?"[103] Jesus replied, "What does your heart say?"[104] Then Jesus said, "I hope you do come, Nicodemus."[105] Jesus then tells Nicodemus, "Blessed are those who take refuge in Him."[106] Jesus and Nicodemus hug.
31:29	✚	Matthew is in his tax booth. Jesus and His disciples walk by. Jesus and Matthew make eye contact again. Jesus invites Matthew to follow Him. Matthew does.

The meeting between Jesus and Nicodemus started so strong. In Jesus' meeting with Nicodemus, eight verses from John 3 are directly quoted from the Bible. Two heretical statements[107] outweighed all that good by contradicting Scripture. Jesus asks Nicodemus, "What does your heart say?" and "I hope you do come Nicodemus." These are both things Jesus would not say. The Bible tells us over and over not to trust our hearts, for they are evil. Additionally, since Jesus was fully God, He would have known whether or not Nicodemus would have followed Him. This supports the Mormon view

---

[101] John 3:14-15, "And as Moses lifted up the serpent in the wilderness, so must the Son of Man be lifted up, 15 that whoever believes in him may have eternal life."

[102] John 3:16-17, "For God so loved the world, that He gave His only Son, that whoever believes in Him should not perish but have eternal life. 17 For God did not send is Son into the world to condemn the world, but in order that the world might be saved through im."

[103] This is not recorded as being part of their conversation.

[104] This is blatant heresy and goes against Scripture. Jeremiah 17:9, "The heart is deceitful above all things, and desperately sick; who can understand it?" Genesis 6:5, "The LORD saw that the wickedness of man was great in the earth, and that every intention of the thoughts of his heart was only evil continually." Matthew 15:19, "For out of the heart come evil thoughts, murder, adultery, sexual immorality, theft, false witness, slander." And plenty of additional verses speak of the evil of the heart. Jesus would never ask someone what their heart tells them. However, LDS missionaries use this type of statement to evangelize. The missionaries explain their beliefs and then ask the person to whom they are witnessing, "What does your heart tell you?" The emphasis is not on what is true but based on what is felt.

[105] Again, something that is not Scriptural. Jesus would know if Nicodemus would join Him or not. He wouldn't hope. Jesus is omniscient (all-knowing). 1 John 3:20 says, "For whenever our heart condemns us, God is greater than our heart, and he knows everything." See also Psalm 147:5, Hebrews 4:13, and Proverbs 15:3. So, to say that Jesus hopes something will happen violates this omniscience of God. This promotes the Mormon doctrine that states that Jesus was not God during His time on earth.

[106] Psalm 2:12, "Kiss the son, lest he be angry, and you perish in the way, for his wrath is quickly kindled. Blessed are all who take refuge in him."

[107] Heretical means that it contradicts Scripture or a basic tenet of the Christian faith.

of Jesus—He was only a man during His time on earth. If Christ had been only a man, He would have said something like, "I hope you do."

⌒⌒

Episode 8 – "I am He"

In this episode, Jesus and His disciples leave Capernaum for Samaria. Jesus meets with a suffering woman at Jacob's Well and announces that He is the Messiah.

1:8 Plot Summary		
0:00	➕	Canaan, 1952 BC. Jacob and his sons dig his well.
3:00	➕	Jacob's well, 26 AD. A woman is drawing water from the well and brings it home.
5:40	➕	The woman meets with her husband to request a divorce. He refuses.
8:33	👍 ➕	Feast at Matthew's house. The Pharisees arrive and are invited in, but they refuse. They ask Matthew, "Why does your master eat with tax collectors and sinners?" Jesus answers for Matthew, "It's not the healthy who need a doctor, but the sick. I desire mercy more than sacrifice. I have not come to call the righteous, but sinners."[108] Gaius arrives and tries to talk Matthew into returning to his job as a tax collector.
13:26	➕	Nicodemus and his wife discuss returning to Jerusalem.
18:03	➕	Quintus and Gaius discuss Matthew's resignation.
18:57	➕	At camp, Jesus and Simon discuss Simon's family issues.

---

[108] Matthew 9:10-13, "And as Jesus reclined at table in the house, behold, many tax collectors and sinners came and were reclining with Jesus and his disciples. 11 And when the Pharisees saw this, they said to His disciples, "Why does your teacher eat with tax collectors and sinners?" 12 But when He heard it, He said, "Those who are well have no need of a physician, but those who are sick. 13 Go and learn what this means: 'I desire mercy and not sacrifice.' For I came not to call the righteous, but sinners."

20:28	👍 ➕	Nicodemus and Shmuel speak about false prophecy. Shmuel quotes Daniel 7:14[109] word for word.
23:59	Ⓜ ➕	Simon's mother-in-law is running a fever and coughing. Jesus arrives and talks to Eden. Simon and Andrew arrive and check on Simon's mother-in-law. Jesus tells Eden, "I cannot make everything about this easier for you."[110] Jesus then clasps Simon's mother-in-law's hands and heals her.[111] She immediately gets up and serves Jesus and His disciples.
29:38	➕	In the Samaritan market, a vendor refuses to sell to a woman.
30:23	➕	Quintus outlaws all religious gatherings outside of the temple or schools.
30:52	➕	The disciples leave their homes to travel with Jesus. Nicodemus and his wife also pack up. Jesus and the disciples meet at a fountain while Nicodemus waits in the wings. Simon finds some gold left by Nicodemus for them. Jesus looks in Nicodemus' direction and whispers, "You came so close." Nicodemus weeps but doesn't leave with Jesus.
34:08	➕	Gaius visits Matthew's parents and drops Matthew's house keys and dog off.
37:30	👍 ➕	Jesus and His disciples walk, and He tells them they will travel through Samaria. In Samaria, they approach Jacob's well. Jesus sends the disciples to buy some food. The Samaritan woman arrives, and Jesus asks her for a drink. She replies, "How is it that you, a Jew, ask for a drink from me, a woman of Samaria?"[112] Jesus replied,

---

[109] Daniel 7:14, "And to Him was given dominion and glory and a kingdom, that all peoples, nations, and languages should serve Him; His dominion is an everlasting dominion, which shall not pass away, and His kingdom one that shall not be destroyed."

[110] This is a false statement about Jesus Christ. As Christians, we believe He is omnipotent, and for Him to say He cannot do something runs counter to that attribute. Verses on omnipotence include Matthew 19:26, Luke 1:37, and Hebrews 1:3.

[111] Matthew 8:14-15, "And when Jesus entered Peter's house, He saw his mother-in-law lying sick with a fever. 15 He touched her hand, and the fever left her, and she rose and began to serve Him."

[112] John 4:9, "The Samaritan woman said to Him, "How is it that you, a Jew, ask for a drink from me, a woman of Samaria?" (For Jews have no dealings with Samaritans.)"

		"If you knew who I am, you would ask me for a drink."[113] The conversation between them quotes John 4:11-14[114] exactly, but John 4:15[115] is replaced with "Prove it." The next part of the conversation is loosely based on John 4:16-26.[116] Jesus begins naming her husbands as she walks away. As the disciples return, she exclaims, "This man told me everything I've done! He must be the Christ."[117] She runs to tell the townspeople. The disciples and Jesus head into town.

Episode 8 has quite a few positive aspects. The feast at Matthew's house quotes Matthew 9:10-13 exactly. Daniel 7:14 is quoted word-for-word from the ESV in the conversation between Nicodemus and Shmuel. In the final scene, large chunks of John 4 are quoted directly. However, in the ninth scene, Jesus states, "I cannot make everything about this easier for you." If Jesus were fully man and fully God, He would have been able to do so. However, Mormon theology mandates that Jesus was only a man while he was human and, therefore, would not have been able to make everything easier for her.

Additionally, much of John 4 is loosely quoted. The writers could have stayed closer to John 4 than they did. Again, there was a significant amount of extra-Biblical content, but much of this was needed for plot development.

Season 1 Assessment

Season 1 was well-written and produced. Quality-wise, the show is far better than most other Christian television shows and movies. The writers and producers did an excellent job at showing Nicodemus remaining unbiased in

---

[113] This is a loose summary of John 4:10, which reads, "Jesus answered her, "If you knew the gift of God, and who it is that is saying to you, 'Give me a drink,' you would have asked Him, and He would have given you living water."

[114] John 4:11-14, "The woman said to him, "Sir, you have nothing to draw water with, and the well is deep. Where do you get that living water? [12] Are you greater than our father Jacob? He gave us the well and drank from it himself, as did his sons and his livestock." [13] Jesus said to her, "Everyone who drinks of this water will be thirsty again, [14] but whoever drinks of the water that I will give him will never be thirsty again. The water that I will give him will become in him a spring of water welling up to eternal life."

[115] John 4:15, "The woman said to him, "Sir, give me this water, so that I will not be thirsty or have to come here to draw water."

[116] This is disappointing because the writers could have stayed true to John 4 but they chose to paraphrase most of it instead.

[117] John 4:29, "Come, see a man who told me all that I ever did. Can this be the Christ?" In the show, this sentence is a statement, whereas in the gospel of John, it is an invitation.

Jesus' actions. While the other Pharisees were openly antagonistic toward Jesus, Nicodemus was not. The writers also did a fantastic job of showing how hated the tax collectors were by the rest of Jewish society. The development of individuals in the story is almost exclusively based on extra-Biblical content. Although much of this did not contradict Scripture, some sections stood in direct opposition to Scripture. Therein lies the problem. While the show is primarily faithful to Scripture, there are occasional lines that are not. This is how the enemy works. He tells 99 truths and slips in one lie. We must carefully compare what we watch with what the gospels teach. The problem is that most people will get their theology from the show rather than from their Bibles. They replace reading the gospels with watching a television show.[118] So that one falsehood has become a theological truth for them.

---

[118] One fan of the show said, "Watching this show is studying the Bible. Glory to God." It is not. It is studying man's interpretation of the Bible. Since the show is not 100% true to Scripture, it is not the same as studying the Bible.

7

Season 2

⌒⌐

THE SECOND SEASON OF *THE Chosen* shows how the disciples become unified as they begin to follow Jesus. There is animosity between the disciples, specifically Simon and Matthew. There is a power struggle between them as Jesus' ministry on earth picks up steam. The season begins with Jesus and the disciples heading to Samaria and finishes with preparations for the Sermon on the Mount. The second season deals with much of the prejudice between different cultures: the Jews and Samaritans, the religious elite and Jesus, and the Romans and Jews.

Disclaimer
Please be advised that the content of this chapter will contain spoilers. If you don't want the plot revealed to you, do not read further. Instead of reading the chapter before watching each episode, read the chapter as you watch the episode. That will allow you to critique each episode from a Biblical standpoint. For your convenience, most Bible references are included in the footnotes. In this chapter, the plot summaries will use different symbols to assist the reader in understanding the source for each scene.

⊕   means that the scene is not found in Scripture but doesn't specifically conflict with it.

👍   means that the scene is Scriptural or is grounded in Scripture.

👎   means that the scene runs contrary to Scripture.

Ⓜ   means that the scene presents Mormon theology.

Episode 1 – "Thunder"

In this episode, the disciples worry about Jesus' increasing fame.

2:1 Plot Summary		
0:34	⊕	45 AD Followers of Jesus are being interviewed by a middle-aged apostle, John, after the death of his brother James.[1] John is collecting information for his gospel.[2] During her interview, Salome said to John, "If you try to write every single thing He did, the world itself could not contain the books that would be written."[3] She also quoted Jesus saying, "Heaven and earth may pass away, but my words will never pass away."[4]
9:46	⊕	John and James are plowing a field and sowing seeds.
11:48	⊕	Thomas and Ramah are lost on a road in Samaria. They are trying to catch up with Jesus.
13:11	⊕	The disciples lose Jesus, so they search for him. We find him repairing a chariot.
17:04	⊕	Matthew and Mary Magdalene welcome Thomas and Ramah.
19:46	👍	Jesus is teaching the parable of the lost sheep. He says, "It is not the will of my Father that one of these should perish. There will be more joy in heaven over one sinner

---

[1] According to Acts 12:2, James, the Son of Alphaeus (Big James in the show) died a martyr. This occurred in approximately 44 AD.

[2] The writers have taken some liberty here because the Gospel of John wasn't written until 90-100 AD, after all the other disciples had died.

[3] John 21:25, "Now there are also many other things that Jesus did. Were every one of them to be written, I suppose that the world itself could not contain the books that would be written." Scripture does not indicate that Salome said this to John.

[4] Matthew 24:35, "Heaven and earth will pass away, but My words will not pass away."

		who repents than over ninety-nine righteous persons who need no repentance."[5]
21:18	⊕	A man with a broken leg limps up to the plowed and planted field crying tears of joy.
21:46	⊕	Jesus meets Thomas, Ramah, and her father, Kafni. He agrees to meet privately with Kafni the following day.
23:28	⊕	Jesus thanks James and John for working the field.
24:06	⊕	The disciples walk and discuss Jesus' plans for the day.
28:33	⊕	Ramah talks to her father (Kafni) about Jesus. Jesus and Kafni talk. Kafni gives money to Ramah and leaves.
33:55	⊕	Jesus and the disciples look at the plowed field. Jesus tells James and John, "Well done."
34:28	👎 ⊕	Jesus and His disciples visit the house of the man with the broken leg. The man thanks Jesus for the work done in his field. John and James say, "We were told it was for travelers."[6] They have brought food and will share a meal with the man and his family. During dinner, Jesus says, "I am here to preach the good news of the Kingdom of Heaven, a kingdom that is not of this world. A kingdom that is coming soon where yes, sorrow and suffering will flee away." "I will make a way for people to access this kingdom. But, in this world, bones will still break; hearts will still break. But in the end, the light will overcome darkness.[7] The lame man says to Jesus, "If you knew who I am, you never would have helped me." The man then confesses to killing a Jew on the road to Jericho and stealing his horse. Jesus tells him that the man did not

[5] Luke 15:3-7, "So He told them this parable: [4] "What man of you, having a hundred sheep, if he has lost one of them, does not leave the ninety-nine in the open country, and go after the one that is lost, until he finds it? [5] And when he has found it, he lays it on his shoulders, rejoicing. [6] And when he comes home, he calls together his friends and his neighbors, saying to them, 'Rejoice with me, for I have found my sheep that was lost.' [7] Just so, I tell you, there will be more joy in heaven over one sinner who repents than over ninety-nine righteous persons who need no repentance."

[6] This implies that either Jesus did not know who it was for or that he lied to James and John. Either option is problematic.

[7] According to Scripture, Jesus never said this. This is a significant problem, as the writers add things that Jesus never said to their story. Many viewers will not know the difference.

		die. Jesus encourages him to return to the synagogue. Jesus hugs him and leaves.[8]
44:07	➕	Jesus and His disciples spend the night at the Samaritan woman's house.
45:24	➕	The following morning, the lame man wakes up with a healed leg.
46:14	➕	Jesus speaks to James and John about the healed leg. Before breakfast, Jesus prays, "I am thankful before You, living and enduring King, for you have mercifully restored my soul within me. Great is Your faithfulness."[9]
47:37	👎 ➕	Jesus and His disciples eat breakfast and Jesus leaves to be alone. The disciples argue about the plans for the day. James and John catch up with Jesus and are spit upon and stoned by a group of Samaritans. Jesus tells James and John that their work planting seeds is akin to planting seeds for the Kingdom of God. He tells them, "As we gather others, I need you to show the way."[10]
54:44	➕	The other disciples join Jesus, James, and John, along with the priest from the synagogue in Sychar. The priest invites Jesus to the synagogue to read from the Torah.[11]
55:39	Ⓜ	This scene takes place at the temple in Sychar. The disciples serve as greeters and ushers. The Samaritan Woman and her husband arrive. The priest leads Jesus to the Torah Ark,[12] where the Torah is kept. Jesus asks for John to be sent in. Jesus says to John, "The five books of Moses and no more." John replies, "They are missing out on so much."[13] Jesus asks John to tell Him what to read. John replies that he is not worthy. Jesus says, "Who is

---

[8] These lines by Jesus from *The Chosen* are found nowhere in Scripture.

[9] This prayer is a daily Jewish prayer. (See Appendix A for more information) We don't know if Jesus prayed this or not. There certainly is no Scriptural support that He did.

[10] Also, according to Scripture, Jesus never said this. Once again, most viewers will not know the difference.

[11] The Torah is the first five books of the Bible – the ones written by Moses: Genesis, Exodus, Leviticus, Numbers, and Deuteronomy.

[12] The Torah Ark is where the Torah is stored in the synagogue. It was frequently located near the front of the synagogue facing Jerusalem.

[13] John is referring to historical books and writings (the rest of the Jewish Scriptures). But it could also be understood that John is talking about the three Mormon books that they have added to Scripture.

		worthy of anything?" John replies, "You." Jesus responds, "I am a man, John.[14] I am who I am."[15] John explains to Jesus what "word" means in Greek.
59:49	👍 ➕	Jesus enters the sanctuary. The man whose leg was healed arrives. Jesus winks at him. Jesus reads from Genesis 1:1-5.[16] As Jesus reads, John is writing John 1:1-5 in his head. The scene closes with middle-aged John again sitting at a desk writing his gospel.

This episode displays the animosity between the Samaritans and the Jews quite well. One example is the scene where the Samaritans spit upon James and John. The disciples also make derogatory comments about the Samaritans, emphasizing the hatred between the two groups. Finally, the episode shows the tremendous cost of following Jesus—leaving family and home. But it also shows how Jesus came to earth to return things to their right by healing the sick and forgiving the sinners.

The primary issue with this episode is that there are three sentences said by Jesus that are not found anywhere in Scripture. The first erroneous statement comes in the 34:28 scene, when Jesus says, "I will make a way for people to access this kingdom. But, in this world, bones will still break; hearts will still break. But in the end, the light will overcome darkness." The second statement comes in the scene that starts at 47:37. Jesus says to James and John, "As we gather others, I need you to show the way." The third sentence is troubling, as it promotes Mormon theology. It appears in the scene which

---

[14] Jesus, while implying that He was only a man, never made this statement. This is blatant Mormon theology, which believes that Jesus started as a man and, through His works, became a god. According to the Mormon website, www.churchofjesuschrist.org, "We believe that Jesus was fully human in that He was subject to sickness, to pain and to temptation." Most viewers will have no idea that this is unscriptural.

[15] Jesus is quoting how Yahweh referred to himself in Exodus 3:14, "God said to Moses, "I AM WHO I AM." And he said, "Say this to the people of Israel: 'I AM has sent me to you.'" However, there is no Biblical record of Jesus ever saying this.

[16] Jesus reads Genesis 1:1-5a word for word, "In the beginning, God created the heavens and the earth. ² The earth was without form and void, and darkness was over the face of the deep. And the Spirit of God was hovering over the face of the waters. ³ And God said, "Let there be light," and there was light. ⁴ And God saw that the light was good. And God separated the light from the darkness. ⁵ God called the light Day," John thinks John 1:1-5 out loud, "In the beginning was the Word, and the Word was with God, and the Word was God. ² He was in the beginning with God. ³ All things were made through Him, and without Him was not anything made that was made. ⁴ In Him was life, and the life was the light of men. ⁵ The light shines in the darkness, and the darkness has not overcome it."

begins at 55:39. In this scene, Jesus says, "I am a man, John. I am who I am." While all three of these statements seem innocent enough, the issue is that the show is beginning to slip in non-Scriptural statements by Jesus. With so many people watching the show instead of reading their Bibles, unbiblical statements by Jesus will be taken as truth. While Jesus was a man, He was also truly God. Mormons believe that Jesus became a god after His life on earth. These sorts of things open the door to more unbiblical things that Jesus said on the show. It is heresy to attribute statements to Jesus that He never made. We must be cautious not to do that.

Episode 2 – "I Saw You"
The disciples must accept Jesus' increasing fame and notoriety in this episode. Philip and Nathaniel also join Jesus' group of disciples.

2:2 Plot Summary		
0:30	➕	The scene opens at a construction site. Nathaniel and the foreman are arguing when an accident occurs outside. Nathaniel is blamed for the accident.
3:12	👍	The disciples are bringing firewood. Philip, a former disciple of John the Baptist, approaches them. Philip wants to speak with Jesus. Philip is brought to camp. After a bit, Ezekiel 39:9-10a[17] is recited by the disciples word for word.
8:37	➕	Nathaniel enters a tavern, asks for a drink, and talks to the bartender for a bit.
11:33	➕	Matthew and Philip talk about Matthew's past. Philip said to him, "Once you've met the Messiah, 'am' is all that matters.
15:20	👍	Nathaniel rests under a fig tree. He begins one Jewish prayer, "Blessed are you, Lord our God, King of the

---

[17] Ezekiel 39:9-10a, "Then those who dwell in the cities of Israel will go out and make fires of the weapons and burn them, shields and bucklers, bow and arrows, clubs and spears; and they will make fires of them for seven years, [10] so that they will not need to take wood out of the field or cut down any out of the forests, for they will make their fires of the weapons."

		universe. Then he quotes Deuteronomy 6:4 word for word.[18]
18:11	➕ 👎	Matthew and Philip are stripping wood while they talk. Philip says, "Jesus doesn't love everything about religion."[19]
21:20	➕	Nathaniel is mourning by the fig tree. He pours ashes on himself and leaves.
22:22	➕	Philip and Jesus talk. Philip goes to bed for the night.
27:08	➕	Camp the following day. Mary Magdalene and Ramah talk. Ramah prays the morning prayer.[20] The disciples talk among themselves.
30:50	➕	Matthew is writing in his book. Thaddeus approaches and sits and talks with Matthew.
33:18	➕	The disciples leave camp and talk as they walk. Simon and Jesus talk, and Jesus says, "Every one of these people I have called for a reason."[21]
41:35	👍	Caesarea Philippi. Philip goes to speak with Nathaniel and wakes him. They talk about the construction accident. Philip then tells Nathaniel about Jesus. Nathaniel says, "Can anything good come out of Nazareth?" Philip invites Nathaniel to meet Jesus. [22]
46:59	👍	Jesus runs into Philip and Nathaniel on the road. He speaks with them and tells Nathaniel, "I saw you under the fig tree."[23] Their conversation follows John 1:50-51.

---

[18] Deuteronomy 6:4, "Hear, O Israel: The LORD our God, the LORD is one."

[19] We cannot validate the truth of that statement. Jesus may or may not love everything about religion. What Jesus does hate is self-righteousness.

[20] "I am thankful before You, living and enduring King, for you have mercifully restored my soul within me. Great is Your faithfulness."[20] This is a traditional Jewish prayer. There are different variations of it based on the time of prayer. For example, one version is said before drinking wine and another that is said before meals. (See Appendix A for more information on daily Jewish prayers.)

[21] While this statement is likely true, there is no record of Jesus ever saying it.

[22] John 1:46, "Nathanael said to him, "Can anything good come out of Nazareth?" Philip said to him, "Come and see."

[23] John 1:50-51, "Jesus answered him, "Because I said to you, 'I saw you under the fig tree,' do you believe? You will see greater things than these. And He said to him; truly, truly, I say to you, you will see heaven opened, and the angels of God ascending and descending on the Son of Man."

This episode contains a lot of extra-Biblical character development for Philip and Nathaniel. For the most part, it does not conflict with Scripture, though. There are three incidents where God's Word is quoted or followed directly – Ezekiel 39:9-10a, Deuteronomy 6:4, and John 1:46-51. Jesus' conversation with Philip was very Biblically accurate. The writers would do well to have more scenes adhere to Scripture like this one.

Episode 3 – "Matthew 4:24"[24]

This episode highlights Jesus' healing ministry. He has a long line of people waiting to be cured of various ailments. The disciples cannot do much to help Him. He sees people until late in the night.

2:3 Plot Summary		
1:28	👍 ➕	Syria: The episode opens with many injured and sick people waiting to see Jesus. Philip and Matthew walk and talk, and Philip teaches Matthew Psalm 139:8[25] to Matthew. He then says to Matthew, "He is always right here, right now, for you."[26]
4:25	➕	Camp. The disciples take turns performing crowd control for Jesus. Matthew, Ramah, and Mary Magdalene speak. They discuss Jesus' increasing fame. Matthew and Ramah and Mary Magdalene speak. They paraphrase Zechariah 14:1-4.[27] An extra-Biblical rabbinic prayer is

---

[24] Matthew 4:24, "So his fame spread throughout all Syria, and they brought Him all the sick, those afflicted with various diseases and pains, those oppressed by demons, those having seizures, and paralytics, and He healed them."

[25] Psalm 139:8, "If I ascend to heaven, you are there! If I make my bed in Sheol, you are there!"

[26] Romans 8:28-31, "And we know that for those who love God all things work together for good, for those who are called according to His purpose. [29] For those whom He foreknew He also predestined to be conformed to the image of His Son, in order that He might be the firstborn among many brothers. [30] And those whom He predestined He also called, and those whom He called He also justified, and those whom He justified He also glorified. [31] What then shall we say to these things? If God is for us, who can be against us?"

[27] Zechariah 14:1-4. "Behold, a day is coming for the LORD, when the spoil taken from you will be divided in your midst. [2] For I will gather all the nations against Jerusalem to battle, and the city shall be taken and the houses plundered and the women raped. Half of the city shall go out into exile, but the rest of the people shall not be cut off from the city. [3] Then the LORD will go out and fight against those nations as when He fights on a day of battle. [4] On that day His

		also said. As the disciples continue to talk, Thomas states that he feels that people believe in Jesus because He heals them. Mary, mother of Jesus arrives. The disciples finish setting up camp, wash up, and eat dinner.
15:40	➕	The disciples sit around the campfire, talking about Jesus. Mary, the mother of Jesus, is asked about his birth. The conversation turns to talking about their past sins and intentional violations of Jewish law. Because of Matthew's past, Simon and the other disciples focus their anger on him. Jesus returns and is so exhausted that He goes to bed. Mary, the mother of Jesus, washes His feet as He lies down.

Episode 3 emphasizes Jesus' healing ministry. It consumes an entire day. It also shows the physical toll that ministry had on Jesus. The episode is best summarized in Matthew 4:24.[28] Outside of Jesus healing people, there is not much other Biblical content in this episode. The episode's purpose is further character development, which relies on extra-Biblical sources. There is not much theological depth in this one.

~~~~~

Episode 4 – "The Perfect Opportunity"
In this episode, Jesus and His disciples travel to Jerusalem to celebrate the Feast of Tabernacles. While in Jerusalem, Jesus heals Jesse, a man who has been lame for 38 years.

2:4 Plot Summary		
0:26	➕	A young boy named Jesse falls out of a tree. His father brings him to a doctor who declares that the boy is lame.
1:41	➕	The boys' mother dies in childbirth, giving birth to Jesse's younger brother, Simon. The father remarries. The boys grow up together.

---

feet shall stand on the Mount of Olives that lies before Jerusalem on the east, and the Mount of Olives shall be split in two from east to west by a very wide valley, so that one half of the Mount shall move northward, and the other half southward."

[28] Matthew 4:24, "So His fame spread throughout all Syria, and they brought Him all the sick, those afflicted with various diseases and pains, those oppressed by demons, those having seizures, and paralytics, and He healed them."

4:14	⊕	Simon wheels Jesse into town where they witness Roman violence. Simon enlists to become a zealot.
5:00	⊕	The brothers go to sleep. In the morning, Simon is gone. He has left a note for Jesse.
5:32	⊕	Simon walks in the mountains. Jesse reads Simon's note.
5:57	⊕	Jesse is sitting near the pool at Bethesda with other sick people. When the fountain comes on, all the sick people hurry to be first to touch it so that they may be healed. Being lame, Jesse is unable to do be the first.
7:00	⊕	Simon trains to become a Zealot. The zealots learn martial arts. The scene alternates between martial arts and Jesse at the pool.
10:21	⊕	In the marketplace, Simon the Zealot stops an argument.
12:45	⊕	The disciples build a tabernacle for the Feast of Tabernacles.[29]
14:27	👍 ⊕	Simon the Zealot meets with the head zealot. They quote Exodus 22:20[30] word for word. Simon is instructed to travel to Jerusalem to kill Rufus.
16:10	👍	Zealot trainees quote part of Zephaniah 3:15-18[31]
16:38	⊕	Shmuel is in the Jerusalem market preparing to street preach.
18:05	⊕	Jesse is still by the pool and is unable to get in.
19:16	⊕	Simon the Zealot approaches the gate to Jerusalem. Men are being crucified.
21:14	⊕	Several disciples are at the market where Shmuel is preaching against false prophets.
23:36	⊕	Simon the Zealot meets with other zealots to plan Rufus' assassination.

[29] The Feast of Tabernacles (Sukkot) is a seven-day agricultural festival. It commemorates God's protection of the Israelites during their 40 years of wandering in the desert. During the festival, the Jews build temporary shelters and eat their meals in them for seven days.

[30] Exodus 22:20, "Whoever sacrifices to any god, other than the LORD alone, shall be devoted to destruction."

[31] Zephaniah 3:15-18, "The LORD has taken away the judgments against you; He has cleared away your enemies. The King of Israel, the LORD, is in your midst; you shall never again fear evil. [16] On that day it shall be said to Jerusalem: "Fear not, O Zion; let not your hands grow weak. [17] The LORD your God is in your midst, a mighty one who will save; He will rejoice over you with gladness; He will quiet you by his love; He will exult over you with loud singing. [18] I will gather those of you who mourn for the festival, so that you will no longer suffer reproach."

26:24	👍 ⊕	At the camp, the disciples finish the work on their tabernacle. They sit down for dinner, and one disciple quotes Zechariah 14:16.[32]
30:40	⊕	John and Simon meet with Jesus and discuss Shmuel.
31:47	👍	At the temple, a Levite reads Zephaniah 3:17-19.[33] Simon the Zealot is in the crowd.
32:30	⊕	Simon the Zealot walks on the walls of Jerusalem and stares at the men being crucified.
33:12	⊕	Jesus, Simon, John, and Matthew walk to Jerusalem. They speak of the pool at Bethesda. They walk past the crucifixions. Jesus stares at them knowingly.
34:51	👍 ⊕	At the Jerusalem market, Atticus (Roman secret intelligence agent) meets with Petronius, Rufus' assistant. Simon the Zealot speaks with Jesse at the Bethesda pool. Simon quotes Ecclesiastes 3:3[34] and Zephaniah 3:19.[35]
43:29	⊕	Simon the Zealot disguises himself.
44:40	⊕	Jesus, Matthew, Simon, and John enter the pool area. Jesus speaks compassionately to Jesse and tells him, "Let's go. Pick up your mat and walk." Jesse does so as Jesus and His disciples leave. The Pharisees approach Jesse and scold him for picking up his mat on the Sabbath.
51:10	⊕	Rufus and his wife enter the restaurant. While about to kill Rufus, Simon the Zealot sees his brother, Jesse, walk by. Jesse decides not to assassinate Rufus. The zealots flee the scene. Simon the Zealot and Jesse hug.

[32] Zechariah 14:16, "Then everyone who survives of all the nations that have come against Jerusalem shall go up year after year to worship the King, the LORD of hosts, and to keep the Feast of Booths."

[33] Zephaniah 3:17-19, "The LORD your God is in your midst, a mighty one who will save; He will rejoice over you with gladness; He will quiet you by His love; He will exult over you with loud singing. [18] I will gather those of you who mourn for the festival, so that you will no longer suffer reproach. [19] Behold, at that time I will deal with all your oppressors. And I will save the lame and gather the outcast, and I will change their shame into praise and renown in all the earth."

[34] Ecclesiastes 3:3, "a time to kill, and a time to heal; a time to break down, and a time to build up."

[35] Zephaniah 3:19, "Behold, at that time I will deal with all your oppressors. And I will save the lame and gather the outcast, and I will change their shame into praise and renown in all the earth."

| 55:01 | ➕ | Jesus, Simon, John, and Matthew leave Jerusalem. |

Very little of episode 4 is based on the Bible. However, there are five places where Old Testament prophecy is quoted word for word. Most of the episode is used for character development and to show how much the Romans were involved in policing the Jewish people. This episode shows the viewer the zealots' training. Once again, we are at risk because of extra-Biblical content being added to Scripture.

Episode 5 – "Spirit"

In this episode, Shmuel, Atticus, and Simon the Zealot pursue Jesus. John the Baptist visits Jesus and His disciples.

2:5 Plot Summary		
0:25	➕	Mary Magdalene gathers fruit. She prays the Jewish daily prayer but then continued with parts that were not Psalm 139.
2:47	➕	Members of the Sanhedrin[36] question Jesse about Jesus.
4:16	➕	Atticus questions Jesse, who says of his brother, Simon the Zealot, "He believes the man responsible (for his healing) has to be our Messiah."
6:22	➕	Simon the Zealot prays. He then practices martial arts. He hears howling and screaming and checks it out. He finds a demon-possessed man, Caleb. They talk.
10:17	➕	Simon, Andrew, Jesus, and another disciple are walking. John the Baptist jumps out from a bush and frightens them. They speak with John the Baptist.
11:29	👍	Mary Magdalene and Ramah read Psalm 7:1 and part of 7:2.[37]
13:00	➕	Matthew and Thomas chop vegetables and talk.
14:44	➕	Simon the Zealot spies on Mary Magdalene.

---

[36] The Sanhedrin was the highest council of the Jews. It was headed up by the High Priest and had religious, civil, and criminal jurisdiction.
[37] Psalm 7:1-2, "O LORD my God, in you do I take refuge; save me from all my pursuers and deliver me, ² lest like a lion they tear my soul apart, rending it in pieces, with none to deliver."

14:56	➕	John the Baptist and Jesus talk. John quotes Leviticus 20:21.[38] Jesus tries to talk John the Baptist out of speaking against Herod. Jesus says, "I'm always ready to do my Father's will, but that doesn't make it easy."[39]
20:44	➕	The scene alternates between Mary Magdalene and Ramah reading and Thomas and Matthew chopping vegetables.
22:15	➕	Mary Magdalene, Ramah, Thomas, and Matthew hear the demoniac (Caleb) scream. He then enters the camp. Mary Magdalene and Caleb talk. Caleb attacks Mary Magdalene, but Simon the Zealot jumps in and saves her. While Caleb and Simon the Zealot fight, Jesus enters the camp and commands the demon, "Out! Out of him!"[40] Jesus then speaks to Caleb compassionately.
28:25	➕	Shmuel and a member of the Sanhedrin meet. Shmuel wants to open another investigation into Jesus, but he is shut down.
30:19	➕ 👎	Jesus and Simon the Zealot speak about Jesse. Jesus confirms He is the Messiah.[41] Simon the Zealot promises allegiance to Jesus. Jesus throws Simon's dagger into the river. Jesus tells Simon the Zealot, "No one buys their way into our group with special skills."
33:25	➕	Atticus approaches the river and retrieves Simon the Zealot's dagger.
33:48	➕	Mary Magdalene walks toward Jericho, crying. She enters Jericho and heads to a bar.
36:02	➕	Jesus and John the Baptist talk. John leaves. Jesus cries softly. Jesus and Simon the Zealot return to camp.
38:13	➕	Shmuel meets with another member of the Sanhedrin. They discuss politics and how to reopen the case against Jesus.
41:57	➕	Mary Magdalene is in a bar in Jericho.

[38] Leviticus 20:21, "If a man takes his brother's wife, it is impurity. He has uncovered his brother's nakedness; they shall be childless."

[39] This line appears nowhere in Scripture.

[40] Jesus cast out demons 12 times in the gospels. The writers have taken some liberty as none of the instances match this one. This episode may be a summary of some of them.

[41] The only time in Scripture where Jesus answered the question, "Are you the Messiah?" was in front of Caiaphas, the High Priest, where Jesus replied, "I am."

| 42:33 | ➕ | The disciples are sitting around the campfire. Simon introduces Simon the Zealot to everyone when they realize that Mary Magdalene is missing. |
| 43:24 | 👍 ➕ | When Simon approaches, Jesus is preparing a sermon. Simon tells Jesus that Mary Magdalene is missing. Jesus asks Matthew to recite Psalm 139:8,[42] which Matthew does word for word. Jesus sends Simon and Matthew to find Mary Magdalene in Jerusalem. |

Once again, this episode contains very little Biblical content. Old Testament verses are recited four times, but the same verse is repeated one of those times. Jesus' exorcism of the demon appears nowhere in Scripture, but it is similar to other exorcisms. While nothing in this episode contradicts the Bible, most is not found in it. One would think that a "Christian" television show might have more Scripture in it.

⁓

Episode 6 – "Unlawful"

In this episode, Simon and Matthew search for Mary Magdalene, and the Pharisees challenge Jesus with breaking the Sabbath rules and blasphemy.

2:6 Plot Summary		
0:06	➕	The episode opens in Nob, Israel, in 1008 BC. Ahimelech, the High Priest, is preparing showbread with a young boy. David bursts in and asks for the showbread, which Ahimelech gives him.
4:42	➕	Simon wakes up in a barn in Jericho. Matthew is looking at maps. They talk.
8:30	👍 ➕	Mary, the mother of Jesus, and Ramah walk and talk about Mary Magdalene. Mary quotes Psalm 20:7[43] word for word.
11:21	➕	Mary Magdalene is in the tavern, drinking and gambling. She leaves the tavern, forgetting her winnings.

---

[42] Psalm 139:8, "If I ascend to heaven, you are there! If I make my bed in Sheol, you are there!"
[43] Psalm 20:7, "Some trust in chariots and some in horses, but we trust in the name of the LORD our God."

13:30	➕	Thomas is preparing a meal. He and Andrew discuss this meal using up the last of their resources. Simon the Zealot practices martial arts.
17:55	➕	Simon and Matthew enter the tavern. Matthew quotes Psalm 139:8.[44] They ask the patrons about Mary Magdalene. Simon and Matthew leave the tavern and come across Mary. However, Mary has relapsed and is ashamed to return to Jesus. She says, "I do have faith in Him, just not in me." Simon and Matthew encourage her to return.
22:49	➕	Shmuel and Yussif meet with another Sanhedrin member to garner support for their case against Jesus. They are shut down again, and the Sanhedrin member leaves. They decide to bring their case to Shammai, a rival Sanhedrin member.
26:43	➕	The disciples are in camp. Mary Magdalene, Simon, and Matthew return. The disciples talk about John the Baptist being imprisoned. Mary Magdalene approaches Jesus, ashamed. "You redeemed me, but I threw it all away."[45] Jesus replied, "That's not much of a redemption if it can be lost in a day, can it? I just want your heart, Mary. The Father just wants your heart. Did you think you'd never struggle or sin again? I forgive you. It's over."
31:06	➕	Thomas approaches Jesus and appraises Him of the low rations. Jesus suggests that they pray.
33:48	👍 ➕	Jesus and His disciples go to the synagogue. The rabbi reads from Deuteronomy 23:2-4[46] word for word. Jesus goes to heal a man with a withered hand. The Pharisee tells Him that it is not lawful to heal on the Sabbath. Jesus

[44] Psalm 139:8, "If I ascend to heaven, you are there! If I make my bed in Sheol, you are there!"
[45] How many of us feel that way at one time or another?
[46] Deuteronomy 23:2-4, "No one born of a forbidden union may enter the assembly of the LORD. Even to the tenth generation, none of his descendants may enter the assembly of the LORD. ³"No Ammonite or Moabite may enter the assembly of the LORD. Even to the tenth generation, none of them may enter the assembly of the LORD forever, ⁴ because they did not meet you with bread and with water on the way, when you came out of Egypt, and because they hired against you Balaam the son of Beor from Pethor of Mesopotamia, to curse you."

		loosely quotes Matthew 12:9-12.[47] They argue with the Pharisees and leave.
37:39	👍	While returning to camp, Simon picks some wheat on the Sabbath. He spits it out when someone reminds him that it is the Sabbath. Jesus tells the disciples, "You may." The disciples all start picking wheat. The Pharisees approach and yell at Jesus for allowing His disciples to pick grain on the Sabbath. Jesus responds by quoting Matthew 12:3-7.[48] Jesus then quotes Mark 2:27-28.[49] The Pharisees accuse Jesus of blasphemy. Jesus and the disciples return to camp.
40:24	⊕	The Pharisees plan to notify the Sanhedrin of Jesus' blasphemy.

The bulk of this episode is extra-Biblical. Even though four scenes include quotations from Scripture, most of which are accurate, those scenes are overrun with content that is not from the Bible. The six passages quoted include Psalm 20:7, Psalm 139:8, Deuteronomy 23:3-4, Matthew 12:9-12, Psalm 12:3-7, and Mark 2:27-28. Again, this episode could have been so much more Scriptural.

[47] Matthew 12:9-14, "He went on from there and entered their synagogue. [10] And a man was there with a withered hand. And they asked Him, "Is it lawful to heal on the Sabbath?"—so that they might accuse Him. [11] He said to them, "Which one of you who has a sheep, if it falls into a pit on the Sabbath, will not take hold of it and lift it out? [12] Of how much more value is a man than a sheep! So, it is lawful to do good on the Sabbath." [13] Then He said to the man, "Stretch out your hand." And the man stretched it out, and it was restored, healthy like the other. [14] But the Pharisees went out and conspired against Him, how to destroy Him."
[48] Matthew 12:3-7, "Have you not read what David did when he was hungry, and those who were with him: [4] how he entered the house of God and ate the bread of the Presence, which it was not lawful for him to eat nor for those who were with him, but only for the priests? [5] Or have you not read in the Law how on the Sabbath the priests in the temple profane the Sabbath and are guiltless? [6] I tell you, something greater than the temple is here. [7] And if you had known what this means, 'I desire mercy, and not sacrifice,' you would not have condemned the guiltless."
[49] Mark 2:27-28, "The Sabbath was made for man, not man for the Sabbath. [28] So the Son of Man is Lord even of the Sabbath."

Episode 7 – "Reckoning"

In this episode, Jesus is arrested by Roman soldiers. He is brought to Quintus, who questions and releases him. Throughout the entire episode, the disciples quarrel among themselves.

2:7 Plot Summary		
0:25	⊕	Atticus meets Quintus. They talk.
3:01	⊕	Simon, Andrew, James, and John argue on the shore of the Sea of Galilee.
4:41	⊕	Jesus and some disciples are planning the Sermon on the Mount. Jesus tells them, "What makes this sermon so important is each person who will be there." "This (sermon) will define our whole ministry."[50]
6:24	⊕	Shmuel meets with another Pharisee. They argue about Jesus.
9:00	⊕	Simon and Andrew fish and argue.
10:00	⊕	Shmuel attempts to meet with Quintus. He is denied.
11:39	⊕	Atticus, Gaius, and other Roman soldiers head to find Jesus.
14:15	⊕	Simon and Andrew are fishing. They talk of Mary Magdalene's disappearance. They see Roman soldiers on the shore.
17:20	⊕	Jesus and some disciples plan the Sermon on the Mount. The soldiers arrive and take Jesus in for questioning.
20:50	⊕	In the camp, the disciples argue about what to do about Jesus' arrest.
22:00	⊕	Shmuel and Yussif look for the Ethiopian woman (Tamar).
23:17	⊕	The disciples are at camp still arguing about Jesus' arrest.
24:45	⊕	Philip and Andrew arrive in the city of Jotapata, where they come across Tamar and the formerly lame man who was lowered through the roof of Zebedee's house.
27:22	⊕	Jesus before Quintus. Quintus does not know what to make of Jesus and sets Him free.
33:07	⊕	Shmuel and Yussif are in Jotapata. They meet with the local Pharisees and talk about Jesus.

[50] We can place these two statements into the file marked "things Jesus never said."

34:00	➕	Andrew, Philip, Tamar, and the former lame man talk about Jesus. A Pharisee named Yussif (a pupil of Nicodemus) arrives and warns them about Shmuel.
36:15	➕	The disciples are at camp. Jesus returns and begins to teach them the Lord's prayer,[51] but the scene fades out after two lines.
39:30	➕ 👎	Jesus wakes Matthew in the middle of the night, needing help organizing His sermon.[52]

Except for the last few minutes, the entire episode has no Scripture references. And that Scripture reference is cut short. Additionally, there is no evidence that the disciples assisted Jesus with writing the Sermon on the Mount. The author's primary question at almost two seasons into the show is, "how can you write a television show about Jesus that contains almost no lines from Scripture?" While *The Chosen* is supposedly about Jesus Christ, there has been so little truth that the show might be better considered historical fiction.

～

Episode 8 – "Beyond Mountains"

In this episode, Jesus and Matthew continue to work on the Sermon on the Mount while the disciples continue to argue amongst themselves. Everyone prepares for the Sermon on the Mount. A member of the Sanhedrin takes up Shmuel's case. We meet Judas Iscariot.

2:8 Plot Summary		
0:29	➕	An old man is debating selling his land to two men who wish to "build tombs" in the mountains.
5:02	➕	The disciples are sawing and chopping wood. They pray their daily prayer before eating breakfast. They then argue about preparation for the Sermon on the Mount.

---

[51] Matthew 6:9-10, "Our Father in heaven, hallowed be your name. [10] Your kingdom come; your will be done…"

[52] Matthew did not help Jesus write the Sermon on the Mount. This is completely unbiblical.

7:21	👍	Ramah and Mary Magdalene study. Ramah reads Psalm 139:15-16[53] word-for-word with the ESV.
9:16	⊕	Tamar and Mary, the mother of Jesus, talk. Thomas joins them. The disciples argue.
11:07	⊕	In the tavern, the two men from the first scene talk of deceiving the old man.
14:12	⊕	Nathaniel, James, and Thaddeus scout out a location for the Sermon on the Mount.
15:43	⊕	Shmuel and Yussif meet with Shammai, who agrees to take their case and use it for political reasons.
19:07	👎 ⊕	Jesus and Matthew work on the sermon and discuss the disciples' arguments. Jesus asks Matthew which parts to cut. Jesus tells him, "It's a manifesto, Matthew. I'm not here to be sentimental and soothing. I'm here to start a revolution…I want my followers to be a people who hold back the evil over the world… I want my followers to renew the world and be part of its redemption… these things will make sense to some but not to others."[54]
25:17	⊕	Nathaniel, James, and Thaddeus meet a landowner in a tavern to discuss using his land for the sermon. The men from the opening scene convince him to do so.
28:00	👎 ⊕	Montage: The disciples hand out invitations to the sermon, others build a stage for the sermon,[55] Matthew and Jesus work on the sermon, and Gaius gives Quintus an invitation.
29:47	⊕	The disciples return to camp to find Jesus and Matthew still gone.

---

[53] Psalm 139:15-16, "My frame was not hidden from you, when I was being made in secret, intricately woven in the depths of the earth. ¹⁶ Your eyes saw my unformed substance; in your book were written, every one of them, the days that were formed for me."

[54] In the entire conversation with Matthew, nothing Jesus said is Biblical.

[55] There is no indication that Jesus rehearsed for the Sermon on the Mount, or that the disciples passed out invitations or built a stage. The Son of God would not have needed to rehearse a sermon. The fact that He does so emphasizes His humanity over His divinity, which fits in well with the Mormon doctrine of Christ being only human during His time on earth. The sub-plot that Jesus' disciples handed out invitations and built Him a stage contradicts Scripture. Matthew 5:1 says that Jesus *sat down* with His disciples, indicating that a stage was not used to deliver the Sermon on the Mount.

30:44	➕ 👎	Matthew and Jesus are working on the Sermon on the Mount. Jesus dictates the beatitudes word-for-word from Matthew 5:3-12a[56] from the ESV.
34:23	Ⓜ	People begin arriving for the Sermon on the Mount. The two businessmen, Eden, Simon's wife, and Gaius, Atticus, and Roman soldiers also arrive. Jesus, talking to His mother, Mary, says, "In case I mess up in front of such a big crowd." Speaking of the sermon, He says, "It's pretty good actually." One of the two men from the opening scene introduces himself as Judas. Jesus steps out on stage and looks out at thousands of people.

The season two finale contains the show's most significant Scripture quotation thus far. Jesus quotes the Beatitudes word-for-word out of the ESV. Additionally, Ramah reads Psalm 139:15-16 out loud. However, outside of those two passages, very little of the balance of the episode is Scriptural. Mormon theology enters the scene in the conversation between Jesus and his mother, Mary. In that conversation, Jesus says, "In case I mess up in front of such a big crowd." While Jesus was fully man, he was also fully God. He would not mess up His words in a sermon. The problem lies in the Mormon belief that Jesus was a man who became a god. A mere man could make mistakes in a sermon. God would not. In adding this line to what Jesus said, the writers emphasize Jesus' humanity while downplaying His divinity. It is a fundamental Christian concept that Jesus was fully God and fully man. That is a non-negotiable, and *The Chosen* doesn't promote that.

---

[56] Matthew 5:3-12a, "Blessed are the poor in spirit, for theirs is the kingdom of heaven. [4]Blessed are those who mourn, for they shall be comforted. [5]Blessed are the meek, for they shall inherit the earth. [6]Blessed are those who hunger and thirst for righteousness, for they shall be satisfied. [7]Blessed are the merciful, for they shall receive mercy. [8]Blessed are the pure in heart, for they shall see God. [9]Blessed are the peacemakers, for they shall be called sons of God. [10]Blessed are those who are persecuted for righteousness' sake, for theirs is the kingdom of heaven. [11]Blessed are you when others revile you and persecute you and utter all kinds of evil against you falsely on my account. [12]Rejoice and be glad, for your reward is great in heaven." The problem is that the writers left off the last part of verse 12, "for so they persecuted the prophets who were before you."

Season 2 Assessment

Season 2, like season 1, is extremely well made. The characters have depth, the sets are well-done, and the dialogue is easy to understand. Season 2 moved at the right pace, packing only a little material into the allotted time and not dragging out the content. Some excellent scenes present Scripture, but sadly, most content does not. *The Chosen* develops character backstories using content not found in the New Testament. The writers claim to do so to present the gospels in a human and relatable way. However, whatever the reason, they are still adding to Scripture, which is forbidden in Revelation 22:18-19.[57] This is one of the most problematic issues with the Mormon church – they have added to Scripture with their three books, *The Book of Mormon*, *The Pearl of Great Price*, and *Doctrines and Covenants*. The Bible tells us these are not Scripture, yet the Mormon church believes they are. Bible-believing Christians cannot accept those in the Church of Jesus Christ of Latter-Day Saints as Christians, for they are not.

---

[57] Revelation 22:18-19, "I warn everyone who hears the words of the prophecy of this book: if anyone adds to them, God will add to him the plagues described in this book, [19] and if anyone takes away from the words of the book of this prophecy, God will take away his share in the tree of life and in the holy city, which are described in this book."

8

Season 3

~

THE THIRD SEASON OF *THE Chosen* continues the story of Jesus and His disciples as they cope with the stress of a growing ministry. We are introduced to some new characters: Jairus, Judas, and Joanna. Often, throughout season 3, the disciples argue among themselves. Some face personal battles that ultimately bring them closer to Jesus. The Pharisees and Roman authorities become increasingly aware of Jesus and the threat that He has become to their way of life. As with the previous two seasons, this one is full of miracles and teachings from Jesus.

Disclaimer
Please be advised that the content of this chapter will contain spoilers. If you don't want the plot revealed to you, do not read further. Instead of reading the chapter before watching each episode, read the chapter as you watch the episode. That will allow you to critique each episode from a Biblical standpoint. For your convenience, most Bible references are included in the

footnotes. In this chapter, the plot summaries will use different symbols to assist the reader in understanding the source for each scene.

- ➕   means that the scene is not found in Scripture but doesn't specifically conflict with it.
- 👍   means that the scene is Scriptural or is grounded in Scripture.
- 👎   means that the scene runs contrary to Scripture.
- Ⓜ   means that the scene presents Mormon theology.

Episode 1 – "Homecoming"

In this episode, Jesus and the disciples prepare for and deliver the Sermon on the Mount.

3:1 Plot Summary		
0:25	➕	AD 24 – A Roman soldier knocks on the door of Matthew's father's house. He begins to arrest him when Matthew intervenes. Matthew and his parents argue. His mother quotes Proverbs 3:5.[1] Matthew's father disowns him.
3:50	👍	Jesus preaches the Sermon on the Mount. He quotes: (all from Matthew and in this order) 5:21-22a,[2] 5:23-24,[3]

---

[1] Proverbs 3:5, "Trust in the LORD with all your heart, and do not lean on your own understanding."

[2] Matthew 5:21-24, "You have heard that it was said to those of old, 'You shall not murder; and whoever murders will be liable to judgment.' [22] But I say to you that everyone who is angry with his brother will be liable to judgment."

[3] Matthew 5:23-24, "So if you are offering your gift at the altar and there remember that your brother has something against you, [24] leave your gift there before the altar and go. First be reconciled to your brother and then come and offer your gift."

		6:25-27,[4] 6:31-33[5], 7:12,[6] 7:1,[7] 5:38-40,[8] 5:43-45a,[9] 6:28b,[10] 7:3,[11] 6:9[12] 5:41,[13] 6:10-11,[14] 5:42,[15] 6:12-13,[16] 6:19-21,[17] 7:26-27,[18] 7:24-25.[19]
10:21	✚	Yussif overhears people talking about the Sermon on the Mount; Judas tells his friend that he is going with Jesus. Gaius and Atticus talk. Judas tells Jesus he wants to follow him. The disciples clap for Jesus. Jesus prays the

---

[4] Matthew 6:25-27, "Therefore I tell you, do not be anxious about your life, what you will eat or what you will drink, nor about your body, what you will put on. Is not life more than food, and the body more than clothing? [26] Look at the birds of the air: they neither sow nor reap nor gather into barns, and yet your heavenly Father feeds them. Are you not of more value than they? [27] And which of you by being anxious can add a single hour to his span of life?"

[5] Matthew 6:31-33, "Therefore do not be anxious, saying, 'What shall we eat?' or 'What shall we drink?' or 'What shall we wear?' [32] For the Gentiles seek after all these things, and your heavenly Father knows that you need them all. [33] But seek first the kingdom of God and His righteousness, and all these things will be added to you."

[6] Matthew 7:12, "So whatever you wish that others would do to you, do also to them, for this is the Law and the Prophets."

[7] Matthew 7:1, "Judge not, that you be not judged."

[8] Matthew 5:38-40, "You have heard that it was said, 'An eye for an eye and a tooth for a tooth.' [39] But I say to you, Do not resist the one who is evil. But if anyone slaps you on the right cheek, turn to him the other also. [40] And if anyone would sue you and take your tunic, let him have your cloak as well."

[9] Matthew 5:43-45a, "You have heard that it was said, 'You shall love your neighbor and hate your enemy.' [44] But I say to you, 'Love your enemies and pray for those who persecute you, [45] so that you may be sons of your Father who is in heaven.'"

[10] Matthew 6:28b, "Consider the lilies of the field, how they grow: they neither toil nor spin."

[11] Matthew 7:3, "Why do you see the speck that is in your brother's eye, but do not notice the log that is in your own eye?"

[12] Matthew 6:9, "Pray then like this: "Our Father in heaven, hallowed be your name."

[13] Matthew 5:41, "And if anyone forces you to go one mile, go with him two miles."

[14] Matthew 6:10-11, "Your kingdom come, your will be done, on earth as it is in heaven. [11] Give us this day our daily bread."

[15] Matthew 5:42, "Give to the one who begs from you, and do not refuse the one who would borrow from you."

[16] Matthew 6:12-13, "and forgive us our debts, as we also have forgiven our debtors. [13] And lead us not into temptation but deliver us from evil."

[17] Matthew 6:19-21, "Do not lay up for yourselves treasures on earth, where moth and rust destroy and where thieves break in and steal, [20] but lay up for yourselves treasures in heaven, where neither moth nor rust destroys and where thieves do not break in and steal. [21] For where your treasure is, there your heart will be also."

[18] Matthew 7:26-27, "And everyone who hears these words of mine and does not do them will be like a foolish man who built his house on the sand. [27] And the rain fell, and the floods came, and the winds blew and beat against that house, and it fell, and great was the fall of it."

[19] Matthew 7:24-25, "Everyone then who hears these words of mine and does them will be like a wise man who built his house on the rock. [25] And the rain fell, and the floods came, and the winds blew and beat on that house, but it did not fall, because it had been founded on the rock."

		Aaronic blessing (Numbers 6:23-26).[20] Disciples disburse, each to their own home.
19:08	➕	Joanna is the wife of one of Herod's advisors. In this scene, she meets Mary Magdalene, Tamar, and Ramah. Joanna tells Jesus and Andrew about the imprisoned John the Baptist. Andrew leaves with Joanna, hoping to visit John.
26:41	➕	Yussif meets Jairus.
31:03	➕	Simon and Eden return home. Nathaniel unexpectedly drops by looking for a place to stay, and Simon the Zealot also arrives looking for accommodations.
34:00	➕	James and John walk home. Thomas joins them.
36:50	➕	Tamar, Ramah, and Mary Magdalene arrive at Mary's home. They discuss Joanna.
40:27	👍 ➕	Joanna and Andrew visit John the Baptist. John quotes Isaiah 61:1c.[21] Andrew quotes Matthew 6:33.[22] John the Baptist tells Andrew to obey Jesus.
45:46	➕	The next morning, Judas gets ready for his day and leaves home.
46:49	➕	Judas visits his sister, Dvorah.
51:21	➕	Yussif revisits Jairus. He leaves an unsealed scroll with Jairus.
52:17	➕	Andrew visits Mary Magdalene and apologizes to her.
55:04	➕	Matthew knocks on his parents' door. His father greets him with a single word, "son."

Episode 1 contains more Scripture than any of the previous episodes. It should, for it includes the Sermon on the Mount. While the show quotes the Sermon on the Mount from Matthew 5-7 word for word, it jumps around between verses. This makes sense since the scene is a montage. Some of the circumstances surrounding the sermon were silly. It is not likely that Jesus

---

[20] Numbers 6:24-26, "The LORD bless you and keep you; [25] the LORD make His face to shine upon you and be gracious to you; [26] the LORD lift up his countenance upon you and give you peace."

[21] Isaiah 61:1, "The Spirit of the Lord GOD is upon me, because the LORD has anointed me to bring good news to the poor; He has sent me to bind up the brokenhearted, to proclaim liberty to the captives, and the opening of the prison to those who are bound."

[22] Matthew 6:33, "But seek first the kingdom of God and His righteousness, and all these things will be added to you."

stood on a stage built by his disciples or that His disciples clapped for Him after the sermon. If you look at this from a Biblical point of view, these are issues. However, these are not issues if you consider the show historical fiction. The scene where Andrew and Joanna visit John the Baptist contains two word-for-word Scripture quotations. Once again, in this episode, most of the plot and action are not Biblical.

Episode 2 – "Two by Two"
In this episode, squatters establish a tent city outside Capernaum. Jesus sends his disciples to share the gospel.

3:2 Plot Summary		
0:23	➊	Atticus and Gaius stand on the wall of Capernaum, looking at a shanty town that has sprung up outside of the city wall.
2:02	➊	People in the tent city wash clothes and prepare food. Simon the Zealot and Nathaniel walk through the tents.
5:38	👍	Matthew is at his parents' house. He quotes Matthew 5:23-24.[23] Matthew and his parents make up.
13:22	➊	Atticus and Gaius appear before Quintus. They discuss the squatters in Capernaum.
18:31	Ⓜ	John, James, and Thomas talk. Thomas announces that he wants to marry Ramah. He says, "I've searched my heart and know it's right. Jesus will make it work."[24]
20:34	➊	Eden and Simon are talking while she kneads some dough.
22:07	➊	Gaius and Julius (another soldier) walk through the tent city.

[23] Matthew 5:23-24, "So if you are offering your gift at the altar and there remember that your brother has something against you, [24] leave your gift there before the altar and go. First be reconciled to your brother and then come and offer your gift."
[24] There are two significant issues with these statements. Firstly, Scripture is abundantly clear that we are not to trust our hearts. Jeremiah 17:9 says, "The heart is deceitful above all things, and desperately sick; who can understand it?" Genesis 6:5, "The LORD saw that the wickedness of man was great in the earth, and that *every intention of the thoughts of his heart was only evil continually.*" (Italics added.) By having Thomas say this line, the show promotes the unbiblical idea of trusting one's heart. Secondly, by saying that "Jesus will make it work," the show is making it seem that Jesus will do whatever our hearts desire. This is false.

23:28	➕	Simon the Zealot and Atticus talk.
28:39	➕	Simon and Eden sit in front of a fire and talk.
31:10	👎	Mary Magdalene, Tamar, and Ramah discuss moving to Matthew's old house. Tamar says, "Jews, Gentiles – love is love!"[25]
35:05	Ⓜ	Jesus meets with His disciples at Simon's house. He reveals His plans of sending the disciples out two by two. He tells them, "But I have chosen you twelve as my apostles."[26] Jesus loosely quotes Matthew 10:6-14.[27] He then quotes Matthew 10:28a.[28] The disciples choose Judas to be in charge of their finances. Thomas then says to Jesus, "Thank you for believing in me," to which Jesus replied, "I do."[29]
50:25	➕	Thomas and Ramah discuss his *mission*[30] and how to ask for her father's permission to marry.
53:09	👎	Little James[31] and Jesus discuss how Little James is supposed to heal people when he needs to be healed himself. He asks Jesus to heal him and Jesus refuses.[32]

---

[25] This is a very dangerous statement to make because it is a common refrain in the LGBTQ+ community. By having Tamar say this, the producers to be supporting that sinful lifestyle.

[26] Judas was not considered an apostle because he did not see the resurrected Jesus.

[27] Matthew 10:6-8, "But go rather to the lost sheep of the house of Israel. 7 And proclaim as you go, saying, 'The kingdom of heaven is at hand. 8 Heal the sick, raise the dead, cleanse lepers, cast out demons. You received without paying; give without pay. 9 Acquire no gold or silver or copper for your belts, 10 no bag for your journey, or two tunics or sandals or a staff, for the laborer deserves his food. 11 And whatever town or village you enter, find out who is worthy in it and stay there until you depart. 12 As you enter the house, greet it. 13 And if the house is worthy, let your peace come upon it, but if it is not worthy, let your peace return to you. 14 And if anyone will not receive you or listen to your words, shake off the dust from your feet when you leave that house or town."

[28] Matthew 10:28a, "And do not fear those who kill the body but cannot kill the soul."

[29] This statement would be acceptable if Jesus were merely a man. (Therefore, it is permissible in Mormon circles.) However, since Jesus is more than a man, He would not believe in Simon. Simon would believe in Him.

[30] It is concerning that the producers are calling the sending out of the disciples a *mission*, as this is the term that Mormon missionaries use for their two years of service. By using this term, the show may be inadvertently promoting Mormon phrases to subtly convince believers that Mormon *missions* and the *mission* of the disciples are the same thing when, in fact, they are not. This appears to be another manner in which the show is convincing Christians that Mormons are fellow believers.

[31] Little James is the disciple/apostle known as James, son of Alphaeus.

[32] Nowhere in Scripture does Jesus ever deny healing anyone that came to him to be healed. This is heresy to state that Jesus refused.

59:43	👎 ➕	Matthew returns to his old house. He runs into Gaius, and they talk. The other disciples show up and discuss their *mission*. The disciples recite Psalm 3[33] almost word-for-word.

Of the episodes thus far, season 3, episode 2 had the worst theology thus far. In the fifth scene, Thomas says, "I've searched my heart and know it's right. Jesus will make it work." This is very errant theology, as Jeremiah 17:9[34] instructs us that our hearts are evil. We should not trust our hearts at any time because we will likely be deceived. The second part of Thomas' statement, "Jesus will make it work," is also horrible theology because it makes Jesus seem a bit like He is at the bidding of Thomas' heart.

In the penultimate scene, Jesus refused to heal Little James when he came to Jesus to be healed. Nowhere in Scripture does Jesus ever refuse to heal someone that came to Him for healing. Matthew 4:23[35] is clear that Jesus healed every person who came to Him. The producers of The Chosen have taken liberties that were not theirs to take.

In the tenth scene, Tamar says, "Jew, Gentile – love is love." This is dangerous in today's culture because that is one of the slogans of LGBTQ+ supporters. By including it in a show about Jesus, it is implying that Jesus supports the LGBTQ+ lifestyle when He, indeed, does not. In the next scene, Thomas says to Jesus, "Thank you for believing in me," Jesus replies, "I do." Jesus, being fully God and fully man, would know better than to believe in Thomas. After all, as we just discussed, Thomas' heart, like ours, is deceitful above all things. A divine Jesus would never believe in Thomas. However, if Jesus were a man who would eventually become a god, He would say that. Jesus did not say it because He was is, and always will be, fully God and fully man. The episode does end on a high note. The disciples recite almost all of

---

[33] Psalm 3, "O LORD, how many are my foes! Many are rising against me; ² many are saying of my soul, "There is no salvation for him in God." *Selah* ³ But you, O LORD, are a shield about me, my glory, and the lifter of my head. ⁴ I cried aloud to the LORD, and he answered me from His holy hill. *Selah* ⁵ I lay down and slept; I woke again, for the LORD sustained me. ⁶ I will not be afraid of many thousands of people who have set themselves against me all around. ⁷ Arise, O LORD! Save me, O my God! For you strike all my enemies on the cheek; you break the teeth of the wicked. ⁸ Salvation belongs to the LORD; your blessing be on your people!"

[34] Jeremiah 17:9, "The heart is deceitful above all things, and desperately sick; who can understand it?"

[35] Matthew 4:23, "And he went throughout all Galilee, teaching in their synagogues and proclaiming the gospel of the kingdom and healing *every* disease and *every* affliction among the people." (Italics added.)

Psalm 3 in its entirety. Simon begins to say it, and the other disciples join in. It was a good way to end a theologically terrible episode.

Episode 3 – "Physician, Heal Yourself"

In this episode, Jesus returns to Nazareth, His childhood home, to celebrate the Jewish New Year. While there, He must address the rumors surrounding His ministry.[36]

3:3 Plot Summary		
0:24	➕	Lazarus, Jesus, Mary, and Martha are small children playing with their mothers.
2:40	➕	Jesus visits His mother. He prays the daily prayer before they share a meal. His brothers are not home. In the conversations with Mary, Jesus asks a lot of questions of her.[37]
10:48	➕	Jesus goes to the bedroom to rest. He opens a box with a harness in it.
13:37	➕	The next morning, in a field, people are singing, dancing, and playing. Lazarus, Mary, and Martha arrive and talk to Jesus. Jesus and Lazarus play a game with the other men. Jesus loses.
24:02	Ⓜ	Evening at the synagogue. The rabbi prays the daily prayer.[38] Jesus reads from Luke 4:18-19 and 21.[39] Jesus and Rabbi Benjamin argue. When the Pharisees invoke

---

[36] In the plot summary on BYUTV, which airs *The Chosen* for free, producers say "the rumors that surround His *mission* and ministry," once again promoting the distinctly Mormon concept of a *mission*.

[37] This emphasizes Jesus' human nature over His divine nature. Because of His divine nature, Jesus would know the answers to these questions. However, if He were only a man, He would not. Again, Mormon theology is showing.

[38] See Appendix A for more on daily prayers.

[39] Luke 4:18-19, 21, "The Spirit of the Lord is upon me, because He has anointed me to proclaim good news to the poor. He has sent me to proclaim liberty to the captives and recovering of sight to the blind, to set at liberty those who are oppressed, [19] to proclaim the year of the Lord's favor. And He began to say to them, "Today this Scripture has been fulfilled in your hearing."

		the law of Moses, Jesus says to them, "I am the law of Moses."[40] The people bring Jesus to a cliff to kill Him. Jesus tells them, "This isn't going to happen today," and walks away.[41]
38:25	➕	Jesus walks to Joseph's (His father) tomb.
39:40	➕	Flashback to Jesus learning to read Isaiah 61:1.[42] Joseph teaches Jesus how to hammer a nail. Joseph gives Jesus a bit and bridle that has been passed down through the family for generations.
46:15	➕	Jesus at Joseph's tomb again. His mother and Lazarus arrive. They talk about what Jesus said in the temple.

Of the eight scenes in episode 3, only two contained Scripture: the synagogue scene and the scene where a young Jesus learns to read. The synagogue scene was particularly well done, as it stayed true to Luke 4:18-30. However, the writers still took liberty and had Jesus say things that were not Scriptural. The most significant offense takes place at 35:17, when Jesus says, "I am the law of Moses." This statement is taken directly from *The Book of Mormon*. It is not found in the Bible at all. When confronted with this problem, Dallas Jenkins doubled down and refused to credit *The Book of Mormon* for the line, instead choosing to use social media to promote it. In the scene where Jesus is learning to read, only two lines of Isaiah 61:1 are said. The rest of the episode, again, is sadly unbiblical. The disturbing thing about Jesus' ministry on the show is how the writers and producers continue referring to it as a *mission*. This is a distinctly Mormon phrase that refers to young Mormon missionaries' two years of service. By calling Jesus' work a *mission*, they are making it appear as though Jesus was a practicing Mormon.

---

[40] This statement is particularly problematic. It is found nowhere in Scripture. In addition to adding words to what Jesus said, the phrase, "I am the law," comes from 3 Nephi 15:9 in the *Book of Mormon*. The verse reads, "Behold, *I am the law*, and the light. Look unto me, and endure to the end, and ye shall live; for unto him that endureth to the end will I give eternal life." (Italics added.) (This verse is even more of an issue because it endorses salvation by works.)

[41] This entire scene stays true to Luke 4:22-30.

[42] Isaiah 61:1, "The Spirit of the Lord GOD is upon me, because the LORD has anointed me to bring good news to the poor; he has sent me to bind up the brokenhearted, to proclaim liberty to the captives, and the opening of the prison to those who are bound."

Dallas Jenkins
October 17, 2022 · 🌐

"I am the law of Moses."

#ChosenSeason3trailer

👍❤️ 7.4K   1.2K comments 171 shares

👍 Like   💬 Comment   ↪ Share

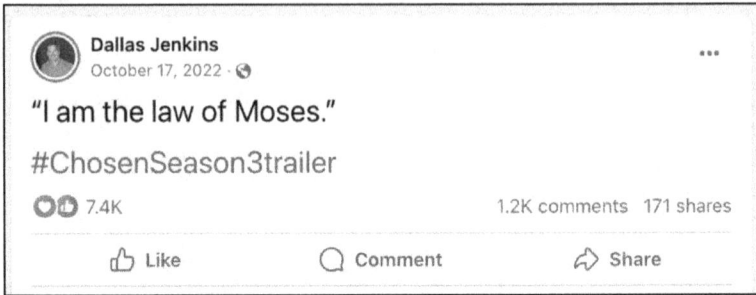

Episode 4 – "Clean Part 1"

In this episode, the disciples return from their work around Israel. Capernaum's water supply has become contaminated. Simon and Eden argue. Jairus' daughter becomes ill, and we meet Veronica, a woman with a bleeding disorder.

3:4 Plot Summary		
0:21	➕	Montage of the disciples preaching, teaching, healing, and casting out demons. They teach the Lord's prayer[43] word-for-word.
9:13	👎 ➕	Zebedee, James, and John are in the synagogue. Zebedee refers to James and John's *missions*. The rabbi reads from Leviticus 15:7-11[44] word-for-word.
10:37	➕	Capernaum's cistern is contaminated. Yussif and the soldiers argue.
12:12	➕	Jairus and Yussif discuss Jesus as well as Shmuel's request for more information on Jesus.

---

[43] Matthew 6:9-13, "Our Father in heaven, hallowed be your name. [10] Your kingdom come, your will be done, on earth as it is in heaven. [11] Give us this day our daily bread, [12] and forgive us our debts, as we also have forgiven our debtors. [13] And lead us not into temptation but deliver us from evil."

[44] Leviticus 15:7-11, "And whoever touches the body of the one with the discharge shall wash his clothes and bathe himself in water and be unclean until the evening. [8] And if the one with the discharge spits on someone who is clean, then he shall wash his clothes and bathe himself in water and be unclean until the evening. [9] And any saddle on which the one with the discharge rides shall be unclean. [10] And whoever touches anything that was under him shall be unclean until the evening. And whoever carries such things shall wash his clothes and bathe himself in water and be unclean until the evening."

17:43	⊕	Women travel out of town to collect water.
18:23	⊕	Simon returns home. He talks with Eden.
21:34	⊕	Eden meets a stranger (Veronica) who takes her to a secret spring outside Capernaum.
22:50	⊕	Jairus arrives home. His daughter has terrible stomach pain.
24:54	⊕	Eden and Veronica arrive at the spring. All of Veronica's clothes are blood-stained.
26:15	⊕	Tamar and Mary Magdalene arrive at Matthew's old house. Zebedee arrives and asks them to critique his oil. Tamar and Mary leave to meet with Judas.
31:39	⊕	The disciples gather at Simon's house to discuss their work.
35:56	⊕	Zebedee sells his boat.[45]
36:55	⊕	Veronica and Eden wash clothes together.
39:50	⊕	Jairus and Yussif speak about Jairus' daughter.
41:09	⊕	The Sanhedrin meets to discuss false prophets.
43:55	⊕	Veronica is declared unclean by a man in Capernaum.
45:18	⊕	Eden and Simon talk. Jesus arrives with the disciples. A crowd gathers outside. Simon goes for a walk.
46:48	⊕	Simon runs into Gaius. They discuss the water problem. Gaius pulls out a flask and takes a drink. He offers some to Simon, who refuses. They talk.
54:41	⊕	Jairus' wife checks on their daughter. She screams as the episode ends.

Episode 4 is a set-up for episode 5. It provides the back story for the woman with the bleeding disorder and Jairus' daughter. Only one part of Scripture is contained in the episode, Leviticus 15:7-11, which a rabbi reads. The problem is that people are talking over it, so it is sometimes difficult to understand. Almost the entire episode is extra-Biblical, to the point that this episode has nearly nothing to do with the Bible.

---

[45] This is neither Scriptural nor likely. Nowhere in Scripture does Zebedee sell the family's boat, their only means of income. Typically, in the time of Christ, families stayed in same occupation for generations. According to John 21:1-3, after Jesus' crucifixion, Peter, James, and John, among others, went fishing on a boat. Since James and John were business partners with Peter and Andrew, the boat likely belonged to the four of them. Therefore, it is highly unlikely that Zebedee sold the boat.

⌒﹏

Episode 5 – "Clean Part 2"

In this episode, Simon and Gaius work together to repair Capernaum's cistern. Jairus searches for Jesus so that his daughter may be healed. Jesus heals the woman (Veronica) with the bleeding disorder.

3:5 Plot Summary		
0:28	➕	Two weeks before this episode, Eden visits the doctor. She is pregnant but loses the baby.
3:36	➕	Jairus' daughter is at the doctor with a weak heart. The doctor tells Jairus to make funeral arrangements. Jairus leaves to find Jesus.
5:05	➕	Simon and Eden barely speak to each other.
6:25	➕	Zebedee, James, and John are talking. Zebedee announces that he has sold the boat and is purchasing an olive grove.
10:14	➕	Nathaniel and Thaddeus carry water. They come across fresh blood on the ground and follow its trail. This leads them to Veronica's camp, where they agree to take her to find Jesus.
15:10	➕	Judas, Zebedee, Tamar, and Mary Magdalene look at the olive grove.
16:44	➕	Simon and Gaius work on the cistern. They talk.
20:24	➕	Yussif finds Jairus in his office, looking frantically for a scroll. They discuss Jesus healing Jairus' daughter. They go to Andrew's house to see Jesus but are sent to Simon's.
22:42	➕	Jesus and a few disciples meet at Simon's house. Jesus prays the daily prayer. They talk about fasting. Jesus loosely quotes Luke 5:33-38[46] as part of the conversation.

---

[46] Luke 5:33-38, "And they said to Him, "The disciples of John fast often and offer prayers, and so do the disciples of the Pharisees, but yours eat and drink." [34] And Jesus said to them, "Can you make wedding guests fast while the bridegroom is with them? [35] The days will come when the bridegroom is taken away from them, and then they will fast in those days." [36] He also told them a parable: "No one tears a piece from a new garment and puts it on an old

		Jesus then says, "The ways of the kingdom I am bringing into this world will not fit into old containers or frameworks."[47]
26:30	➕	Jairus and Yussif run to Simon's house. They burst in and talk with Jesus. Jesus replies with Matthew 9:18b.[48] They head to Jairus' house.
29:15	➕	Simon and Gaius are still working on the cistern. They follow the crowd to Jairus' house. Along the way, a large crowd gathers around Jesus. Veronica slips through the crowd and touches the tassel of Jesus' garment. Jesus stops everyone and asks, "Who touched me?" Jesus speaks to her compassionately, but much of what he says is not Scriptural. They continue to Jairus' house but hear mourners coming from his house.
43:01	👍	In Jairus' daughter's bedroom, Jesus lifts the veil off the girl and prays. She comes to life. Jesus then instructs everyone not to talk about this. Jairus says, "Whatever you command, we will do."
46:54	➕	Veronica cuts off the extra clothing which has been tied to her to catch the blood. She throws it into the fire.
47:49	➕	Veronica is on the beach. She purifies herself by jumping into the water.
48:45	➕	A Pharisee questions Jesus about the healing of Jairus' daughter and Veronica. Jesus and the disciples also go to the beach and play in the water.

Episode 5 of season 3 stays pretty accurate to Mark 5:21-43. A few things are not Biblical: the contaminated cistern, Eden's miscarriage, the sale of Zebedee's boat, and the subsequent purchase of the olive grove. Most of what Jesus says to Veronica (the woman with the bleeding disorder) is not Biblical.

---

garment. If he does, he will tear the new, and the piece from the new will not match the old. [37] And no one puts new wine into old wineskins. If he does, the new wine will burst the skins and it will be spilled, and the skins will be destroyed. [38] But new wine must be put into fresh wineskins."

[47] Jesus' statement fits in with what He has been saying; however, this statement is not Scriptural. Once again, the writers are putting words into Jesus' mouth.

[48] Matthew 9:18, "While he was saying these things to them, behold, a ruler came in and knelt before him, saying, "My daughter has just died, but come and lay your hand on her, and she will live."

However, the plot line of Mark 5 shows through, specifically in the healing of Veronica and Jairus' daughter. It's more Biblical than most of the previous episodes.

~

Episode 6 – "Intensity in Tent City"

In this episode, some of the disciples receive word that their preaching may have caused problems. Jesus returns to Capernaum and begins healing people. Two of John the Baptist's disciples question Jesus.

3:6 Plot Summary		
0:23	✚	Pontius Pilate's wife is having nightmares. She and Pilate talk.
4:19	✚	Jesus' disciples are sharpening their knives, talking about protecting Jesus.
9:21	✚	Quintus and Gaius talk. Quintus instructs Gaius to get rid of the tent city.
12:26	✚	A young man breaks into where the disciples are sleeping. He tells them that their preaching in the Decapolis has caused problems there. They need to return to the Decapolis. They are told that their *mission* cannot be over.[49]
16:09	✚	Mary Magdalene and Tamar talk. They leave and head to a vineyard.
25:23	✚	Atticus meets with Pilate. They talk about Quintus.
28:25	✚	Tamar and Mary Magdalene meet with Zebedee to talk about the olive grove. Mary Magdalene attempts to retrieve money from the disciples' safe, but it is missing.
31:51	✚	Atticus and Pilate continue talking.
33:44	✚	Simon and Eden eat. James and John arrive and speak to Simon. Eden leaves.
37:01	✚	John the Baptist's disciples have a message for Jesus. They tell Simon.

---

[49] Again, writers and producers use the Mormon phrase *mission*. While it may not be intentional, the constant repetition of it and its use within the Mormon church is Christianizing Mormon terms.

38:05	➕	Simon the Zealot hides in the tent city. Other zealots discover him, and he finds himself surrounded by them. Gaius walks through the tent city. Simon speaks to the zealots.
43:43	👍	Jesus returns to Capernaum. He heals people as a crowd gathers. Those in the crowd include Gaius, the zealots, Pharisees, Jairus, and Yussif. John the Baptist's disciples ask Jesus if He is the Messiah. Jesus loosely quotes Matthew 11:2-11.[50] Jesus speaks to the crowd about John the Baptist. He then quotes Luke 7:33-35.[51] The crowd disburses.
58:36	➕	While Jesus, James, John, and Simon are walking through the streets, they are approached by Barnaby and Shula, two of Jesus' supporters. Jesus returns sight to Shula's eyes and heals Barnaby's leg.
64:30	➕	Simon returns home to Eden, who tells him that she was pregnant and miscarried. Simon replied, "You're upset that I was on a *mission*."[52] They make up and hug.

Episode 6 does a great job with character and story development. The disciples' reaction to Jesus' miracles is perfect. The storyline about Gaius becoming more compassionate is very warming. However, only one scene contained anything Scriptural, and even that was not quoted precisely. The word *mission* was used four times during the episode to refer to the disciples being sent out across the country. Again, this is a Mormon term that refers to

---

[50] Matthew 11:2-6, "Now when John heard in prison about the deeds of the Christ, he sent word by his disciples [3] and said to Him, "Are you the one who is to come, or shall we look for another?" [4] And Jesus answered them, "Go and tell John what you hear and see: [5] the blind receive their sight and the lame walk, lepers are cleansed and the deaf hear, and the dead are raised up, and the poor have good news preached to them. [6] And blessed is the one who is not offended by me." As they went away, Jesus began to speak to the crowds concerning John: "What did you go out into the wilderness to see? A reed shaken by the wind? [8] What then did you go out to see? A man dressed in soft clothing? Behold, those who wear soft clothing are in kings' houses. [9] What then did you go out to see? A prophet? Yes, I tell you, and more than a prophet. [10] This is he of whom it is written, "'Behold, I send my messenger before your face, who will prepare your way before you.' [11] Truly, I say to you, among those born of women there has arisen no one greater than John the Baptist."

[51] Luke 7:33-34, "For John the Baptist has come eating no bread and drinking no wine, and you say, 'He has a demon.' [34] The Son of Man has come eating and drinking, and you say, 'Look at him! A glutton and a drunkard, a friend of tax collectors and sinners!' [35] Yet wisdom is justified by all her children."

[52] Again, this is another referral to the disciples' journeys as *missions*.

the two-year period that their missionaries do. Scripture does not use it that way at all.

⌒〜つ

Episode 7 – "Ears to Hear"

This episode shows plenty of drama and fighting among the disciples. Jesus and the disciples travel to the Decapolis to try to rectify the unrest brought about by Philip and Andrew's teaching.

3:7 Plot Summary		
0:22	👍	Jairus tells the story of Esther. He quotes Esther 7:7-8a[53] and Esther 9:19.[54]
1:37	➕	Music and dancing outside. Simon is angry.
3:46	➕	Philip and Andrew return from the Decapolis. Philip exclaims, "We failed in our *mission*!"
6:07	👍	Philip and Andrew get home. Judas makes lunches for the homeless. Philip tells the story of the banquet.[55]

---

[53] Esther 7:7-8a, "And the king arose in his wrath from the wine-drinking and went into the palace garden, but Haman stayed to beg for his life from Queen Esther, for he saw that harm was determined against him by the king. **8** And the king returned from the palace garden to the place where they were drinking wine, as Haman was falling on the couch where Esther was. And the king said, "Will he even assault the queen in my presence, in my own house?"

[54] Esther 9:19, "Therefore the Jews of the villages, who live in the rural towns, hold the fourteenth day of the month of Adar as a day for gladness and feasting, as a holiday,"

[55] Philip and Andrew tell the parable in their own words. The parable text is Luke 14:16-24, "But He said to him, "A man once gave a great banquet and invited many. **17** And at the time for the banquet he sent his servant to say to those who had been invited, 'Come, for everything is now ready.' **18** But they all alike began to make excuses. The first said to him, 'I have bought a field, and I must go out and see it. Please have me excused.' **19** And another said, 'I have bought five yoke of oxen, and I go to examine them. Please have me excused.' **20** And another said, 'I have married a wife, and therefore I cannot come.' **21** So the servant came and reported these things to his master. Then the master of the house became angry and said to his servant, 'Go out quickly to the streets and lanes of the city and bring in the poor and crippled and blind and lame.' **22** And the servant said, 'Sir, what you commanded has been done, and still there is room.' **23** And the master said to the servant, 'Go out to the highways and hedges and compel people to come in, that my house may be filled. **24** For I tell you, none of those men who were invited shall taste my banquet.'"

Time		Description
10:54	👍 ⊕	Matthew and Tamar talk. Thomas returns without Ramah. Simon the Zealot enters with ash for the olive grove. Philip quotes Isaiah 42:1[56] and Matthew 12:21.[57]
15:22	⊕	Mary Magdalene and Matthew discuss a box of prayer tassels that Mary found in Matthew's house. Matthew gets angry and storms out.
16:42	⊕	Shmuel interviews a man whom a false Christ swindled.
18:23	⊕	In the Capernaum marketplace, Atticus speaks to the Pharisees.
20:23	⊕	Simon walks through the Roman quarter. Before leaving the Roman quarter, Gaius takes Simon to his home to protect him. While in Gaius' home, Simon sees Gaius' servant, who is deathly ill.
23:37	⊕	Matthew apologizes to Mary Magdalene for his previous outburst.
25:00	⊕	Flashback to Matthew in his tax collector's booth, talking to an old man who gives Matthew the prayer tassels.
32:36	⊕	Matthew and Mary Magdalene discuss the prayer tassels in more detail.
36:59	⊕	Gaius and Simon leave the Roman quarter. They discuss Gaius' servant.
40:07	⊕	Thaddeus teaches Matthew to tie the prayer tassels to his garment.
42:11	👍 ⊕	Andrew and Philip discuss the issues in the Decapolis with Jesus. Jesus says, "He who has ears, let him hear."[58]
44:45	⊕	Jesus tells John to stay behind and wait for Simon.
47:16	⊕	Jesus and the disciples (without John and Simon) walk along a dusty road.
48:14	⊕	Mary Magdalene and Tamar prepare food. Simon arrives. John and Simon leave for the Decapolis.

---

[56] Isaiah 42:1, "Behold my servant, whom I uphold, my chosen, in whom my soul delights; I have put my Spirit upon Him; He will bring forth justice to the nations."

[57] Matthew 12:21, "and in His name the Gentiles will hope."

[58] Matthew 11:15, "He who has ears, let him hear."

| 50:36 | 👍 | Jesus and his disciples are on the road. Leander (a Greek) approaches them with a blind and deaf man. Jesus heals him.[59] On the road, crowds gather around Jesus. |
| 57:32 | 👎 | Simon and John argue while they walk. John says that Jesus said, "In this world, bones will still break, hearts will still break. "[60] John continues, "But He is making a way for people to access a better kingdom."[61] They catch up with Jesus and His disciples. |

While this episode contained more Scripture than most previous episodes, there was also plenty of non-Biblical content. The most concerning statement occurs in the final scene, where Jesus is attributed to saying, "In this world, bones will break. Hearts will break. (But He is) making a way for people to access a better kingdom." This is problematic, as Jesus is saying things He did not actually say. People who watch the show rather than read the Bible will attribute these false teachings to Jesus. Additionally, Mormons believe that there are different levels of heaven, so Jesus saying a better kingdom could refer to that. Regardless, Jesus would have said "the kingdom of God," not "a better kingdom."

---

[59] This scene follows Mark 7:31-37 pretty closely, "Then He returned from the region of Tyre and went through Sidon to the Sea of Galilee, in the region of the Decapolis. [32] And they brought to Him a man who was deaf and had a speech impediment, and they begged Him to lay His hand on him. [33] And taking him aside from the crowd privately, He put His fingers into his ears, and after spitting touched his tongue. [34] And looking up to heaven, He sighed and said to him, "Ephphatha," that is, "Be opened." [35] And his ears were opened, his tongue was released, and he spoke plainly. [36] And Jesus charged them to tell no one. But the more He charged them, the more zealously they proclaimed it. [37] And they were astonished beyond measure, saying, "He has done all things well. He even makes the deaf hear and the mute speak."

[60] Having Jesus say things like this on the show when they do not appear in Scripture is problematic. Many viewers will watch this and believe that Jesus said these things. This is loosely based on John 16:33, "I have said these things to you, that in me you may have peace. In the world you will have tribulation. But take heart; I have overcome the world."

[61] Jesus came to earth to spread the gospel message – "repent and believe." He did not come to grant access to "a better kingdom." He brings salvation so those who believe in Him may spend eternity with Him. It is heretical and dangerous to change Jesus' purpose on earth.

Episode 8 – "Sustenance"

In this episode, Jesus and His disciples visit the Decapolis to rectify the damage caused by Andrew and Philip's preaching. Jesus feeds a crowd of thousands of hungry people since no food is nearby. Jesus and Simon walk on the water on the Sea of Galilee.

3:8 Plot Summary		
0:24	👍	King David addresses his musicians. They perform Psalm 77:1-6,[62] and 10-11.[63]
4:25	👍 ⊕	People from the Decapolis question Jesus. John and Simon arrive. Jesus quotes Luke 17:5-6[64] and Matthew 17:20-21,[65] but then He says, "It's not about size, Philip, it's about who your faith is in."[66] A man with a leg infection arrives. Jesus heals him in front of the crowd.
10:58	⊕	Eden is in the market, where she runs into Zebedee, Salome, and Mary Magdalene. They step inside Eden's house. Eden tells them about her miscarriage and cries.
16:53	👍 ⊕	Crowds are gathering around Jesus in the field outside the Decapolis. People of different nationalities begin to argue with each other. One of the Jewish men quotes Jeremiah 6:16.[67] Jesus responds with Isaiah 43:18.[68]

[62] Psalm 77:1-6, "I cry aloud to God, aloud to God, and he will hear me. [2] In the day of my trouble I seek the Lord; in the night my hand is stretched out without wearying; my soul refuses to be comforted. [3] When I remember God, I moan; when I meditate, my spirit faints. *Selah* [4] You hold my eyelids open; I am so troubled that I cannot speak. [5] I consider the days of old, the years long ago. [6] I said, "Let me remember my song in the night; let me meditate in my heart."

[63] Psalm 77:10-11, "Then I said, "I will appeal to this, to the years of the right hand of the Most High." [11] I will remember the deeds of the LORD; yes, I will remember your wonders of old."

[64] Luke 17:5-6, "The apostles said to the Lord, "Increase our faith!" [6] And the Lord said, "If you had faith like a grain of mustard seed, you could say to this mulberry tree, 'Be uprooted and planted in the sea,' and it would obey you."

[65] Matthew 17:20-21, "He said to them, "Because of your little faith. For truly, I say to you, if you have faith like a grain of mustard seed, you will say to this mountain, 'Move from here to there,' and it will move, and nothing will be impossible for you."

[66] This is not something Jesus ever said in the Bible. It's a modified Tim Keller quote from his book *Reason for God*, "It is not the strength of your faith but the object of your faith that actually saves you."

[67] Jeremiah 6:16, "Thus says the LORD: "Stand by the roads, and look, and ask for the ancient paths, where the good way is; and walk in it and find rest for your souls. But they said, 'We will not walk in it.'"

[68] Isaiah 43:18, "Remember not the former things, nor consider the things of old."

		Jesus tells the parable of the sower.[69] The crowd continues to grow.
26:43	👍 ➕	Jesus preaches repentance to the crowd. He quotes Matthew 11:25-27.[70] Jesus says, "What is stirring in your hearts, in the midst of such division and unrest is Father God being revealed to you."[71] He then quotes Matthew 11:28-30.[72] Jesus then dismisses the crowd for the evening.
33:24	➕	Jesus and His disciples head to camp. They discuss the crowd's hunger. At one point in the conversation, John says, "Jesus said, "The success of this *mission* depends on Simon."
35:47	➕	Pharisees travel to the Decapolis in a covered wagon.
39:04	👍	Jesus preaches to a large crowd. He tells the parable of the two sons.[73] Andrew asks people in the crowd about food, and a young boy offers him some. Jesus, in preaching, quotes Matthew 13:44-45.[74] Jesus explains the meanings of the parables. The disciples pull Jesus aside and explain the food shortage. Andrew arrives with

---

[69] Matthew 13:3-9, "A sower went out to sow. [4] And as he sowed, some seeds fell along the path, and the birds came and devoured them. [5] Other seeds fell on rocky ground, where they did not have much soil, and immediately they sprang up, since they had no depth of soil, [6] but when the sun rose, they were scorched. And since they had no root, they withered away. [7] Other seeds fell among thorns, and the thorns grew up and choked them. [8] Other seeds fell on good soil and produced grain, some a hundredfold, some sixty, some thirty. [9] He who has ears, let him hear."

[70] Matthew 11:25-27, "At that time Jesus declared, "I thank you, Father, Lord of heaven and earth, that you have hidden these things from the wise and understanding and revealed them to little children; [26] yes, Father, for such was your gracious will. [27] All things have been handed over to me by my Father, and no one knows the Son except the Father, and no one knows the Father except the Son and anyone to whom the Son chooses to reveal him."

[71] This is not anything Jesus ever said.

[72] Matthew 11:28-30, "Come to me, all who labor and are heavy laden, and I will give you rest. [29] Take my yoke upon you, and learn from me, for I am gentle and lowly in heart, and you will find rest for your souls. [30] For my yoke is easy, and my burden is light."

[73] Matthew 21:28-31, "What do you think? A man had two sons. And he went to the first and said, 'Son, go and work in the vineyard today.' [29] And he answered, 'I will not,' but afterward he changed his mind and went. [30] And he went to the other son and said the same. And he answered, 'I go, sir,' but did not go. [31] Which of the two did the will of his father?" They said, "The first."

[74] Matthew 13:44-45, "The kingdom of heaven is like treasure hidden in a field, which a man found and covered up. Then in his joy he goes and sells all that he has and buys that field. [45] "Again, the kingdom of heaven is like a merchant in search of fine pearls, [46] who, on finding one pearl of great value, went and sold all that he had and bought it."

		five barley loaves and two fish.[75] Jesus tells the disciples to distribute the food in twelve baskets. They do so.
49:16	👍 ➕	Eden and another woman visit Rabbi Yussif. He quotes them Psalm 77:2-4[76] and 7-15.[77]
55:05	➕	The disciples return to Jesus with their baskets overflowing. Simon storms off. The crowd disburses as the Pharisees arrive. They are upset that Jesus breaks bread with Gentiles.
59:05	➕	Simon rents a boat while the disciples break camp. Jesus tells them to take the boat while He stays and prays. Atticus observes from a distance while the Pharisees wander through the remaining crowd. One Pharisee runs into Jesus, and they talk. The Pharisee quotes Psalm 13:2.[78] Jesus and the Pharisee head off to pray.
63:42	➕	The disciples are in a boat on the sea in a storm. They spot the figure of a man on the horizon. It is Jesus. Simon asks if he can step out onto the sea. Jesus quotes Matthew 11:28.[79] Simon steps out of the boat and walks toward Jesus. Jesus says to him, "Why do you think I allow

---

[75] This miracle can be found in Matthew 14:15-21, "Now when it was evening, the disciples came to him and said, "This is a desolate place, and the day is now over; send the crowds away to go into the villages and buy food for themselves." [16] But Jesus said, "They need not go away; you give them something to eat." [17] They said to him, "We have only five loaves here and two fish." [18] And he said, "Bring them here to me." [19] Then he ordered the crowds to sit down on the grass, and taking the five loaves and the two fish, he looked up to heaven and said a blessing. Then he broke the loaves and gave them to the disciples, and the disciples gave them to the crowds. [20] And they all ate and were satisfied. And they took up twelve baskets full of the broken pieces left over. [21] And those who ate were about five thousand men, besides women and children."

[76] Psalm 77:2-4, "In the day of my trouble I seek the Lord; in the night my hand is stretched out without wearying; my soul refuses to be comforted. [3] When I remember God, I moan; when I meditate, my spirit faints. *Selah* [4] You hold my eyelids open; I am so troubled that I cannot speak."

[77] Psalm 77:7-15, "Will the Lord spurn forever, and never again be favorable? [8] Has His steadfast love forever ceased? Are His promises at an end for all time? [9] Has God forgotten to be gracious? Has He in anger shut up His compassion?" *Selah* [10] Then I said, "I will appeal to this, to the years of the right hand of the Most High." [11] I will remember the deeds of the LORD; yes, I will remember your wonders of old. [12] I will ponder all your work and meditate on your mighty deeds. [13] Your way, O God, is holy. What god is great like our God? [14] You are the God who works wonders; you have made known your might among the peoples. [15] You with your arm redeemed your people, the children of Jacob and Joseph."

[78] Psalm 13:2, "How long must I take counsel in my soul and have sorrow in my heart all the day? How long shall my enemy be exalted over me?"

[79] Matthew 11:28, "Come to me, all who labor and are heavy laden, and I will give you rest."

		trials? They prove the genuineness of your faith. They strengthen you."
68:46	➕	Montage of Eden going through a purification ritual and Simon walking on water toward Jesus. Both go under the water at the same time. Jesus reaches down and pulls Simon to safety. Simon repeatedly says, "Don't let me go." At the same time, Eden prays, "Don't let him go." Jesus says, "I let people go hungry but I feed them."[80]
73:08	👍 ➕	Asaph recites Psalm 77:10-15.[81] While Asaph reads, there is a montage of various characters culminating with Simon coming home to Eden.
74:56	👍 ➕	Asaph and his musicians before King David. They continue with Psalm 77.[82] Upon the conclusion, David says, "I think it is ready."

The season 3 finale contains far more Biblical content than many previous episodes. It is bookended with Psalm 77, read by Asaph, a court musician and the author of the Psalm. Since most of the lines in the story belong to Jesus, there are plenty of Scriptural references and quotations by Him. Again, a large part of the episode is comprised of extra-Biblical content. However, viewers are exposed to more Scripture than any previous episode, and for that, the writers are to be commended.

---

[80] It does not appear that Jesus said this line in Scripture. However, it sort of comes from Deuteronomy 8:3, "And he humbled you and *let you hunger and fed you* with manna, which you did not know, nor did your fathers know, that he might make you know that man does not live by bread alone, but man lives by every word that comes from the mouth of the LORD." (Italics added.)

[81] Psalm 77:10-15, "Then I said, "I will appeal to this, to the years of the right hand of the Most High." ¹¹ I will remember the deeds of the LORD; yes, I will remember your wonders of old. ¹² I will ponder all your work and meditate on your mighty deeds. ¹³ Your way, O God, is holy. What god is great like our God? ¹⁴ You are the God who works wonders; you have made known your might among the peoples. ¹⁵ You with your arm redeemed your people, the children of Jacob and Joseph. *Selah*"

[82] Psalm 77:16-19, "When the waters saw you, O God, when the waters saw you, they were afraid; indeed, the deep trembled. ¹⁷ The clouds poured out water; the skies gave forth thunder; your arrows flashed on every side. ¹⁸ The crash of your thunder was in the whirlwind; your lightnings lighted up the world; the earth trembled and shook. ¹⁹ Your way was through the sea, your path through the great waters; yet your footprints were unseen."

Season 3 Assessment

Season three was once again well-written and produced. The writers and producers show the stress of Jesus' burgeoning ministry and the growing animosity between the Jewish religious elite and Jesus and His followers. The third season shows how the disciples become close-knit as they struggle with Jesus' ever-increasing ministry. The final two episodes feature far more Scripture quotations than any other. However, the bulk of character development in season three is, again, sadly based on non-Scriptural content. The third season feels rushed, with so much extra-Biblical plot development. The writers, perhaps, should have focused more on Biblical storylines than extra-Biblical material. Additionally, season three has Jesus saying more and more things that are not Biblical at all, and fans of the show are attributing those sayings to the historical Jesus. Facebook groups and fan pages of the show can evidence this.

9

Season 4

⟨⁓⟩

THE FOURTH SEASON OF *THE Chosen* tells the story of Jesus and His disciples slowly progressing toward Jerusalem for the final week of His life before His crucifixion.

Disclaimer

Please be advised that the content of this chapter will contain spoilers. If you don't want the plot revealed to you, do not read further. Instead of reading the chapter before watching each episode, read the chapter as you watch the episode. That will allow you to critique each episode from a Biblical standpoint. For your convenience, most Bible references are included in the footnotes. In this chapter, the plot summaries will use different symbols to assist the reader in understanding the source for each scene.

- ✚ means that the scene is not found in Scripture but doesn't specifically conflict with it.
- 👍 means that the scene is Scriptural or is grounded in Scripture.
- 👎 means that the scene runs contrary to Scripture.
- Ⓜ means that the scene presents Mormon theology.

Episode 1 – "Promises"

In this episode, Salome's dance leads Herod to behead John the Baptist.

4:1 Plot Summary		
1:21	➕	An unknown couple guides a pregnant Mary to visit her cousin Elizabeth.
1:39	👍	Mary arrives at Zechariah and Elizabeth's home. Zechariah cannot speak, so he writes on a hand-held chalkboard. As Mary approaches, John leaps in Elizabeth's womb. Elizabeth quotes Luke 1:42-45[1] and Luke 1:16-17.[2] The only deviation from Scripture is that they call angels messengers."
5:46	➕	Salome is taking dance lessons as her mother looks on.
9:04	➕	James, John, and Zebedee load oil into a wagon. Ramah arrives. Tamar and Ramah talk. Zebedee prays one of the Jewish prayers.
12:17	➕	Joanna arrives at her husband's (Chuza) home. (They are separated since Chuza took a mistress. Chuza and Joanna talk about the banquet Herod is going to hold. They also discuss John the Baptist.
15:26	➕	Judas and Simon the Zealot wash clothes near a river. Judas is worried about finances and talks about them with Simon. Judas quotes Isaiah 2:2.[3]

---

[1] Luke 1:42-45, "Blessed are you among women, and blessed is the fruit of your womb! [43] And why is this granted to me that the mother of my Lord should come to me? [44] For behold, when the sound of your greeting came to my ears, the baby in my womb leaped for joy. [45] And blessed is she who believed that there would be a fulfillment of what was spoken to her from the Lord."

[2] Luke 1:16-17, "And he will turn many of the children of Israel to the Lord their God, [17] and he will go before Him in the spirit and power of Elijah, to turn the hearts of the fathers to the children, and the disobedient to the wisdom of the just, to make ready for the Lord a people prepared."

[3] Isaiah 2:2, "It shall come to pass in the latter days that the mountain of the house of the LORD shall be established as the highest of the mountains and shall be lifted up above the hills; and all the nations shall flow to it."

21:54	➕	James, John, Zebedee and Tamar arrive at the temple with the oil. Tamar is refused entry. The rabbis inspect Zebedee's oil and agree to purchase it.
25:10	➕	Preparation for the banquet. Herodias and the dance instructor discuss John the Baptist.
26:45	➕	Joanna visits John the Baptist in prison, but she is not allowed to see him because they are moving him which means that John will either be freed or executed. John loosely quotes Matthew 11:5.[4]
28:32	➕	Thomas and Ramah sit and discuss marriage.
33:50	👎	Herod's banquet. Herodias is getting him drunk. Scripture does not say that Herod was drunk. It is implied, but it does not state it.
35:30	➕	The scene cuts to Joanna in a carriage.
35:50	👎	The banquet is in full swing. A chair is brought for Herod and placed in the middle of the dance floor. Salome dances for him. Herod and the crowd cheer. Herod offers her up to half of his kingdom. Salome whispers her request in his ear.
40:39	👍	Flashback: John is presented in the temple.
40:58	➕	John is led to his execution. The platter is being polished. John looks out the window and sees a lamb and whispers "thank you." He then says, "I've never been to a wedding banquet, but I am on my way to one."
		For the rest of the episode, scenes cut in and out. I will state the highlights of these scenes.
43:30	➕	Flashback: Zechariah can speak again.
45:12	➕	As John is beheaded, Jesus weeps.
46:43	➕	Joanna's carriage travels to Capernaum
48:33	➕	Joanna arrives and tells the disciples of John's death.
51:31	➕	Jesus arrives and talks to the disciples.

Episode 1 was very light on Scripture quotations. Most of the scene is fiction. There are three minor deviations from Scripture: Throughout the episode, Herod's party is called a (wedding) banquet, when, according to Matthew 14,

---

[4] Matthew 11:5, "The blind receive their sight and the lame walk, lepers are cleansed and the deaf hear, and the dead are raised up, and the poor have good news preached to them."

it was Herod's birthday party. Another issue is that Herodias and Salome have already decided that they want the head of John the Baptist on a platter. In Mark 6:24, Salome asks her mother what she should ask of Herod. This did not happen on the show. Additionally, according to Matthew 14:9, Herod was grieved by John' execution. He was not even upset in episode 1.

⌒‿⌒

Episode 2 – "Confessions"

In this episode, Simon's name is changed to Peter. Matthew asks Peter for forgiveness for his past sins against him. Peter eventually forgives him.

4: 2 Plot Summary		
:30	➕	50 second zoom in on Jesus, who sees John the Baptist.
2:24	➕	Jesus wakes up. It was just a dream. Andrew enters and they talk about John's death. Jesus said, "This bread tastes like Elisha's bones." Andrew calls Jesus a mystery.
8:05	👎	Shmuel quotes Ecclesiastes 1:2,[5] 1:14,[6] 3:6-7,[7] 5:10[8]
9:39	➕	Shmuel and Nathaniel talk. Yussif enters and discuses Shmuel's appointment to the Sanhedrin.
12:12	➕	Quintus is having a bust made of himself. Atticus enters and asks Quintus for information about the Jews.
14:49	➕	Jesus and His disciples travel down a road. Thomas and Ramah speak to Jesus. They ask Jesus for His permission to marry. Ramah asks Jesus to give her away. Jesus quotes Matthew 10:34.[9] Jesus says that he will not

---

[5] Ecclesiastes 1:2, "Vanity of vanities, says the Preacher, vanity of vanities! All is vanity."
[6] Ecclesiastes 1:14, "I have seen everything that is done under the sun, and behold, all is vanity and a striving after wind."
[7] Ecclesiastes 3:6-7, "A time to seek, and a time to lose; a time to keep, and a time to cast away;
[7] a time to tear, and a time to sew; a time to keep silence, and a time to speak."
[8] Ecclesiastes 5:10, "He who loves money will not be satisfied with money, nor he who loves wealth with his income; this also is vanity."
[9] Matthew 10:34, "Do not think that I have come to bring peace to the earth. I have not come to bring peace, but a sword." Except on the show, instead of "a sword," Jesus says, "division."

		approve of the marriage because it will tear apart Ramah's family. Jesus quotes Matthew 10:37a.[10]
21:17	➕	Yussif gets measured by a tailor.
23:41	➕	Jesus and the disciples continue on their journey. They pass a crumbling altar for Baal. They stop at the "gates of hell."
26:35	➕	The Sanhedrin meets. They declare Jesus to be as evil as Ahab and Jezebel. Caiaphas enters and leads the conversation to the matter of trapping and capturing Jesus. Shmuel feels guilty for his part.
32:52	👎 ➕	Jesus and the disciples are at the "gates of hell." Jesus askes them, "Who do people say the Son of Man is?" Matthew 16:13-20[11] is quoted fairly accurately, but a lot of non-Scriptural things have been added. Jesus changed Simon's name to Peter.
40:45	➕	Shmuel and Yussif speak in front of the temple in Jerusalem.
42:24	➕	Jesus and the disciples are in camp. The disciples sit around a campfire and argue over who is the most important. Jesus and Matthew speak at another campfire. Jesus tells Matthew to ask for Peter's forgiveness, then goes to bed.
50:35	➕	The disciples continue to argue around the campfire.
52:52	➕	Jesus and His disciples walk along a road. Jesus buys pistachios for everyone. Andrew and Peter talk. They discuss the circumcision of Moses' boys from Exodus 4. Matthew apologizes to Peter, but Peter does not forgive him.

---

[10] Matthew 10:37, "Whoever loves father or mother more than me is not worthy of me, and whoever loves son or daughter more than me is not worthy of me."

[11] Matthew 16:13-20, "Now when Jesus came into the district of Caesarea Philippi, he asked his disciples, "Who do people say that the Son of Man is?" [14] And they said, "Some say John the Baptist, others say Elijah, and others Jeremiah or one of the prophets." [15] He said to them, "But who do you say that I am?" [16] Simon Peter replied, "You are the Christ, the Son of the living God." [17] And Jesus answered him, "Blessed are you, Simon Bar-Jonah! For flesh and blood has not revealed this to you, but my Father who is in heaven. [18] And I tell you, you are Peter, and on this rock, I will build my church, and the gates of hell shall not prevail against it. [19] I will give you the keys of the kingdom of heaven, and whatever you bind on earth shall be bound in heaven, and whatever you loose on earth shall be loosed in heaven." [20] Then he strictly charged the disciples to tell no one that he was the Christ."

60:30	➕	At the Capernaum temple, the rabbis receive an edict from the Sanhedrin. Yussif opens a metal safe with a metal key. He then leaves for Jerusalem.
62:54	➕	Peter is home, in bed with his wife, Eden. They talk and Peter gets up and leaves.
64:55	👎 ➕	Peter walks to Jesus' camp. Peter lists seven sins that Matthew has committed against him. Jesus quotes Matthew 18:22.[12]
70:09	➕	Quintus and Gaius discuss the pilgrim camp outside of Capernaum.
71:30	➕	Gaius runs into Matthew on the street. Matthew invites Gaius to meet Jesus and listen to Him speak.
74:01	➕	The disciples load oil into a cart. Thomas, James, and John head off to the market.
75:16	➕	Peter and Matthew hug. Peter forgives him.

The biggest problem with episode 2 is that Jesus quotes Scripture and then says a bunch of things that are not in Scripture. He then goes back and forth between Scripture and fiction. This is problematic for someone who doesn't know the Bible.

The story that Zebedee, James, and John gave up their fishing jobs and began an olive grove is ludicrous. It is completely unscriptural.

One of the larger issues with episodes 1 and 2 are the anachronisms.[13] For example, in episode 1, Zechariah communicates by writing on a chalkboard. In episode 2, Shmuel unlocks a metal safe with a metal key. When the safe is closed, you can see the locking mechanism. In several of the scenes, there are city signs that tell people when they have reached Jerusalem. In episode 5, Jesus and his mother are discussing cabinet making and Mary mentions dovetail joints. Dovetail joints did not exist until the 1500's.

~∿

---

[12] Matthew 18:22, "Jesus said to him, 'I do not say to you seven times, but seventy-seven times.'"

[13] An anachronism is something that is out of place in time, such as an event, object, or person that is from a future historical period.

Episode 3 – "Moon to Blood"

In this episode, the religious leaders confront Jesus about healing a blind man on the Sabbath. Quintus becomes personally involved in attempting to arrest Jesus and kills Ramah.

4:3 Plot Summary		
		Disclaimer: "This episode contains violent images. Parental discretion strongly advised."
:27	👍	Two men look at a praying King David, who is prostrate on the floor.
2:00	👍	David's newborn baby dies. David gets up and cleans up.
3:57	👍 ⊕	David and Bathsheba talk. She asks him why he no longer grieves. He answers from 2 Samuel 12:21-23[14]
7:26	⊕	Quintus is using an abacus. He flies into a rage because his district is in the red. He takes to the streets as an outlet for his anger.
11:42	👍 ⊕	James and John sit down with Salome and Zebedee. They discuss Peter's "promotion." They quote Matthew 7:7-8[15] word for word.
16:52	⊕	Thomas puts on a backpack with a blanket.
17:17	⊕	Thomas, James, and John enter a room so Thomas can speak to Ramah. He asks if they can go for a walk. Andrew will chaperone.
18:44	⊕	Thomas and Ramah sit in a field and talk. He gives her a sundial.
22:33	⊕	A rabbi at the Capernaum temple lectures other rabbis to keep their eyes open for Jesus.

---

[14] According to the show, Bathsheba asks David the question instead of David's attendants in 2 Samuel 12:21-23, "His attendants asked him, "Why are you acting this way? While the child was alive, you fasted and wept, but now that the child is dead, you get up and eat!" [22] He answered, "While the child was still alive, I fasted and wept. I thought, 'Who knows? The LORD may be gracious to me and let the child live.' [23] But now that he is dead, why should I go on fasting? Can I bring him back again? I will go to him, but he will not return to me." While this is a minor deviation from Scripture, it is a deviation, nonetheless.

[15] Matthew 7:7-8, "Ask, and it will be given to you; seek, and you will find; knock, and it will be opened to you. [8] For everyone who asks receives, and the one who seeks finds, and to the one who knocks it will be opened."

23:35	➕	Jesus and Peter talk. John and James discuss their position in the disciples. Peter and Matthew talk.
26:12	👍	Jesus and the disciples walk down a street in Capernaum. They speak to Shula and Barnaby. Jesus sees a blind man. The Pharisees ask, "Who sinned, this man or his parents?" Quotes John 9:2-5.[16] The blind man can now see. Crowds begin to form around Jesus. People begin to leave the tent city to hear Jesus.
32:39	👍	A Rabbi takes the formerly blind man to the temple. The Pharisees are upset that Jesus has healed him on the Sabbath. This section follows John 9:13-34 closely.
35:25	👍	Jesus preaches to a crowd. Someone shouts, "Blessed is the womb that bore you, and the breasts at which you nursed!" Jesus speaks from a variety of passages, including Luke 11:27-28,[17] Matthew 12:48-50,[18] and Matthew 12:28-32.[19] Atticus tells Gaius to alert Quintus to the situation. The rabbis openly accuse Jesus of violating the Sabbath. Jesus then quotes Matthew 23:23-28,[20] but not in the order of the text. The crowd begins to

[16] John 9:2-5, "And his disciples asked Him, "Rabbi, who sinned, this man or his parents, that he was born blind?" [3] Jesus answered, "It was not that this man sinned, or his parents, but that the works of God might be displayed in him. [4] We must work the works of Him who sent me while it is day; night is coming, when no one can work. [5] As long as I am in the world, I am the light of the world." Another discrepancy is that on the television show, the Pharisees ask the question, but in Scripture, the disciples ask it.

[17] Luke 11::27-28, "As He said these things, a woman in the crowd raised her voice and said to Him, "Blessed is the womb that bore you, and the breasts at which you nursed!" [28] But He said, "Blessed rather are those who hear the word of God and keep it!"

[18] Matthew 12:48-50, "But He replied to the man who told Him, "Who is my mother, and who are my brothers?" [49] And stretching out His hand toward His disciples, He said, "Here are my mother and my brothers! [50] For whoever does the will of my Father in heaven is my brother and sister and mother."

[19] Matthew 12:28-32, "But if it is by the Spirit of God that I cast out demons, then the kingdom of God has come upon you. [29] Or how can someone enter a strong man's house and plunder his goods, unless he first binds the strong man? Then indeed he may plunder his house. [30] Whoever is not with me is against me, and whoever does not gather with me scatters. [31] Therefore I tell you, every sin and blasphemy will be forgiven people, but the blasphemy against the Spirit will not be forgiven. [32] And whoever speaks a word against the Son of Man will be forgiven, but whoever speaks against the Holy Spirit will not be forgiven, either in this age or in the age to come."

[20] Matthew 23:23-38, "Woe to you, scribes and Pharisees, hypocrites! For you tithe mint and dill and cumin and have neglected the weightier matters of the law: justice and mercy and faithfulness. These you ought to have done, without neglecting the others. [24] You blind guides,

		get unruly, and Gaius tells Matthew to "Get Jesus out of here." The disciples try to keep Jesus safe from the crowd. Jesus quotes Luke 12:1b-3[21] He then quotes a changed version of Matthew 10:34.[22] Jesus makes a paste of mud and saliva, puts it on the man's eyes and has him wash his face in a bucket of water.[23]
45:18	✚	Quintus arrives on the scene and tells Gaius to arrest Jesus. When Gaius refuses, Quintus has Gaius arrested. He then orders others to arrest Jesus. Jesus and some of the disciples escape. The crowd is getting more unruly. Quintus draws his sword and shouts, "Where is Jesus?" In a fit of rage, he stabs Ramah and kills her. Jesus watches as Ramah dies. Despite Thomas' repeated request for Jesus to heal her or save her, Jesus refuses. Jesus apologies for not saving her. Thomas weeps.

Of almost all of the episodes thus far, season 4, episode 3 contained the most Scripture references. Most of them were word for word from the ESV.

The final scene in the episode presents a situation similar to that of Little John asking to be healed. (Season 3, episode 2.) In that scene Jesus refused to heal Little James[24] when he came to Jesus to be healed. *Nowhere in Scripture does Jesus ever refuse to heal someone that came to Him for healing.* Here again, we have a similar situation in that Jesus refused to heal Ramah when Thomas asked Him to. Jesus healed everyone who came to Him and asked for

---

straining out a gnat and swallowing a camel! [25] "Woe to you, scribes and Pharisees, hypocrites! For you clean the outside of the cup and the plate, but inside they are full of greed and self-indulgence. [26] You blind Pharisee! First clean the inside of the cup and the plate, that the outside also may be clean. [27] "Woe to you, scribes and Pharisees, hypocrites! For you are like whitewashed tombs, which outwardly appear beautiful, but within are full of dead people's bones and all uncleanness. [28] So you also outwardly appear righteous to others, but within you are full of hypocrisy and lawlessness."

[21] Luke 12:1b-3 "Be on your guard against the yeast of the Pharisees, which is hypocrisy. [2] There is nothing concealed that will not be disclosed or hidden that will not be made known. [3] What you have said in the dark will be heard in the daylight, and what you have whispered in the ear in the inner rooms will be proclaimed from the roofs."

[22] Matthew 10:34, "Do not suppose that I have come to bring peace to the earth. I did not come to bring peace, but a sword." However, instead of "a sword," on the show, Jesus says, "division." The producers have taken liberty that should not have been taken here.

[23] This is not accurate, as Scripture says that he was to wash his face in the pool of Siloam. John 9:7, "and said to him, "Go, wash in the pool of Siloam" (which means "sent"). So, he went and washed and came back seeing."

[24] Little James the disciple on the show was the actual disciple named James of Alphaeus.

healing. By refusing to heal her, Jesus appears callous and indifferent, and that is not who He was.

Episode 3 provides several concerns. The show's producers are more and more frequently deviating from Scripture. In the scene beginning at 26:12, the Pharisees ask Jesus a question. But in John 9:2,[25] the disciples asked the question. In the same scene, the blind man is told to wash his face in the pool of Siloam, but on the show, he washes his face in a bucket of water. Matthew 10:34 has Jesus saying, "Do not suppose that I have come to bring peace to the earth. I did not come to bring peace, but a sword." On the show, however, instead of "a sword," Jesus says, "division." While these are small discrepancies, the issue is that the show's producers are taking liberty and deviating from God's holy, inerrant Word.

Episode 4 – "Calm Before"

In this episode, Jesus, Thomas, and the rest of the disciples take Ramah's body to her family. This episode begins the final weeks of Jesus' ministry. Also, the centurion comes to Jesus to beg for the healing of his servant/son.

4:4 Plot Summary		
:30	➕	The episode opens with Quintus under arrest for killing Ramah. He is demoted. Gaius is then brought in and is promoted to Quintus' old position.
2:45	➕	Ramah's funeral possession. Jesus and Peter talk. Thomas grieves deeply.
7:21	➕	Mary Magdalene expresses guilt over Ramah's death. She was the one charged with watching her before she died.
8:52	➕	Peter, James, and John talk about Thomas. They question why Jesus brought Jairus' daughter back to life, but didn't bring Ramah back to life. They quote Isaiah 55:8-

[25] John 9:2, "And His disciples asked Him, 'Rabbi, who sinned, this man or his parents, that he was born blind?'"

		9[26] word for word. Peter says, "I trust in a God that walks on water."
13:26	⊕	The scene returns to the funeral procession. There are flashbacks of Thomas and Ramah. Thomas is still grieving. Kafni (Ramah's father) meets them on the road. He is angry and blames Jesus and Thomas for her death. He then curses Jesus. They part ways.
22:26	⊕	Tamar, Mary Magdalene, and Zebedee are returning from Jerusalem. The see a sign for Jerusalem that has been vandalized. It says, "Jesus is Messiah."
22:45	⊕	Tamar and Mary give money from the sale of oil to Judas.
23:05	⊕	Jesus, His disciples, and many other followers travel down the road. Jesus comes across a demoniac, which He heals without speaking a word.
24:05	⊕	Yussif arrives in Jerusalem.
24:21	⊕	Thomas continues grieving.
24:47	⊕	Jesus passes a blind beggar and heals him. Kafni is telling people how evil Jesus is. Jesus preaches to a small crowd.
26:16	⊕	Gaius is brought a message which he promptly burns.
26:44	⊕	Jesus and His disciples sit around a table talking. Peter and Thomas talk. Simon the Zealot brings food. The disciples discuss pomegranates. Jesus leaves.
30:04	⊕	Jesus goes outside and talks to Little John and another disciple. They discuss Jesus' future suffering in Jerusalem. Peter comes in. Roman soldiers arrive asking for Matthew. Peter and Matthew leave with them. Jesus tells the other disciples to prepare for a journey.
35:58	⊕	Matthew and Peter travel to see Gaius.
37:09	⊕	They arrive and are ushered into Gaius' office. He warns them of the Pharisees plot to eliminate Jesus. They talk to Gaius about his sick servant/son. They hug and leave.

---

[26] Isaiah 55:8-9, "For my thoughts are not your thoughts, neither are your ways my ways, declares the LORD. [9] For as the heavens are higher than the earth, so are my ways higher than your ways and my thoughts than your thoughts."

45:18	➕	Andrew tells James and John that Jesus wants them to prepare for a journey. John and James talk to Salome about sitting at Jesus' right and left sides in heaven.
46:25	👍	Peter and Matthew take Gaius to see Jesus. Gaius begs Jesus on bended knee to heal his servant/son. Jesus loosely quotes Matthew 8:5-13.[27] Jesus then sends Gaius on his way.
50:50	👎	John and James ask Jesus if He remembered when He preached, "Ask for anything and it will be given to you." Jesus lies and tells them "No." Then He says, "Just kidding." They ask to sit at his right and left sides in heaven. Except for the part of Jesus lying, the scene follows Mark 10:35-40[28] fairly closely.
53:13	➕	Gaius is in the market, buying toys for his servant/son.
53:55	👍	Jesus tells his disciples, "When we go to Jerusalem, the Son of Man will be delivered over to priests and scribes and they will condemn Him to death. Jesus quotes Mark 10:33-34.[29] The disciples become indignant. He then

---

[27] Matthew 8:5-13, "When He had entered Capernaum, a centurion came forward to Him, appealing to Him, **6** "Lord, my servant is lying paralyzed at home, suffering terribly." **7** And He said to him, "I will come and heal him." **8** But the centurion replied, "Lord, I am not worthy to have you come under my roof, but only say the word, and my servant will be healed. **9** For I too am a man under authority, with soldiers under me. And I say to one, 'Go,' and he goes, and to another, 'Come,' and he comes, and to my servant, 'Do this,' and he does it." **10** When Jesus heard this, He marveled and said to those who followed him, "Truly, I tell you, with no one in Israel have I found such faith. **11** I tell you; many will come from east and west and recline at table with Abraham, Isaac, and Jacob in the kingdom of heaven, **12** while the sons of the kingdom will be thrown into the outer darkness. In that place there will be weeping and gnashing of teeth." **13** And to the centurion Jesus said, "Go; let it be done for you as you have believed." And the servant was healed at that very moment."

[28] Mark 10:35-40, "And James and John, the sons of Zebedee, came up to Him and said to Him, "Teacher, we want you to do for us whatever we ask of you." **36** And He said to them, "What do you want me to do for you?" **37** And they said to Him, "Grant us to sit, one at your right hand and one at your left, in your glory." **38** Jesus said to them, "You do not know what you are asking. Are you able to drink the cup that I drink, or to be baptized with the baptism with which I am baptized?" **39** And they said to Him, "We are able." And Jesus said to them, "The cup that I drink you will drink, and with the baptism with which I am baptized, you will be baptized, **40** but to sit at my right hand or at my left is not mine to grant, but it is for those for whom it has been prepared."

[29] Mark 10:33-34, "Saying, "See, we are going up to Jerusalem, and the Son of Man will be delivered over to the chief priests and the scribes, and they will condemn Him to death and deliver Him over to the Gentiles. **34** And they will mock Him and spit on Him and flog Him and kill Him. And after three days, He will rise."

		quotes Matthew 20:25-28.[30] Jesus tells the disciples to head toward Jerusalem without Him. He will catch up with them. Jesus begins to grieve over what is coming.
57:29	✚	Gaius returns home to a healed son. He teaches his sons the word *shalom*.
58:37	✚	Jesus walking alone, whispering to Himself. He comes across Mary Magdalene, Zebedee and Salome making oil. He watches as they press the oil. Gaius approaches and hugs Jesus.

Episode 4 was almost all fiction. There was very little Scripture in it. However, the episode does a good job at making the disciples not understand Jesus very much. In that, it is true to Scripture. However, it appears that Peter is the disciple Jesus loved instead of John.

The scene at 46:25 of Gaius acknowledging Jesus as his Savior is a tear jerker. And it is true to Scripture. However, the scene beginning at 50:50 is problematic in several areas. John and James ask Jesus if He remembers when He preached on "ask for anything and it will be given to you." Jesus lies to them and says no. Then He says that He is just kidding. It was not in Jesus' nature to lie, even if for a joke.

~

Episode 5 – "Sitting, Serving, Scheming"

In this episode, the disciples carry Roman armor and Jesus teaches them to go the extra mile. Jesus tells the parable of the laborers.

4:5 Plot Summary		
:23	✚	A man on horseback meets the disciples on a road. He gives Andrew a box from Joanna. It contains many

---

[30] Matthew 20:25-28, "But Jesus called them to him and said, "You know that the rulers of the Gentiles lord it over them, and their great ones exercise authority over them. [26] It shall not be so among you. But whoever would be great among you must be your servant, [27] and whoever would be first among you must be your slave, [28] even as the Son of Man came not to be served but to serve, and to give His life as a ransom for many.""

		valuable gifts. The disciples split up the gifts and go to sell them.
6:40	➕	The Pharisees and Sadducees debate the resurrection of the dead.
9:40	➕	Shmuel and Yussif speak outside.
11:14	➕	Disciples eat breakfast. They are trying to figure out lodging in Jerusalem. Jesus arrives and says that they will stay with Lazarus, Mary, and Martha.
13:01	➕	Jesus and the disciples head toward Jerusalem. Along the way, they run into a regiment of Roman soldiers and are asked to carry the Roman soldiers' armor and belongings. The disciples drop their bags and do so.
15:30	➕	Shmuel and Yussif speak in Jerusalem.
18:51	➕	Jesus and the disciples carry the armor and supplies for the Roman army. They reach a mile and are no longer required to carry it. Jesus insists that they take it another mile to the soldiers' final destination. As they do so, the Romans begin to take some of the things and help carry them.
22:24	➕	The Sanhedrin discusses Pilate's harsh treatment of the Jews.[31] Shmuel and Yussif step out to discuss various committees.
28:04	➕	Jesus and his disciples walk back to collect their belongings. They head off to Bethany. Mary runs ahead to greet them.
30:06	➕	When they arrive at the house, Martha is in the kitchen preparing everything. She is quite stressed. Lazarus enters and talks with Jesus and the disciples.
32:17	➕	Shmuel introduces Yussif to the others rabbis in the Sanhedrin.
34:19	👍	Jesus and the disciples relax at Lazarus' house. While they are talking, Martha is in the kitchen, anxiously

---

[31] According to Jewish historian Josephus, everything the Sanhedrin says about Pilate in this scene is true.

		preparing food. Jesus tells the parable of the laborers from Matthew 20:1-16[32] word for word.
43:06	⊕	Mary the mother of Jesus arrives. The disciples are playing instruments and singing. Jesus leaves to greet His mother. Judas leaves to go see his old business partner.
46:25	👎	They talk about the disciples while she washes His hair. At one point in the conversation, Jesus tells Mary, "I am human." Later on, Mary tells him "You'll figure it out." Jesus agreed with her. They go inside.
52:35	⊕	Judas enters the home of his old partner. They speak of Jesus being a revolutionary. Judas admits that he is angry that he doesn't fully understand Jesus.
59:20	⊕	Shmuel introduces Yussif to other rabbis in the Sanhedrin. They speak of putting Jesus to death.
63:25	⊕	Jesus and the disciples prepare to leave Bethany to head to Jerusalem. Judas steals from the disciples' money.

Episode 5 is not very Scriptural in the sense that Scripture is quoted. However, there are times where the story follows things that happened in Scripture. For example, the scene where Mary complains about Martha is from Luke 10:38-

---

[32] Matthew 20:1-16, "For the kingdom of heaven is like a master of a house who went out early in the morning to hire laborers for his vineyard. [2] After agreeing with the laborers for a denarius a day, he sent them into his vineyard. [3] And going out about the third hour he saw others standing idle in the marketplace, [4] and to them he said, 'You go into the vineyard too, and whatever is right I will give you.' [5] So they went. Going out again about the sixth hour and the ninth hour, he did the same. [6] And about the eleventh hour he went out and found others standing. And he said to them, 'Why do you stand here idle all day?' [7] They said to him, 'Because no one has hired us.' He said to them, 'You go into the vineyard too.' [8] And when evening came, the owner of the vineyard said to his foreman, 'Call the laborers and pay them their wages, beginning with the last, up to the first.' [9] And when those hired about the eleventh hour came, each of them received a denarius. [10] Now when those hired first came, they thought they would receive more, but each of them also received a denarius. [11] And on receiving it they grumbled at the master of the house, [12] saying, 'These last worked only one hour, and you have made them equal to us who have borne the burden of the day and the scorching heat.' [13] But he replied to one of them, 'Friend, I am doing you no wrong. Did you not agree with me for a denarius? [14] Take what belongs to you and go. I choose to give to this last worker as I give to you. [15] Am I not allowed to do what I choose with what belongs to me? Or do you begrudge my generosity?' [16] So the last will be first, and the first last."

42.[33] The scene with Judas stealing from the disciples' money is not specifically found in Scripture, but when Mary washed Jesus' feet with her hair, it is mentioned that Judas did help himself from time to time.

The scene where Mary the mother of Jesus washes Jesus' hair really shows her deep love for Him. There is the feeling of a mother taking care of her child. However, in the same scene, Jesus says to her, "I am human." There is no mention of His divinity. This is typical of Mormon theology, because they do not believe that Jesus was God until after he died. Christians believe that He always has been and always will be God. In the same scene, Mary tells Jesus, "You'll figure it out," and Jesus agrees with her. If Jesus is God, he would be omniscient. He would know everything. Therefore, He is either lying or He is not God. This is more of the Mormon theology about the humanity of Christ leaking through.

Episode 6 – "Dedication"

In this episode, Jesus and His disciples celebrate Hanukkah together. Matthew confronts Judas about money missing from the purse. Jesus preaches in Jerusalem and is stoned by the Pharisees. They receive word that Lazarus is dead.

4:6 Plot Summary		
:20	➕	The disciples and Jesus burst into a room. Several of them are hurt. James has a serious head injury.
2:59	👎 ➕	Thomas lights a piece of wood and prays. Jesus and His disciples have gathered to celebrate Hannukah. Everyone

---

[33] Luke 10:38-42, "Now as they went on their way, Jesus entered a village. And a woman named Martha welcomed Him into her house. [39] And she had a sister called Mary, who sat at the Lord's feet and listened to his teaching. [40] But Martha was distracted with much serving. And she went up to Him and said, "Lord, do you not care that my sister has left me to serve alone? Tell her then to help me." [41] But the Lord answered her, "Martha, Martha, you are anxious and troubled about many things, [42] but one thing is necessary. Mary has chosen the good portion, which will not be taken away from her."

		in the room recites Psalm 113:2-4[34] word for word. Jesus recounts the story of Alexander the Great while three of the disciples act it out. He then spoke of the Abomination of Desolation. Everyone recites Psalm 114:7-8.[35]
6:39	👎	The disciples exchange gifts. Matthew and John talk about what they are writing. Jesus continues with Jewish history, with the disciples acting out the story. They recite Psalm 116:15-17[36] word for word. They sing together, then recite Psalm 118:8-9[37] word for word. Andrew and John arm wrestle. Andrew wins. Someone says to Jesus, "I can't believe Andrew won." Jesus replied, "Even I didn't see that coming." Jesus announces that on the last day of the feast that they will go to Jerusalem where He will preach. Thomas disagrees with this plan and says so.
14:03	➕	James, John, Matthew, and Simon the Zealot talk. They ask Matthew if there is enough money to buy Thomas new sandals. Matthew opens the purse and realizes that there is money missing.
15:50	➕	Matthew confronts Judas about the missing money. Judas gets angry, changes the subject, and leaves.
18:06	➕	Yussif is reading scrolls in an office. His father comes in, and Yussif loosely quotes Matthew 7:7-11[38] to him. They speak a bit more, then his father leaves.

[34] Psalm 113:2-4, "Blessed be the name of the LORD from this time forth and forevermore! 3 From the rising of the sun to its setting, the name of the LORD is to be praised! 4 The LORD is high above all nations, and his glory above the heavens!"

[35] Psalm 114:7-8, "Tremble, O earth, at the presence of the Lord, at the presence of the God of Jacob, 8 who turns the rock into a pool of water, the flint into a spring of water."

[36] Psalm 116:15-17, "Precious in the sight of the LORD is the death of his saints. 16 O LORD, I am your servant; I am your servant, the son of your maidservant. You have loosed my bonds. 17 I will offer to you the sacrifice of thanksgiving and call on the name of the LORD."

[37] Psalm 118:8-9, "It is better to take refuge in the LORD than to trust in man. 9 It is better to take refuge in the LORD than to trust in princes."

[38] Matthew 7:7-11, "Ask, and it will be given to you; seek, and you will find; knock, and it will be opened to you. 8 For everyone who asks receives, and the one who seeks finds, and to the one who knocks it will be opened. 9 Or which one of you, if his son asks him for bread, will give him a stone? 10 Or if he asks for a fish, will give him a serpent? 11 If you then, who are evil, know how to give good gifts to your children, how much more will your Father who is in heaven give good things to those who ask him!"

21:39	➕	The disciples are in the market. Peter and Thomas talk about how Thomas is feeling. Thomas questions why Jesus didn't save Ramah. Peter quotes Isaiah 55:8[39] word for word.
27:17	➕	Jairus receives a scroll from Yussif.
27:42	👎 ➕	The disciples recite Psalm 115:1-3[40] word for word. Everyone hangs out talking. They give Thomas his sandals. A woman enters and gives Jesus a message. The message says that Lazarus is very sick. Jesus leaves to go to bed and the disciples and women sing Miriam's song.[41]
31:29	➕	Jesus is in bed, visibly upset about Lazarus.
31:49	➕	The next morning, the disciples are outside threshing grain. Judas has an idea to put collection boxes in each town the visit. The disciples disagree with him. Little John quotes Ecclesiastes 3:1[42] to him. John talks to Judas and tells Judas to talk to Jesus.
36:28	➕	Jesus and Judas watch as a shepherd tends to his sheep. They talk. Judas quotes Matthew 10:16.[43] Jesus tells Judas to pay close attention to his sermon the next day.
38:54	➕	Zebedee pulls a cart loaded with oil. He is called into the temple by Jairus. Jairus tells him about the Pharisees' plot to kill Jesus. Zebedee agrees to tell Jesus. He leaves for Jerusalem.
42:07	➕	Jesus and the disciples pray a Jewish prayer in unison. They leave for Jerusalem.

---

[39] Isaiah 55:8, "For my thoughts are not your thoughts, neither are your ways my ways, declares the LORD."

[40] Psalm 115:1-3, "Not to us, O LORD, not to us, but to your name give glory, for the sake of your steadfast love and your faithfulness! 2 Why should the nations say, "Where is their God?" 3 Our God is in the heavens; He does all that he pleases."

[41] Exodus 15:21, "Sing to the LORD, for He has triumphed gloriously; the horse and his rider He has thrown into the sea."

[42] Ecclesiastes 3:1, "For everything there is a season, and a time for every matter under heaven."

[43] Matthew 10:16, "Behold, I am sending you out as sheep in the midst of wolves, so be wise as serpents and innocent as doves."

43:02	👍	They travel to Jerusalem. When they arrive, Jesus stops at a pen with sheep in it. He quotes John 10:1-5.[44] The disciples don't understand. Jesus then quotes John 10:7-18.[45]
49:24	👍	The Pharisees huddle and discuss Jesus. They accuse Him of being demon-possessed or a madman. When they look up, Jesus and His disciples are gone.
50:33	👍	The Pharisees catch up with Jesus and ask if He is Jesus of Nazareth. Jesus quotes John 10:22-30.[46] The Pharisees begin to stone Jesus and His disciples. James is hit in the head. Jesus quotes John 10:37-38.[47]
53:11	➕	The disciples and Jesus hurry back to their room.

[44]John 10:1-5, "Truly, truly, I say to you, he who does not enter the sheepfold by the door but climbs in by another way, that man is a thief and a robber. [2] But he who enters by the door is the shepherd of the sheep. [3] To him the gatekeeper opens. The sheep hear his voice, and he calls his own sheep by name and leads them out. [4] When he has brought out all his own, he goes before them, and the sheep follow him, for they know his voice. A stranger they will not follow, but they will flee from him, for they do not know the voice of strangers."

[45] John 10:7-18, "So Jesus again said to them, "Truly, truly, I say to you, I am the door of the sheep. [8] All who came before me are thieves and robbers, but the sheep did not listen to them. [9] I am the door. If anyone enters by me, he will be saved and will go in and out and find pasture. [10] The thief comes only to steal and kill and destroy. I came that they may have life and have it abundantly. [11] I am the good shepherd. The good shepherd lays down his life for the sheep. [12] He who is a hired hand and not a shepherd, who does not own the sheep, sees the wolf coming and leaves the sheep and flees, and the wolf snatches them and scatters them. [13] He flees because he is a hired hand and cares nothing for the sheep. [14] I am the good shepherd. I know my own and my own know me, [15] just as the Father knows me and I know the Father; and I lay down my life for the sheep. [16] And I have other sheep that are not of this fold. I must bring them also, and they will listen to my voice. So, there will be one flock, one shepherd. [17] For this reason the Father loves me, because I lay down my life that I may take it up again. [18] No one takes it from me, but I lay it down of my own accord. I have authority to lay it down, and I have authority to take it up again. This charge I have received from my Father."

[46] John 10:22-30, "At that time the Feast of Dedication took place at Jerusalem. It was winter, [23] and Jesus was walking in the temple, in the colonnade of Solomon. [24] So the Jews gathered around Him and said to Him, "How long will you keep us in suspense? If you are the Christ, tell us plainly." [25] Jesus answered them, "I told you, and you do not believe. The works that I do in my Father's name bear witness about me, [26] but you do not believe because you are not among my sheep. [27] My sheep hear my voice, and I know them, and they follow me. [28] I give them eternal life, and they will never perish, and no one will snatch them out of my hand. [29] My Father, who has given them to me, is greater than all, and no one is able to snatch them out of the Father's hand. [30] I and the Father are one."

[47] John 10:37-38, "If I am not doing the works of my Father, then do not believe me; [38] but if I do them, even though you do not believe me, believe the works, that you may know and understand that the Father is in me and I am in the Father."

| 53:56 | 👍 | They burst into the room and tend to their wounds. Jesus finds a note on the floor. Zebedee arrives. Jesus' note informs them that Lazarus has died. Jesus tells them to change and that they will return to Judea. He quotes John 11:7-16.[48] Jesus and Mary Magdalene talk. |
| 60:21 | ➕ | Zebedee, James, and John talk. He tells them of the Pharisees' plot to kill Jesus. |

There is a significant amount of Scripture quoted in episode 6. The script follows John 10 with decent accuracy. Many of the characters' actions and thoughts from Scripture are conveyed well on screen. Despite all of that, there is one major flaw with episode 6. In the scene that begins at 6:39, Andrew and John are arm wrestling. Andrew wins, and one of the disciples turns to Jesus and says, "I can't believe Andrew won." To which Jesus replies, "Even I didn't see that coming." If Jesus is God, He is omniscient (all knowing.) Therefore, He would have seen it coming. But, if He is God, he would have seen it coming and lied about it for the sake of humor. The producers need to be much more careful about having Jesus lie for the sake of a laugh. He never lied and He knew all things.

Episode 7 – "The Last Sign"

In this episode, Jesus brings Lazarus back to life, and begins the final weeks leading up to His death on the cross.

---

[48] John 11:7-16, "Then after this He said to the disciples, "Let us go to Judea again." [8] The disciples said to Him, "Rabbi, the Jews were just now seeking to stone you, and are you going there again?" [9] Jesus answered, "Are there not twelve hours in the day? If anyone walks in the day, he does not stumble, because he sees the light of this world. [10] But if anyone walks in the night, he stumbles, because the light is not in him." [11] After saying these things, He said to them, "Our friend Lazarus has fallen asleep, but I go to awaken him." [12] The disciples said to him, "Lord, if he has fallen asleep, he will recover." [13] Now Jesus had spoken of his death, but they thought that He meant taking rest in sleep. [14] Then Jesus told them plainly, "Lazarus has died, [15] and for your sake I am glad that I was not there, so that you may believe. But let us go to him." [16] So Thomas, called the Twin, said to his fellow disciples, "Let us also go, that we may die with him."

4:7 Plot Summary		
:21	➊	A cart drops off a very old Matthew on a deserted road. He hikes uphill for a bit and comes to a cleft in the rocks. A woman approaches him with a bow drawn. Mary Magdalene comes out and greets him. He hands her a copy of his gospel and asks her to read it. Matthew tells her that Little James (James, the son of Alphaeus) was killed by sword in lower Egypt.[49]
10:54	➊	The disciples prepare to travel to Mary and Martha's house..
12:35	👍 ➊	They begin their journey. Thomas and John talk. Nathaniel and Judas talk. Little John and Mary Magdalene talk. Little John quotes Psalm 13:1,5-6, and 3.[50]
21:56	➊	People are mourning at Mary and Martha's house. Martha and Jesus' mother talk to Lazarus' old business partner and lawyer. They tell her that Jesus is on His way.
24:29	👍	Jesus and the disciples approach Bethany. Martha runs to greet them. The plot loosely follows John 11:20-27.[51] Thomas is upset about what he just heard.,
28:08	👍	Martha arrives at home, gets Mary and they leave. The guests follow. The plot loosely follows John 11:28-37.[52]

[49] Tradition says that James was killed by crucifixion in lower Egypt. But this is not fact.
[50] Psalm 13:1, 5-6, 3 "How long, O LORD? Will you forget me forever? How long will you hide your face from me? [5] But I have trusted in your steadfast love; my heart shall rejoice in your salvation. [6] I will sing to the LORD, because he has dealt bountifully with me. [3] Consider and answer me, O LORD my God; light up my eyes, lest I sleep the sleep of death."
[51] John 11:20-27, "So when Martha heard that Jesus was coming, she went and met Him, but Mary remained seated in the house. [21] Martha said to Jesus, "Lord, if you had been here, my brother would not have died. [22] But even now I know that whatever you ask from God, God will give you." [23] Jesus said to her, "Your brother will rise again." [24] Martha said to him, "I know that he will rise again in the resurrection on the last day." [25] Jesus said to her, "I am the resurrection and the life. Whoever believes in me, though he die, yet shall he live, [26] and everyone who lives and believes in me shall never die. Do you believe this?" [27] She said to him, 'Yes, Lord; I believe that you are the Christ, the Son of God, who is coming into the world.'"
[52] John 11:28-37, "When she had said this, she went and called her sister Mary, saying in private, "The Teacher is here and is calling for you." [29] And when she heard it, she rose quickly and went to Him. [30] Now Jesus had not yet come into the village but was still in the place where Martha had met Him. [31] When the Jews who were with her in the house, consoling her, saw

33:15	👍	They make their way to the tomb. Jesus tells the disciples to remove the stone. They do so. Jesus then commands Lazarus to come out.[53] He does, wrapped in his burial cloths. People start screaming. Jesus tells them to unbind Lazarus. Everyone is amazed. A Sadducee and another man head back to Jerusalem to report to the Sanhedrin.
41:50	➕	James and Matthew ask Jesus why He isn't telling people to keep this quiet. Thomas breaks down. He asks Jesus why He did not resurrect Ramah. Jesus answers, but none of it is grounded in Scripture. Mary Magdalene pauses at the tomb for a moment.
47:02	👎	Mary and Martha tend to Lazarus. Jesus enters and says, "The Father only allows me one miracle per person."
48:50	➕	Mary and Martha sit in the dining room, talking, and drinking wine together.
51:07	👍	Jesus and Lazarus talk. Jesus says that He is out of time, and that this was His last public miracle. Jesus is frustrated with the disciples and angry at the religious leaders. Jesus and Lazarus quote the first half of Isaiah 53:3.[54]
57:42	➕	Thomas is angry at Jesus for not healing Ramah. He throws pottery against the wall. Jesus says that He will discuss it with him at Passover dinner. Judas gives the

Mary rise quickly and go out, they followed her, supposing that she was going to the tomb to weep there. [32] Now when Mary came to where Jesus was and saw Him, she fell at His feet, saying to Him, "Lord, if you had been here, my brother would not have died." [33] When Jesus saw her weeping, and the Jews who had come with her also weeping, He was deeply moved in His spirit and greatly troubled. [34] And He said, "Where have you laid him?" They said to Him, "Lord, come and see." [35] Jesus wept. [36] So the Jews said, "See how He loved him!" [37] But some of them said, "Could not He who opened the eyes of the blind man also have kept this man from dying?"

[53] This part of the story follows John 11:38-44, "Then Jesus, deeply moved again, came to the tomb. It was a cave, and a stone lay against it. [39] Jesus said, "Take away the stone." Martha, the sister of the dead man, said to Him, "Lord, by this time there will be an odor, for he has been dead four days." [40] Jesus said to her, "Did I not tell you that if you believed you would see the glory of God?" [41] So they took away the stone. And Jesus lifted up His eyes and said, "Father, I thank you that you have heard me. [42] I knew that you always hear me, but I said this on account of the people standing around, that they may believe that you sent me." [43] When He had said these things, He cried out with a loud voice, "Lazarus, come out." [44] The man who had died came out, his hands and feet bound with linen strips, and his face wrapped with a cloth. Jesus said to them, "Unbind him, and let him go."

[54] Isaiah 53:3, "He was despised and rejected by men, a man of sorrows and acquainted with grief."

		impression that he believes that Jesus will be the one to overthrow Rome. The question also arises, "Why didn't Jesus heal Little John?"
64:51	👎	Flash forward to an old Mary Magdalene and an old Matthew in Mary's home in the cleft of the rock. Mary says that she felt like she had to write her own songs like David did. She reads a non-scriptural poem.
66:24	➊	This scene is a compilation of a bunch of small scenes. In this scene, the Sadducees arrive in Jerusalem with news of Lazarus' resurrection, Peter bandages James' head wound, Thomas clings to Ramah's sundial, and Jesus holds the broken pottery left over from Thomas' angry outburst.

In episode 7, the producers of the show do an excellent job in beginning to place a wedge between Judas and the other disciples. The viewer gets the keen sense that the other disciples don't really care for him.

In the scene beginning at 47:02, Lazarus jokingly asks Jesus why He didn't fix his knee when He resurrected him. Jesus replied, "The Father only grants me one miracle per person." Again, this is not truthful and is only said for the sake of humor. However, Jesus never lied. He would never have said this, and for Him to say it on the show makes Him seem less divine. It fits with the Mormon narrative that Jesus was only a man while He was alive.

Jesus never denied healing to anyone who asked him for it. Including Little James and Ramah (who is fictitious). The producers have created this false narrative for additional storyline and drama, but it paints an untrue picture of Jesus. They have changed who Jesus truly is and exchanged Him for a more dramatic and entertaining, and humorous Jesus. They have changed Jesus for ratings.

The scene beginning at 64:51 is especially problematic. In the scene, Mary Magdalene, like King David before her, is writing her own poems. This alludes to there being other Scriptures out there that are not included in the Bible. This is a tenant in the Mormon Church. Mormons also believe that there are other Scriptures than the Bible. Specifically, the *Book of Mormon*, *The Pearl of Great Price*, and *Doctrines and Covenants*. As Christians, we believe that the existing books of the Bible are all that we need to have in order for salvation. Anything else is not God's Word.

Episode 8 – "Humble"

In this episode, Jesus enters Jerusalem riding on a donkey instead of a horse like an earthly king would.

4:8 Plot Summary		
:24	➕	King David enters Jerusalem on horseback to waving palms, rose petals, and cloaks laid in his path. The citizens sing, "Hosanna, our king is victorious."
1:33	➕	David enters his palace and hugs his son and Abigail.
1:58	➕	David and his son go examine the Passover lamb. David carries the lamb inside and explains Passover to his son.
3:01	➕	The lamb is in the palace eating with the royal family. David pulls out a bridle to show his son.
4:47	➕	A man is on the temple steps telling of the resurrection of Lazarus. A rabbi argues with him, but the crowd wants to know more about Jesus.
6:20	➕	Pilate and Atticus are on a balcony speaking about Lazarus.
9:31	➕	Mary (Lazarus' sister) is in the market buying oil. She spends a year's wages on one bottle.
12:45	➕	The Sanhedrin discusses Jesus, and Shmuel says, "it bears investigating." There is an uproar. Caiaphas says that he had a prophecy, that "a man will die for our people so that the nation will not perish." He then lays out plans on how to have Jesus killed.
16:44	➕	Shmuel and Yussif meet in a back room and discuss their disdain for some of the members of the Sanhedrin. They agree to pay Lazarus a visit.
18:08	➕	Gaius talks to Eden as she packs for the Passover. Jews from Capernaum begin their journey to Jerusalem.
20:57	➕	Judas wakes in the early morning and steals money from the purse. He doctors the books so he won't be caught.

		He sees Thomas and follows him. Thomas buries Ramah's sundial.
23:32	➕	The streets of Jerusalem are packed. A scroll is delivered to Joanna's husband.
24:18	👎	The disciples share a meal at Lazarus' home. Arnan (Lazarus' business partner) arrives with Shmuel and Yussif. Jesus invites them to join Him at the table. They warn Him of the Sanhedrin's plans. Jesus says, "I would not have expected that." Then He says that He was joking. He recites Matthew 25:31-46,[55] Micah 6:8,[56] and John 13:34-35[57] word for word.
32:47	👍	Mary (Lazarus' sister) enters with her expensive bottle of perfume. She begins to wash Jesus' feet with it. She uses her hair. Judas picks up the bottle and says that it should have been sold and given to the poor. Jesus quotes Mark 14:6-9[58]. Shmuel gets upset and leaves.

---

[55] Matthew 25:31-46, "When the Son of Man comes in his glory, and all the angels with Him, then He will sit on his glorious throne. [32] Before Him will be gathered all the nations, and He will separate people one from another as a shepherd separates the sheep from the goats. [33] And He will place the sheep on His right, but the goats on the left. [34] Then the King will say to those on His right, 'Come, you who are blessed by my Father, inherit the kingdom prepared for you from the foundation of the world. [35] For I was hungry and you gave me food, I was thirsty and you gave me drink, I was a stranger and you welcomed me, [36] I was naked and you clothed me, I was sick and you visited me, I was in prison and you came to me.' [37] Then the righteous will answer Him, saying, 'Lord, when did we see you hungry and feed you, or thirsty and give you drink? [38] And when did we see you a stranger and welcome you, or naked and clothe you? [39] And when did we see you sick or in prison and visit you?' [40] And the King will answer them, 'Truly, I say to you, as you did it to one of the least of these my brothers, you did it to me.' [41] "Then He will say to those on His left, 'Depart from me, you cursed, into the eternal fire prepared for the devil and his angels. [42] For I was hungry and you gave me no food, I was thirsty and you gave me no drink, [43] I was a stranger and you did not welcome me, naked and you did not clothe me, sick and in prison and you did not visit me.' [44] Then they also will answer, saying, 'Lord, when did we see you hungry or thirsty or a stranger or naked or sick or in prison, and did not minister to you?' [45] Then He will answer them, saying, 'Truly, I say to you, as you did not do it to one of the least of these, you did not do it to me.' [46] And these will go away into eternal punishment, but the righteous into eternal life."
[56] Micah 6:8, "He has told you, O man, what is good; and what does the LORD require of you but to do justice, and to love kindness, and to walk humbly with your God?"
[57] John 13:34-35, "A new commandment I give to you, that you love one another: just as I have loved you, you also are to love one another. [35] By this all people will know that you are my disciples, if you have love for one another."
[58] Mark 14:6-9, "But Jesus said, "Leave her alone. Why do you trouble her? She has done a beautiful thing to me. [7] For you always have the poor with you, and whenever you want, you can do good for them. But you will not always have me. [8] She has done what she could; she has anointed my body beforehand for burial. [9] And truly, I say to you, wherever the gospel is proclaimed in the whole world, what she has done will be told in memory of her."

37:17	➕	Shmuel is outside. Judas comes out and talks to him. Judas says, "I'm not like you. I believe He is the one." Arnon, Shmuel, and Yussif leave.
39:00	➕	Pilate, Herod, and others recline for a meal. Herod admits that he is curious about Jesus. They talk about Lazarus rising from the dead. They speak of killing Lazarus.
43:06	➕	Joanna and Claudia (Pilate's wife) talk on a balcony.
47:44	➕	James and John sit at a table. Eden and Salome arrive.
48:50	👍	Jesus, Matthew, and Simon the Zealot are walking on a hill. Jesus tells them to go into town and "borrow a burro." He quotes Matthew 21:2-3[59] word for word. Atticus watches nearby. Mary, the mother of Jesus, brings Jesus His bag. They talk of Jesus' coming death.
52:17	👍	Simon the Zealot and Matthew enter Jerusalem. Atticus is still following them. They find the donkey and the colt just as Jesus said. A man stops them. They tell him that "The Lord has need of it." Simon then quotes Zechariah 9:9.[60] They leave with the colt. The man mounts his horse and leaves.
55:37	➕	The man on horseback rides through the hills. Atticus follows.
55:52	➕	Lazarus says goodbye to the disciples as they leave to go to Jerusalem.
56:15	➕	The man on horseback dismounts and announces to all who can hear that Jesus is coming and will enter Jerusalem through the East Gate.
56:27	➕	Matthew and Simon the Zealot walk with the colt.
56:33	➕	In Jerusalem, two people that Jesus healed are telling others about him. The man tells them Jesus is coming and will enter through the East Gate.
57:07	➕	The disciples and Matthew and Simon the Zealot catch up with Jesus.

---

[59] Matthew 21:2-3, "saying to them, "Go into the village in front of you, and immediately you will find a donkey tied, and a colt with her. Untie them and bring them to me. [3] If anyone says anything to you, you shall say, 'The Lord needs them,' and he will send them at once."

[60] Zechariah 9:9, "Rejoice greatly, O daughter of Zion! Shout aloud, O daughter of Jerusalem! Behold, your king is coming to you; righteous and having salvation is he, humble and mounted on a donkey, on a colt, the foal of a donkey."

57:15	✚	People collect palm branches and head to the East Gate. Joanna joins them.
59:44	✚	Jesus removes the bridle and hands it to Simon the Zealot.
60:14	✚	The crowd heads to the East Gate. Pilate and Claudia watch from their balcony. Caiaphas watches from his.
61:28	✚	Simon the Zealot puts the bridle on the colt. Jesus says, "The time has come," and asks the disciples to come with Him. Peter quotes John 6:68.[61] Jesus mounts the colt and rides it towards Jerusalem. The disciples follow.

Episode 8 had some solid Biblical scenes. The scene of Mary washing Jesus' feet was done exactly to Scripture. The scene of Matthew and Simon the Zealot retrieving the colt are also true to Scripture. However, beyond those two scenes, the episode was mostly fiction.

There is a minor discrepancy with Scripture. According to Mark 14:3, the disciples were reclining at the house of Simon the leper. They were not at Lazarus' home, as shown in the scene beginning at 24:18.

Again, the problem of Jesus lying in order to be funny arises. In the scene beginning at 24:18, Jesus says, "I would not have expected that." He admits that He is joking, but there is never any Scriptural reference stating that Jesus lied in order to be funny. Jesus was fully God. He would not have lied. Even as a joke.

Season 4 Assessment
While Season 4 contained some solid Biblical scenes, the vast majority of the scenes came not from Scripture, but from the writers' imaginations. A few of the themes in Season 4 are especially problematic.

The theme of Jesus refusing to heal those who came and asked Him is especially troubling. While it creates some fantastic drama, it simply is not true, and makes Jesus appear callous and unfeeling. It begins in Season 3 where Little James (James the Son of Alphaeus) asks to be healed and Jesus refuses. Then, in the final scene of Season 4, episode 3, Quintus kills Thomas' fiancé, Ramah. Thomas too begs Jesus to heal her, but Jesus again refuses to do so. This becomes a major issue when Jesus brings Lazarus back to life. Why would Jesus bring one person back to life, and refuse to do so with

---

[61] John 6:68, "Lord, to whom shall we go? You have the words of eternal life."

another? In all of His ministry, Jesus never refused to heal anyone who asked Him.

Additionally, the scene of Mary Magdalene writing her own Psalms is problematic as it introduces the concept of other books of the Bible that are not included in the Bible. This shows the Mormon influence on the show in that they believe that there are other books that are divinely inspired that are not in the Bible.

10

Season 5

⁓

THE FIFTH SEASON OF *THE Chosen* chronicles the beginning of the Passion Week, Christ's final week before His crucifixion. It covers the triumphant entry through Judas' kiss of betrayal.

Disclaimer

Please be advised that the content of this chapter will contain spoilers. If you don't want the plot revealed to you, do not read further. Instead of reading the chapter before watching each episode, read the chapter as you watch the episode. That will allow you to critique each episode from a Biblical standpoint. For your convenience, most Bible references are included in the footnotes. In this chapter, the plot summaries will use different symbols to assist the reader in understanding the source for each scene.

- ✚ means that the scene is not found in Scripture but doesn't specifically conflict with it.
- 👍 means that the scene is Scriptural or is grounded in Scripture.
- 👎 means that the scene runs contrary to Scripture.
- Ⓜ means that the scene presents Mormon theology.

Episode 1 – "Entry"

This episode covers Jesus' triumphant entry into Jerusalem and the events that occurred immediately thereafter.

5:1 Plot Summary		
:02	👍 ➕	The episode opens with Jesus and the disciples at the Lord's Supper. Jesus quotes John 16:16,[62] 16:20-25a,[63] adds non-Biblical text, and returns to John 16:25b-28.[64] The disciples quote John 16:29-30,[65] Jesus replies with John 16:31-32.[66] Non-Biblical text is inserted, and the conversation is finished with John 16:33.[67] The scene mostly follows Scripture. Andrew leads a hymn which is based on Psalm 118:19-20.[68] Jesus quotes John 17:1-4.[69]

---

[62] John 16:16, "A little while, and you will see me no longer; and again, a little while, and you will see me."

[63] John 16:20-25a, "Truly, truly, I say to you, you will weep and lament, but the world will rejoice. You will be sorrowful, but your sorrow will turn into joy. 21 When a woman is giving birth, she has sorrow because her hour has come, but when she has delivered the baby, she no longer remembers the anguish, for joy that a human being has been born into the world. 22 So also you have sorrow now, but I will see you again, and your hearts will rejoice, and no one will take your joy from you. 23 In that day you will ask nothing of me. Truly, truly, I say to you, whatever you ask of the Father in my name, He will give it to you. 24 Until now you have asked nothing in my name. Ask, and you will receive, that your joy may be full. 25 I have said these things to you in figures of speech."

[64] John 16:25b-28, "The hour is coming when I will no longer speak to you in figures of speech but will tell you plainly about the Father. 26 In that day you will ask in my name, and I do not say to you that I will ask the Father on your behalf; 27 for the Father himself loves you, because you have loved me and have believed that I came from God. 28 I came from the Father and have come into the world, and now I am leaving the world and going to the Father."

[65] John 16:29-30, "Ah, now you are speaking plainly and not using figurative speech! 30 Now we know that you know all things and do not need anyone to question you; this is why we believe that you came from God."

[66] John 16:31-32, "Jesus answered them, "Do you now believe? 32 Behold, the hour is coming, indeed it has come, when you will be scattered, each to his own home, and will leave me alone. Yet I am not alone, for the Father is with me."

[67] John 16:33, "I have said these things to you, that in me you may have peace. In the world you will have tribulation. But take heart; I have overcome the world."

[68] Psalm 118:19-20, "Open to me the gates of righteousness, that I may enter through them and give thanks to the LORD. 20 This is the gate of the LORD; the righteous shall enter through it.

[69] John 17:1-4, "When Jesus had spoken these words, He lifted up his eyes to heaven, and said, "Father, the hour has come; glorify your Son that the Son may glorify you, 2 since you have

7:39		Introduction
8:40	➕	Four days earlier – There is a large crowd in the Jerusalem market. Yussif enters the temple and washes his hands. He says, "It's everything I feared."
10:04	➕ 👍	Jesus rides on a colt while the disciples walk with Him. Still a fair distance from Jerusalem, they hear singing, "Hosanna to the Son of David!" (Matthew 21:9)[70] The disciples join in with the singing. They are approached by three Pharisees who encourage them to turn around. Nathanial quotes Zechariah 9:9.[71] The Pharisees implore Jesus to tell His disciples to be quiet. Jesus quotes Luke 19:40.[72] Yussif (a Pharisee) hesitates to leave with the other Pharisees but ultimately joins them.
13:48	➕	Jesus and the disciples enter into the crowd who lays cloaks and palm branches down before Him. Roman soldiers look on. Jesus pauses and sees blood leaking from the wall of Jerusalem. He begins to shake. The crowd chants, "Hosanna to the Son of David!" Atticus appears in the crowd. Joanna is also there.
18:04	➕	Caiaphas surveys the crowd in the Jerusalem market.
18:30	➕	Jesus and His disciples approach the temple. Jesus dismounts. The disciples talk amongst themselves. Peter declares that he will learn to preach. Nicodemus' servant takes notes. He observes Yussif buy clothes and change into them.
22:00	➕	Atticus visits Pilate at Pilate's home. Pilate says, "All that fuss and He rides in on an ass. It's pathetic." Food is brought in. Pilate's wife complains of the smell. A trunk is brought in containing Caiaphas' ceremonial garments (for the Passover.) Caiaphas enters. Pilate offers him

given Him authority over all flesh, to give eternal life to all whom you have given Him. [3] And this is eternal life, that they know you, the only true God, and Jesus Christ whom you have sent. [4] I glorified you on earth, having accomplished the work that you gave me to do."

[70] Matthew 21:9, "And the crowds that went before Him and that followed Him were shouting, "Hosanna to the Son of David! Blessed is He who comes in the name of the Lord! Hosanna in the highest!"

[71] Zechariah 9:9, "Rejoice greatly, O daughter of Zion! Shout aloud, O daughter of Jerusalem! Behold, your king is coming to you; righteous and having salvation is He, humble and mounted on a donkey, on a colt, the foal of a donkey."

[72] Luke 19:40, "He answered, "I tell you, if these were silent, the very stones would cry out.""

		food. Pilate then threatens to touch Caiaphas' garments, thus making them unclean. They discuss the great turnout for Passover. Pilate tells Caiaphas about three executions scheduled for that Friday.
27:05	👍 👎	Jesus is preaching in Jerusalem. He quotes John 12:23-26.[73] Joanna talks with Mary Magdalene and others and offers to let them stay at her friend Phoebe's house. Jesus grasps His heart, leans forward and cries. He quotes John 12:27-28a.[74] Thunder and lightning strike, sounding like the word "glorify." Jesus then loosely quotes verse 30,[75] then some non-Biblical text, then verses 31-32.[76] The disciples ask Him, "What do you mean?" Jesus then quotes verses 35-36.[77] The producers added "and daughters" to verse 36. It thunders and Jesus dismisses the crowd.
32:21	➕	John and Mary Magdalene discuss Jesus appearing troubled.
33:22	👎	Jesus tells the disciples to preach around Jerusalem. They are to repeat anything that He has said. Jesus says, "Time is running out." The disciples head to Phoebe's house. This contradicts Mark 11:11.[78] Peter and Matthew go off to preach.

---

[73] John 12:23-26, "And Jesus answered them, "The hour has come for the Son of Man to be glorified. [24] Truly, truly, I say to you, unless a grain of wheat falls into the earth and dies, it remains alone; but if it dies, it bears much fruit. [25] Whoever loves his life loses it, and whoever hates his life in this world will keep it for eternal life. [26] If anyone serves me, he must follow me; and where I am, there will my servant be also. If anyone serves me, the Father will honor him.""

[74] John 12:27-28a, "Now is my soul troubled. And what shall I say? 'Father, save me from this hour'? But for this purpose, I have come to this hour. [28] Father, glorify your name." Then a voice came from heaven: "I have glorified it and will glorify it again.""

[75] John 12:30, "Jesus answered, "This voice has come for your sake, not mine.""

[76] John 12:31-32, "Now is the judgment of this world; now will the ruler of this world be cast out. [32] And I, when I am lifted up from the earth, will draw all people to myself.""

[77] John 12:35-36, "So Jesus said to them, "The light is among you for a little while longer. Walk while you have the light, lest darkness overtake you. The one who walks in the darkness does not know where he is going. [36] While you have the light, believe in the light, that you may become sons of light." In The Chosen, Jesus said, "that you may become sons and daughters of light." The Greek word for sons is υἱοί, which also means children. This includes daughters. However, rather than translate υἱοί as children, the writers of the show opted to change Scripture instead.

[78] Mark 11:11, "And He entered Jerusalem and went into the temple. And when He had looked around at everything, as it was already late, He went out to Bethany with the twelve."

35:05	👎	Kafni (Ramah's father) leads a group into Jerusalem chanting Psalm 11:5-6.[79] However, in verse 6, they change "wicked" to "false prophet."[80] They are confronted by Nicodemus' servant.
37:22	➕	The disciples enter Phoebe's house. They discuss Jesus' mood. The women discuss the large Passover crowds and the drama they bring to Jerusalem.
40:15	➕	Mary Magdalene leaves and runs into John. They discuss Greek paintings and mythology They discuss Jesus entering Jerusalem through the sheep gate, where Sacrificial lambs are brought in from Bethlehem.[81]
42:28	👍	A crowd and a priest recite Psalm 136:7-14.[82]
43:15	➕	Kafni and others discuss Herod's possible reaction to Jesus' entry. They also discuss Jesus apparent weaknesses.
44:22	➕	Jesus enters a betrothal celebration. There is singing and dancing. Jesus joins in. A young boy exclaims, "Hosanna to the Son of David!" Everyone stares at Jesus, removes their hats and bows to Him. Jesus says, "Thank you. Thank you. There is no need to draw attention. I will leave you to your celebration. This night is not about

[79] Psalm 11:5-6, "The LORD tests the righteous, but His soul hates the wicked and the one who loves violence. 6 Let him rain coals on the wicked; fire and sulfur and a scorching wind shall be the portion of their cup."
[80] The Hebrew word for "wicked" is *rasha`*. It means morally wrong, or an actively bad person. Not once in all of Scripture does it mean "false prophet." The writers of the show have taken liberties to change the inerrant Word of God. Ironically, false prophets in Mormonism are those who change Scripture, among other things.
[81] There is some debate as to which gate of Jerusalem Jesus entered. Zechariah 9:9 implies that Jesus entered through the Golden Gate, which was where kings entered the city, "Rejoice greatly, O daughter of Zion! Shout aloud, O daughter of Jerusalem! Behold, your king is coming to you; righteous and having salvation is He, humble and mounted on a donkey, on a colt, the foal of a donkey." However, there are some who speculate that Jesus entered through the sheep gate, since He was the sacrificial lamb. The show's writers chose the latter interpretation over what is implied by Scripture.
[82] Psalm 136:7-14, "to Him who made the great lights, for His steadfast love endures forever; 8 the sun to rule over the day, for His steadfast love endures forever; 9 the moon and stars to rule over the night, for His steadfast love endures forever; 10 to Him who struck down the firstborn of Egypt for His steadfast love endures forever; 11 and brought Israel out from among them, for His steadfast love endures forever; 12 with a strong hand and an outstretched arm, for His steadfast love endures forever; 13 to Him who divided the Red Sea in two, for His steadfast love endures forever; 14 and made Israel pass through the midst of it, for His steadfast love endures forever.

		me." Before Jesus leaves, the bride asks Him for a blessing. Jesus blesses them with the Jewish wedding prayer. He then blesses everyone, "To all present here tonight, may the light of the paschal feast burn within you, that with heavenly desires and pure minds, you may attain the festival of everlasting light, the kingdom I am bringing into this world."[83] Jesus exits.
48:51	👍	Jesus stands on a balcony overlooking the temple courtyard.[84] He sees the money changers and merchants and begins to get upset. He foresees the fall of Jerusalem and quotes Luke 19:43-44.[85]
53:08	➕	Jesus enters Phoebe's house. The disciples are asleep. Jesus asks Zebedee to take His mother to Lazarus' house for a few days. John wakes up and spies on Jesus as he removes a box with the bridle inside and takes it to His room. He fashions the bridle into a whip.

Season 5, episode 1 had some solid Biblical scenes. The opening scene of the Last Supper quotes much of John 16, and other than a few bits of fiction, stays close to Scripture. The scene of Jesus preaching in Jerusalem also quotes a lot of Scripture, however, there are two problems with this scene. Firstly, Joanna never offered the disciples a place to stay in Jerusalem. They stayed with Lazarus, Martha, and Mary. Secondly, the authors of the show have added "and daughters" to John 12:36. This was not necessary, as the Greek word for sons also means children. They could (and perhaps, should) have used the word "children" instead of adding "and daughters" to the verse. This shows a disregard by the writers for the holiness of Scripture. They add to it when it fits their inclusive agenda. The scene of the priest and the crowd reciting Psalm 136 was perfectly Scriptural.

There are some deviations from Scripture. Kafni (a fictional character) and his men were reciting Psalm 11:5-6, but they changed the word "wicked"

---

[83] This is an Episcopal Easter prayer. It is not Scriptural.

[84] According to Luke 19:45, Jesus "entered the temple and began to drive out those who sold." There is no mention of a balcony overlooking the temple courtyard.

[85] Luke 19:43-44, "For the days will come upon you, when your enemies will set up a barricade around you and surround you and hem you in on every side [44] and tear you down to the ground, you and your children within you. And they will not leave one stone upon another in you, because you did not know the time of your visitation."

to "false prophet." The writers of the show changed Scripture to fit their fictional story. Additionally, Jesus and His disciples stayed at Lazarus, Martha, and Mary's house, not Phoebe's. There is no reason for this deviation, other than to better fit with the fictional story. The writers have disregarded Scripture in favor of fiction.

This would have been a solidly Biblical episode if the writers hadn't changed Scripture and had Jesus and the disciples staying at Lazarus, Martha, and Mary's home instead.

Episode 2 – "House of Cards"

This episode builds up to and covers Jesus' cleansing of the Temple.

5:2 Plot Summary		
0:00	❶	Last Supper – Jesus quotes John 13:38a.[86] He then tells the disciples to listen to Him carefully. He then quotes Luke 22:35,[87] then tells them that they will be going into a hostile world. He says, "The nation has rejected me and now they will reject you." Jesus quotes John 15:19[88] and Luke 22:36.[89] Simon the Zealot says that they have two swords to defend themselves. Jesus replies, Prepare for hostility and persecution. But ultimately, your protection will come from above." Jesus quotes Matthew 26:31.[90] The disciples object. Jesus quotes Luke 22:31-34[91]

[86] John 13:38a, "Jesus answered, "Will you lay down your life for me?"
[87] Luke 22:35, "And he said to them, "When I sent you out with no moneybag or knapsack or sandals, did you lack anything?" They said, "Nothing."
[88] John 15:19, "If you were of the world, the world would love you as its own; but because you are not of the world, but I chose you out of the world, therefore the world hates you."
[89] Luke 22:36, "He said to them, 'But now let the one who has a moneybag take it, and likewise a knapsack. And let the one who has no sword sell his cloak and buy one.'"
[90] Matthew 26:31, "Then Jesus said to them, "You will all fall away because of me this night. For it is written, 'I will strike the shepherd, and the sheep of the flock will be scattered.'"
[91] Luke 22:31-34, "Simon, Simon, behold, Satan demanded to have you, that he might sift you like wheat, [32] but I have prayed for you that your faith may not fail. And when you have turned

		followed by non-Biblical text. Peter swears on his mother's grave that he will never deny Jesus. The disciples all state that they would die with Christ. Jesus quotes John 15:13.[92] Peter replies, Then that's what we will do." Jesus replied, "That is what I will do."
5:08		Introduction
6:10	⊕	Flashback: Ramah receives a necklace from Naomi, her mother.
7:31	⊕	Flashback: Kafni and Thomas load wine on a wagon. They talk. Kafni ends the conversation with "Don't embarrass me or the vineyard." Thomas answers, "You have my word." Kafni and Naomi leave.
9:14	⊕	Flashback: Kafni and Naomi talk, revealing that Thomas was an orphan.
9:51	⊕	People enter Jerusalem.
9:57	⊕	Peter preaches to a crowd of about 100 people. The other disciples are there to help him when he forgets details.[93]
11:00	⊕	Peter, Phillip, Simon the Zealot, and Andrew discuss Peter's sermon. They decide to go get lunch.
12:53	⊕	A woman from the crowd (Dori) reports Peter's preaching to the Pharisees in the temple.
13:11	👍	The disciples are in the Court of Gentiles. They run into Leander, Dion, and Fatiya.[94] (From season 3, episode 7.) The disciples explain Passover, sacrificial animals, and the costs to them. This scene is an excellent primer of the sacrificial system and atonement.
16:40	⊕	They exchange drachmas for shekels. They are appalled at the 45% temple tax.
19:59	⊕	Tamar and Fatiya leave to buy birds. The vendor gives them doves for free.

---

again, strengthen your brothers." [33] Peter said to him, "Lord, I am ready to go with you both to prison and to death." [34] Jesus said, "I tell you, Peter, the rooster will not crow this day, until you deny three times that you know me."

[92] John 15:13, "Greater love has no one than this, that someone lay down his life for his friends."

[93] This contradicts Luke 12:12, in which Jesus says, "for the Holy Spirit will teach you in that very hour what you ought to say."

[94] John 12:20, "Now among those who went up to worship at the feast were some Greeks."

22:30	✚	Zebedee and John arrive at the temple with a wagon full of oil. They meet with Malchus, the chief servant of the high priest. He asks them if they are ritually clean. John admits to having a seminal discharge. He is denied entry into the temple.
25:10	✚	John and Malchus wait outside. They joke about seminal discharge.[95] They speak of Caiaphas's irritation with Jesus.
27:50	✚	Herod Antipas and Caiaphas have lunch. They discuss Jesus. Herod says that Pilate has proposed that Caiaphas have Lazarus killed quietly, putting the rumors of Jesus supposed powers to death. Antipas includes in one of his statements, "your people," to which Caiaphas responds, "Our people. You act like you are not one of us."[96] Herod tells Caiaphas that as far as Rome is concerned, the case against Jesus is weak. Herod expresses a desire to see Jesus perform miracles. He states that he initially thought that Jesus was John the Baptist, back from the dead to avenge him.[97] Herod states that he regrets killing John the Baptist. Caiaphas says that he has had a revelation from God, "One man will die so that our nation will not perish."[98] He then lays out a plan to have Jesus upset Rome so that the Romans will execute Him.
35:25	✚	Thomas and Kafni run into each other in the market. Kafni blames Thomas and Jesus for Ramah's death and threatens them. He vows that this supper will be their last.

---

[95] This scene insinuates that they are joking about masturbation. However, nothing in the show states that directly.

[96] Herod Antipas was a descendant of Esau, so technically, he was not a Jew.

[97] Matthew 14:1-2, "At that time Herod the tetrarch heard about the fame of Jesus, ² and he said to his servants, "This is John the Baptist. He has been raised from the dead; that is why these miraculous powers are at work in Him."

[98] John 11:49-53, "But one of them, Caiaphas, who was high priest that year, said to them, "You know nothing at all. ⁵⁰ Nor do you understand that it is better for you that one man should die for the people, not that the whole nation should perish." ⁵¹ He did not say this of his own accord, but being high priest that year he prophesied that Jesus would die for the nation, ⁵² and not for the nation only, but also to gather into one the children of God who are scattered abroad. ⁵³ So from that day on they made plans to put Him to death."

36:49	✚	Thomas goes off to cool down. He sees and hears a vision of Ramah. But it turns out it is Naomi, Ramah's mother. Thomas apologizes and cries. They talk. Thomas confesses he has been deeply troubled since Ramah's death. John calls out, "Rabbi?" in the crowd. Thomas thanks Naomi and heads into the crowd.
39:35	✚	(See John 2:13-22) Jesus is walking in the Court of Gentiles. He is wearing a leather backpack. A vendor uses the Court of Gentiles as a shortcut but Jesus will not let her pass through. Jesus approaches a vendor and laments about how the temple is now a marketplace. Jesus removes His backpack and takes out a whip. He angrily grabs the whip and returns to the vendor. He overturns the vendor's table and lashes His whip. He releases animals and overturns more tables, telling people to "quit profaning my Father's house."[99] The Pharisees summon the temple guards. Caiaphas hears the commotion and Atticus enters the court.
44:50	✚	Pontius Pilate and Claudia, his wife, are eating and hear the commotion.
45:12	✚	Andrew runs to gather the other disciples, shouting, "He's gone mad!"
45:25	✚	Court of Gentiles – a vendor's tent is on fire. Jesus yells, "This desecration is on your shoulders!" He calls the Pharisees a brood of vipers[100] and snaps His whip at them. Jesus and Caiaphas make eye contact and stare at

---

[99] Scriptural references for this scene can be found in Mark 11:15-19, "And they came to Jerusalem. And He entered the temple and began to drive out those who sold and those who bought in the temple, and He overturned the tables of the money-changers and the seats of those who sold pigeons. [16] And He would not allow anyone to carry anything through the temple. [17] And He was teaching them and saying to them, "Is it not written, 'My house shall be called a house of prayer for all the nations'? But you have made it a den of robbers." [18] And the chief priests and the scribes heard it and were seeking a way to destroy Him, for they feared Him, because all the crowd was astonished at His teaching. [19] And when evening came, they went out of the city." Also, Luke 19:45-48, "And He entered the temple and began to drive out those who sold, [46] saying to them, "It is written, 'My house shall be a house of prayer,' but you have made it a den of robbers." [47] And He was teaching daily in the temple. The chief priests and the scribes and the principal men of the people were seeking to destroy Him, [48] but they did not find anything they could do, for all the people were hanging on His words."

[100] Matthew 23:33, "You serpents, you brood of vipers, how are you to escape being sentenced to hell?

		each other. Judas looks at Jesus and says, "What have you done?"

Season 5, episode 2 is lacking in Scripture. It primarily focuses on the back story behind Jesus' cleansing of the temple. The opening scene has Jesus quote some Scripture, but only in small parts and from various Scripture.

The scene with Herod Antipas and Caiaphas talking contains one non-truth. According to Josephus, Herod the Great and Herod Antipas were descendants of Esau, and were, therefore, not Jewish, as was implied by Caiaphas in that scene. Almost none of what Jesus said during the final three scenes was Scriptural. The writers of the show could have had Jesus follow Scripture in these scenes, and it would have been fine. Instead they have Him say it in the following episode.

Episode 3 – "Woe"

This episode deals with the fallout from Jesus' cleansing of the Court of Gentiles. The Pharisees try to trap Jesus with difficult questions, but Jesus confronts the Pharisees about their hypocrisy.

5:3 Plot Summary		
0:00	👍	The Last Supper – Jesus quotes John 13:36b.[101] He disciples ask why. Jesus quotes John 14:1-6.[102] Philip

---

[101] John 13:36b, "Jesus answered him, "Where I am going you cannot follow me now, but you will follow afterward."

[102] John 14:1-6, "Let not your hearts be troubled. Believe in God; believe also in me. ² In my Father's house are many rooms. If it were not so, would I have told you that I go to prepare a place for you? ³ And if I go and prepare a place for you, I will come again and will take you to myself, that where I am you may be also. ⁴ And you know the way to where I am going." ⁵ Thomas said to him, "Lord, we do not know where you are going. How can we know the way?" ⁶ Jesus said to him, "I am the way, and the truth, and the life. No one comes to the Father except through me."

		quotes John 14:8,[103] Jesus replies with John 14:9-11.[104] Philip says he doesn't understand. Jesus responds with John 14:18,[105] then 17b.[106] The disciples tell Jesus they don't want the Helper; they want Him. Jesus quotes John 14:21,[107] 25-27a[108] and 27c.[109] The middle part of verse 27[110] was omitted. He then quotes verses 28-29.[111] Peter asks Jesus, "Why can I not follow you now? I will lay down my life for you." Jesus replies, "Will you lay down your life for me?"
4:25		Introduction
5:38	✚	Court of Gentiles - (this scene loosely follows John 2:17-22)[112] Jesus and Caiaphas stare at each other. Soldiers come up to Jesus, but Atticus tells them to stand down and let Jesus speak. Jesus quotes Mark 11:17.[113] Simon the Zealot quotes John 2:17. Caiaphas is taken to a secure

---

[103] John 14:8, "Philip said to Him, 'Lord, show us the Father, and it is enough for us.'"

[104] John 14:9-11, "Jesus said to him, "Have I been with you so long, and you still do not know me, Philip? Whoever has seen me has seen the Father. How can you say, 'Show us the Father'? [10] Do you not believe that I am in the Father and the Father is in me? The words that I say to you I do not speak on my own authority, but the Father who dwells in me does his works. [11] Believe me that I am in the Father and the Father is in me, or else believe on account of the works themselves."

[105] John 14:18, "I will not leave you as orphans; I will come to you."

[106] John 14:17b, "You know Him, for he dwells with you and will be in you."

[107] John 14:21, "Whoever has my commandments and keeps them, he it is who loves me. And he who loves me will be loved by my Father, and I will love him and manifest myself to him."

[108] John 145:25-27a, "These things I have spoken to you while I am still with you. [26] But the Helper, the Holy Spirit, whom the Father will send in my name, He will teach you all things and bring to your remembrance all that I have said to you. [27] Peace I leave with you; my peace I give to you."

[109] John 14:27c, "Let not your hearts be troubled, neither let them be afraid."

[110] John 14:27b (omitted from the scene), "Not as the world gives do I give to you."

[111] John 14:28-29, "You heard me say to you, 'I am going away, and I will come to you.' If you loved me, you would have rejoiced, because I am going to the Father, for the Father is greater than I. [29] And now I have told you before it takes place, so that when it does take place you may believe."

[112] John 2:17-22, "His disciples remembered that it was written, "Zeal for your house will consume me."[18] So the Jews said to him, "What sign do you show us for doing these things?" [19] Jesus answered them, "Destroy this temple, and in three days I will raise it up." [20] The Jews then said, "It has taken forty-six years to build this temple, and will you raise it up in three days?" [21] But he was speaking about the temple of his body. [22] When therefore he was raised from the dead, His disciples remembered that He had said this, and they believed the Scripture and the word that Jesus had spoken."

[113] Mark 11:17, "And He was teaching them and saying to them, "Is it not written, 'My house shall be called a house of prayer for all the nations'? But you have made it a den of robbers.""

		location. Jesus announces to the crowd, "No more purchased animals or sacrifices are to be brought through this gate." Peter rolls his eyes. Jesus continues, "Do you hear me?" "But it's Passover." Jesus replies, "I said no more." The Pharisees ask Jesus by whose authority He does these things. He replies, "My own!" There are shouts of heresy. Pharisees ask Him for a sign. Jesus quotes John 2:19, and the Pharisees respond with John 2:20. The crowd begins to shout, "Hosanna to the Son of David!" The disciples lead Jesus out while the Pharisees look on.
8:54	✪	The Pharisees call for a scribe to write down everything that just happened in great detail. They discuss Jesus' statement about destroying the temple and rebuilding it in three days. They discuss Jeremiah's prophecy about the destruction of the temple. They agree to question Jesus the next time they see Him.
12:24	✪	Court of the Gentiles – people pick up coins and restore vendor tables and tents to the way they previously were. Kafni speaks to a vendor who lost his sheep.
13:48	✪	Judas asks Jesus about His statement, "no more sacrifices are to be brought into the temple." Judas asks "How are people supposed to observe Passover?" Jesus leaves to be alone.
14:25	✪	The disciples go inside.
15:02	✪	The disciples discuss Jesus' actions. Judas is upset with Jesus. Mary Magdalene gets up and leaves. Andrew runs after her.
17:17	✪	Mary Magdalene and Andrew talk. Mary leaves to go get help.
18:08	✪	Pilate is getting a message. Atticus and Caiaphas enter. They discuss Jesus' actions and the repercussions for Rome.
21:52	✪	The disciples discuss Jesus cleansing the temple and the crowd's response.
22:37	✪	Matthew and Jesus talk. Jesus tells him to pay attention in the coming days.

| 25:18 | 👍 | Jesus preaches in Jerusalem. He quotes Matthew 25:14-18.[114] The Pharisees again ask Jesus, "On whose authority do you do these things?" Jesus loosely quotes Mark 11:29-33.[115] He then tells the Parable of the Tenants (loosely based on Matthew 21:33-43).[116] While Jesus tells the parable, the disciples act it out. The Pharisees plot to ask Jesus about taxes in front of the Roman soldiers. The scene then follows Matthew 22:15-22[117] loosely. The crowd erupts with shouts for and against Jesus. Jesus begins discussing the Parable of the Talents, when the Pharisees interrupt Him again. "Which |

---

[114] Matthew 25:14-18, "For it will be like a man going on a journey, who called his servants and entrusted to them his property. [15] To one he gave five talents, to another two, to another one, to each according to his ability. Then he went away. [16] He who had received the five talents went at once and traded with them, and he made five talents more. [17] So also he who had the two talents made two talents more. [18] But he who had received the one talent went and dug in the ground and hid his master's money."

[115] Mark 11:29-33, "Jesus said to them, "I will ask you one question; answer me, and I will tell you by what authority I do these things. [30] Was the baptism of John from heaven or from man? Answer me." [31] And they discussed it with one another, saying, "If we say, 'From heaven,' he will say, 'Why then did you not believe him?' [32] But shall we say, 'From man'?"—they were afraid of the people, for they all held that John really was a prophet. [33] So they answered Jesus, "We do not know." And Jesus said to them, "Neither will I tell you by what authority I do these things."

[116] Matthew 21:33-43, "Hear another parable. There was a master of a house who planted a vineyard and put a fence around it and dug a winepress in it and built a tower and leased it to tenants and went into another country. [34] When the season for fruit drew near, he sent his servants to the tenants to get his fruit. [35] And the tenants took his servants and beat one, killed another, and stoned another. [36] Again he sent other servants, more than the first. And they did the same to them. [37] Finally he sent his son to them, saying, 'They will respect my son.' [38] But when the tenants saw the son, they said to themselves, 'This is the heir. Come, let us kill him and have his inheritance.' [39] And they took him and threw him out of the vineyard and killed him. [40] When therefore the owner of the vineyard comes, what will he do to those tenants?" [41] They said to him, "He will put those wretches to a miserable death and let out the vineyard to other tenants who will give him the fruits in their seasons." [42] Jesus said to them, "Have you never read in the Scriptures: "'The stone that the builders rejected has become the cornerstone; this was the Lord's doing, and it is marvelous in our eyes'? [43] Therefore I tell you, the kingdom of God will be taken away from you and given to a people producing its fruits."

[117] Matthew 22:15-22, "Then the Pharisees went and plotted how to entangle Him in His words. [16] And they sent their disciples to Him, along with the Herodians, saying, "Teacher, we know that you are true and teach the way of God truthfully, and you do not care about anyone's opinion, for you are not swayed by appearances. [17] Tell us, then, what you think. Is it lawful to pay taxes to Caesar, or not?" [18] But Jesus, aware of their malice, said, "Why put me to the test, you hypocrites? [19] Show me the coin for the tax." And they brought him a denarius. [20] And Jesus said to them, "Whose likeness and inscription is this?" [21] They said, "Caesar's." Then He said to them, "Therefore render to Caesar the things that are Caesar's, and to God the things that are God's." [22] When they heard it, they marveled. And they left Him and went away."

		is the greatest commandment?" Jesus answers from Matthew 22:36-40[118] (word for word). He then quotes Matthew 23:1-7,[119] 13,[120] 27-33.[121] The Pharisees leave and Jesus exhales. The disciples escort Jesus out of the Court of Gentiles. Jesus pauses, quotes Matthew 24:2,[122] and leaves.
43:06	➕	Jesus announces to His disciples that He is finished preaching to the crowds. He leaves. Peter, Andrew, James, and John follow Him.
44:39	👍	Jesus is sitting on the Mount of Olives. Peter, James, John, and Andrew ask Him about the end times. Jesus

---

[118] Matthew 22:36-40, "Teacher, which is the great commandment in the Law?" [37] And He said to him, "You shall love the Lord your God with all your heart and with all your soul and with all your mind. [38] This is the great and first commandment. [39] And a second is like it: You shall love your neighbor as yourself. [40] On these two commandments depend all the Law and the Prophets."

[119] Matthew 23:1-7, "Then Jesus said to the crowds and to his disciples, [2] "The scribes and the Pharisees sit on Moses' seat, [3] so do and observe whatever they tell you, but not the works they do. For they preach, but do not practice. [4] They tie up heavy burdens, hard to bear, and lay them on people's shoulders, but they themselves are not willing to move them with their finger. [5] They do all their deeds to be seen by others. For they make their phylacteries broad and their fringes long, [6] and they love the place of honor at feasts and the best seats in the synagogues [7] and greetings in the marketplaces and being called rabbi by others."

[120] Matthew 23:13, "But woe to you, scribes and Pharisees, hypocrites! For you shut the kingdom of heaven in people's faces. For you neither enter yourselves nor allow those who would enter to go in"

[121] Matthew 23:27-33, "Woe to you, scribes and Pharisees, hypocrites! For you are like whitewashed tombs, which outwardly appear beautiful, but within are full of dead people's bones and all uncleanness. [28] So you also outwardly appear righteous to others, but within you are full of hypocrisy and lawlessness. [29] "Woe to you, scribes and Pharisees, hypocrites! For you build the tombs of the prophets and decorate the monuments of the righteous, [30] saying, 'If we had lived in the days of our fathers, we would not have taken part with them in shedding the blood of the prophets.' [31] Thus you witness against yourselves that you are sons of those who murdered the prophets. [32] Fill up, then, the measure of your fathers. [33] You serpents, you brood of vipers, how are you to escape being sentenced to hell?"

[122] Matthew 24:2, "But he answered them, "You see all these, do you not? Truly, I say to you, there will not be left here one stone upon another that will not be thrown down."

		quotes Matthew 24:3-14[123] and 24:36.[124] John asks, "Are you really never going back to the temple?" Jesus says that He needs time alone. John kisses Him on the head and tells Him that he loves Him. Jesus replies, "I love you too, John." Jesus weeps over Jerusalem. He repeats Luke 19:42.[125] Sheep approach Jesus. David, the shepherd boy, appears singing Psalm 5:7-11.[126] Jesus looks around, and David is gone. He stands alone with the sheep.

Season 5, episode 3 is definitely one of the more Scriptural episodes. Jesus quotes Scripture in three scenes, albeit somewhat loosely. The initial scene at the Lord's Supper was steeped in Scripture, although it was not in any order presented by the Gospels. Parts of it were taken from other conversations, and still other sentences or phrases were taken out of context. However, the majority of what was said in that scene was based on Scripture. The final scene, with His debate with the Pharisees and telling parables to the people was also based loosely on Scripture. The scene was well done.

---

[123] Matthew 24:3-14, "As He sat on the Mount of Olives, the disciples came to Him privately, saying, "Tell us, when will these things be, and what will be the sign of your coming and of the end of the age?" 4 And Jesus answered them, "See that no one leads you astray. 5 For many will come in my name, saying, 'I am the Christ,' and they will lead many astray. 6 And you will hear of wars and rumors of wars. See that you are not alarmed, for this must take place, but the end is not yet. 7 For nation will rise against nation, and kingdom against kingdom, and there will be famines and earthquakes in various places. 8 All these are but the beginning of the birth pains. 9 "Then they will deliver you up to tribulation and put you to death, and you will be hated by all nations for my name's sake. 10 And then many will fall away and betray one another and hate one another. 11 And many false prophets will arise and lead many astray. 12 And because lawlessness will be increased, the love of many will grow cold. 13 But the one who endures to the end will be saved. 14 And this gospel of the kingdom will be proclaimed throughout the whole world as a testimony to all nations, and then the end will come."
[124] Matthew 24:36, "But concerning that day and hour no one knows, not even the angels of heaven, nor the Son, but the Father only."
[125] Luke 19:42, "saying, "Would that you, even you, had known on this day the things that make for peace! But now they are hidden from your eyes."
[126] Psalm 5:7-11, "But I, through the abundance of your steadfast love, will enter your house. I will bow down toward your holy temple in the fear of you. 8 Lead me, O LORD, in your righteousness because of my enemies; make your way straight before me. 9 For there is no truth in their mouth; their inmost self is destruction; their throat is an open grave; they flatter with their tongue. 10 Make them bear their guilt, O God; let them fall by their own counsels; because of the abundance of their transgressions cast them out, for they have rebelled against you. 11 But let all who take refuge in you rejoice; let them ever sing for joy, and spread your protection over them, that those who love your name may exult in you."

In the scene beginning at 5:38, the Pharisees ask Jesus by whose authority He does these things. He replies, "My own!" This is unscriptural. Jesus never responded with such an answer. Other than that, the episode was solid with no LDS references or serious deviations from Scripture.

~~~~~

Episode 4 – "The Same Coin"

This episode continues the story of the Pharisees' plan to have Jesus killed. Judas is also slowly distancing himself from Jesus and having conflicts with the other disciples. Jesus and His followers relocate to Lazarus' house.

5:4 Plot Summary		
0:00	👍 ➕	Last Supper – Jesus, the disciples, and others[127] recite the Dayenu.[128] Big James tearfully confesses that Christ chose them. They then partake of the bitter herbs, to remember the bitterness of slavery. They recite the Jewish prayer for the bitter herbs. From this point on, the scene follows John 13:21-30.[129] John asks Jesus who will

---

[127] The Gospels imply that only the twelve disciples were present with Jesus at the Last Supper. Matthew 26:20 says, "When it was evening, He reclined at the table with the twelve." However, Matthew does not limit it to the twelve. Therefore, other followers may have been present as well.

[128] The Dayenu is a non-biblical Hebrew song, sung or recited during the Passover meal. Dayenu means "it would have been enough" and expresses thankfulness for the various miracles and blessings experienced by the Israelites during the exodus from Egypt.

[129] John 13:21-30, "After saying these things, Jesus was troubled in his spirit, and testified, "Truly, truly, I say to you, one of you will betray me." [22] The disciples looked at one another, uncertain of whom he spoke. [23] One of his disciples, whom Jesus loved, was reclining at table at Jesus' side, [24] so Simon Peter motioned to him to ask Jesus of whom he was speaking. [25] So that disciple, leaning back against Jesus, said to him, "Lord, who is it?" [26] Jesus answered, "It is he to whom I will give this morsel of bread when I have dipped it." So, when he had dipped the morsel, he gave it to Judas, the son of Simon Iscariot. [27] Then after he had taken the morsel, Satan entered into him. Jesus said to him, "What you are going to do, do quickly." [28] Now no one at the table knew why he said this to him. [29] Some thought that, because Judas had the moneybag, Jesus was telling him, "Buy what we need for the feast," or that he should give something to the poor. [30] So, after receiving the morsel of bread, he immediately went out. And it was night."

		betray Him. Jesus whispers in John's ear, and then gives bread to Judas, who breaks it. Jesus has a short non-biblical conversation with Judas and then tells him, "What you are going to do, do it quickly.[130] Judas gets up from the table and departs. The disciples talk amongst themselves. Jesus quotes John 13:33-35.[131] There is more non-biblical talk, then Peter asks, "Lord, where are you going?"[132]
8:13		Introduction
9:14	➕	Jerusalem marketplace – Atticus watches as Kafni garners support against Jesus. People discuss Jesus. Mary Magdalene speaks with the Pharisees. Yussif enters. The Pharisees leave. Yussif and Mary speak of the Pharisees attempt to have Jesus killed.
13:10	➕	Judas and Peter talk. Judas believes that Jesus is not the right kind of Messiah. He wants one to dethrone Rome. They discuss Judas' lack of belief.
15:35	➕	Caiaphas meets with a Pharisee named Gedera. They speak of Jesus. Caiaphas mentions Jesus' statement about no marriage in heaven.[133] They discuss the Sanhedrin's meeting to undermine Jesus' authority. Caiaphas says he will have Jesus arrested in the middle of the night with no fanfare.
19:07	➕	John is in Phoebe's house, staring at a painting of Agamemnon. Jesus enters and says, "The first commandment didn't exactly make it into this home, did it?"[134] They discuss Jephthah and his tragic vow.[135] They

[130] John 13:27.
[131] John 13:33-35, "Little children, yet a little while I am with you. You will seek me, and just as I said to the Jews, so now I also say to you, 'Where I am going you cannot come.' 34 A new commandment I give to you, that you love one another: just as I have loved you, you also are to love one another. 35 By this all people will know that you are my disciples, if you have love for one another."
[132] John 13:36, "Simon Peter said to him, "Lord, where are you going?" Jesus answered him, "Where I am going you cannot follow me now, but you will follow afterward."
[133] Matthew 22:30, "For in the resurrection they neither marry nor are given in marriage but are like angels in heaven."
[134] This is an extremely serious commandment violation. Jesus would not have joked about it.
[135] Judges 11:29-40.

		quote Judges 21:25.[136] John says, "People still do. Take things into their own hands." They discuss the Greek story of Agamemnon. Jesus asks John, "Does he ever find peace? Can he come to forgive himself for what he did?"[137] John then says, "things are going to change, aren't they?" He then asks about forgiving himself for losing Jesus. Jesus replied, "You don't have to forgive yourself, because I forgive you." They then talk about the coming of the Holy Spirit.
24:40	➕	Caiaphas and Gedera attempt to enter the Sanhedrin's meeting. Gedera is allowed to enter, Caiaphas is not.
25:25	👍 ➕	The Sanhedrin meet to discuss Jesus. They talk about Lazarus' resurrection. Shmuel recommends the death penalty. He quotes Leviticus 24:16a.[138] He then quotes Exodus 31:14a.[139] The Pharisees take a vote.
29:42	➕	Two Pharisees update Caiaphas on the Sanhedrin's proceedings.
31:47	👎	Jesus is at Phoebe's house. Judas enters. He tells Jesus that the window of opportunity to be declared King of Israel is rapidly closing. He tells Jesus to reclaim His birthright. Judas says to Jesus, "If I am of no use to your kingdom, the I am nothing." Jesus tells Judas that he has a choice as to whom to give his heart to. I want it and

[136] Judges 21:25, "In those days, there was no king in Israel. Everyone did what was right in his own eyes."
[137] The Bible does not speak of forgiving oneself. This is a modern concept.
[138] Leviticus 24:16, "Whoever blasphemes the name of the LORD shall surely be put to death. All the congregation shall stone him. The sojourner as well as the native, when he blasphemes the Name, shall be put to death."
[139] Exodus 31:14, "for you shall worship no other god, for the LORD, whose name is Jealous, is a jealous God."

		I've had it before."[140] Jesus holds Judas' outstretched hands, "I will pray for you."[141] Judas leaves. Jesus sobs.
37:21	⊕	Joanna and Tamar are discussing Passover. Mary Magdalene enters and tells them to pack for they are relocating to Bethany.
38:49	⊕	Jesus and His followers walk in a field. Judas speaks to Peter about losing the opportunity to fulfill the prophesies. They walk past a fig tree, which has no figs. Jesus curses the fig tree.[142]
40:44	⊕	Jesus and his followers arrive at Lazarus' house. Jesus sends the women in so that He can talk with the disciples. He tells them to be vigilant and to keep watch.
42:05	⊕	Jesus eats with the women. John keeps watch from outside. Jesus says, "Here we are, my sisters and my mother." He speaks of each of their sacrifices. He asks them to keep their distance from Him over the next few days. The women recite their own Dayenu. Mary Magdalene leaves for Jerusalem.

Despite an abundance of non-biblical storyline and text, episode four has a few high points. The opening scene at the Last Supper follows John 13:21-30 closely. Shmuel's recitation of Leviticus 24:16 and Exodus 31:14 in the scene beginning at 25:25 is also well done.

However, the scene beginning at 19:07 is troubling, in that Jesus and John discuss forgiving oneself. This is not a Biblical concept, but a modern one. Never once does Scripture mention self-forgiveness. The scene is somewhat

---

[140] If Judas had given Jesus his heart, as Jesus says in this scene, Judas would have never been possessed by Satan. John 10:28-30 tells us, "I give them eternal life, and they will never perish, and no one will snatch them out of my hand. [29] My Father, who has given them to me, is greater than all, and no one is able to snatch them out of the Father's hand. [30] I and the Father are one."

[141] Anytime Jesus prayed to God, His prayers were answered. Since Judas became possessed by Satan, either God the Father didn't answer Jesus' prayer or Jesus didn't pray for Judas, which would make Jesus to be a liar.

[142] Mark 11:12-14, "On the following day, when they came from Bethany, He was hungry. [13] And seeing in the distance a fig tree in leaf, He went to see if He could find anything on it. When He came to it, He found nothing but leaves, for it was not the season for figs. [14] And He said to it, "May no one ever eat fruit from you again." And his disciples heard it."

redeemed when Jesus forgives John's future sin of abandonment. Additionally, the scene starting at 31:47 has Jesus telling Judas that He has had Judas' heart before, and He wants it again. This would imply that Judas lost his salvation. John 10:28-30 contradicts this, making this scene contrary to Scripture.

~

Episode 5 – "Because of Me"

This episode continues setting up the story for the arrest of Jesus.

5:5 Plot Summary		
0:00	✚	Last Supper – Jesus attempts to pour a glass of wine, but He is shaking. Little John pours it for Him. Thaddeus enters and states his allegiance to Jesus.
0:30	✚	Last Supper - Simon the Zealot, Philip and Judas discuss who will betray Jesus. Judas suggests Thomas.
1:15	✚	Last Supper - Thomas asks Jesus if it is him who will betray Jesus. Jesus tells him, "You have been faithful despite your anger." The disciples debate who is the greatest among them. Jesus stops it and calls it "foolishness." Jesus tells them to return to their places at the table. He then quotes Luke 22:24-26.[143] Peter interrupts and asks Jesus to show the disciples grace. Jesus says, "Please trust the Father's plan." Jesus quotes Luke 22:28-30.[144] There is some non-biblical dialogue. They continue with the Passover meal and Jesus asks John to lead them in the Dayenu.
6:16		Introduction

[143] Luke 22:24-26, "A dispute also arose among them, as to which of them was to be regarded as the greatest. 25 And He said to them, "The kings of the Gentiles exercise lordship over them, and those in authority over them are called benefactors. 26 But not so with you. Rather, let the greatest among you become as the youngest, and the leader as one who serves."
[144] Luke 22:28-30, "You are those who have stayed with me in my trials, 29 and I assign to you, as my Father assigned to me, a kingdom, 30 that you may eat and drink at my table in my kingdom and sit on thrones judging the twelve tribes of Israel."

7:16	✚	Jerusalem Market – the Pharisees discuss the damage Jesus did to the Court of Gentiles. Barnaby confronts the Pharisees and they walk away. They discuss Matthew 21:3b.[145] They then discuss other statements of Jesus. Annas' son Ananas schemes to become high priest.
10:44	✚	The Pharisees enter Caiaphas' home. His wife, Shoshona greets them. Caiaphas asks why they are there. Ananas quotes from Proverbs 11:14b.[146] They object to Caiaphas' plan to arrest Jesus, claiming there isn't enough time.
12:30	✚	(This scene is based on Matthew 11:20-24.[147]) Jesus and the disciples walk. They come across the withered fig tree. There is some non-biblical discussion, and then Jesus says, "I'm here to tear down what isn't bearing fruit, and the time for that is now." This is followed by more non-biblical talk. Jesus then quotes Matthew 24:9[148] and Matthew 26:2.[149]
17:09	✚	A folk quartet plays for Pilate's wife. She appears distraught. He appears and talks to her. She tells him, "We have to leave." Pilate storms out while the quartet resumes playing.
20:51	✚	Atticus enters Pilate's office and tells Pilate of the Pharisees plan to arrest Jesus.

---

[145] Matthew 21:3, "If anyone says anything to you, you shall say, 'The Lord needs them,' and he will send them at once."

[146] Proverbs 11:14, "Where there is no guidance, a people fall, but in an abundance of counselors there is safety."

[147] Matthew 11:20-24, "Then he began to denounce the cities where most of his mighty works had been done, because they did not repent. [21] "Woe to you, Chorazin! Woe to you, Bethsaida! For if the mighty works done in you had been done in Tyre and Sidon, they would have repented long ago in sackcloth and ashes. [22] But I tell you, it will be more bearable on the day of judgment for Tyre and Sidon than for you. [23] And you, Capernaum, will you be exalted to heaven? You will be brought down to Hades. For if the mighty works done in you had been done in Sodom, it would have remained until this day. [24] But I tell you that it will be more tolerable on the day of judgment for the land of Sodom than for you."

[148] Matthew 24:9, "Then they will deliver you up to tribulation and put you to death, and you will be hated by all nations for my name's sake."

[149] Matthew 26:2, "You know that after two days, the Passover is coming, and the Son of Man will be delivered up to be crucified."

22:41	✚	The Sanhedrin argues over what to do with Jesus. Shmuel quotes Psalm 69:9.[150] Caiaphas says, "The only answer is prayer." They pray and disperse. Shmuel weeps.
27:50	✚	The disciples return to Phoebe's house. They discuss what Jesus said. Judas says that if what Jesus says is literal, they should go on looking for the real Messiah. He also says, "He could strike down His enemies and usher in a Messianic age."
33:56	✚	Simon the Zealot storms out and stumbles on a rock. He sees Atticus coming with Roman soldiers. They turn before they reach him. Simon the Zealot follows them and spies on them. They kick down Kafni's door. Atticus and Kafni stare at each other.
36:28	✚	Shmuel visits Caiaphas. He tells Caiphas that he has someone who knows Jesus' location.
38:09	✚	Mary Magdalene walks through Jerusalem at night. She is accosted by two men. They apologize to her, put a bag over her head, and put her in the back of a cart.
39:59	✚	Shmuel infers that he may need some money to get Jesus' exact whereabouts.
40:06	✚	Mary rides in the cart.
40:22	✚	Caiaphas tells Shmuel that he can handle the money.
40:33	✚	Mary is in the cart. They stop at a house and bring her in.
42:07	✚	Judas enters Caiaphas' house.
42:17	✚	Mary is brought to the owner of the house. He turns around and she realizes that it is Nicodemus. She smiles warmly at him.[151]

---

[150] Psalm 69:9, "For zeal for your house has consumed me, and the reproaches of those who reproach you have fallen on me."

[151] Nowhere in Scripture do Mary Magdalene and Nicodemus ever meet, much less converse.

Episode 5 was a disappointment. Most of the episode focused on fictitious characters. Scripture was only mentioned six times. The rest of the episode was non-Scriptural.

~

Episode 6 – "Because of Me"

This episode has Mary Magdalene speaking with Nicodemus at length. Judas and Caiaphas iron out their agreement. Atticus takes matters into his own hands when Pilate fails to step up.

5:6 Plot Summary		
0:00	👍	Last Supper. Jesus tells the disciples that "this is our last Passover together on this earth." Jesus prays, breaks bread and passes it around. "Tonight, we celebrate your redemption from sin because of me. He quotes Luke 22:19.[152] He prays, followed by non-biblical dialogue. He then quotes 1 Corinthians 11:25,[153] John 15:1-2,[154] 4-

[152] Luke 22:19, "And He took bread, and when He had given thanks, He broke it and gave it to them, saying, 'This is my body, which is given for you. Do this in remembrance of me.'"
[153] 1 Corinthians 11:25, "In the same way also He took the cup, after supper, saying, "This cup is the new covenant in my blood. Do this, as often as you drink it, in remembrance of me."
[154] John 15:1-2, "I am the true vine, and my Father is the vinedresser. ² Every branch in me that does not bear fruit He takes away, and every branch that does bear fruit He prunes, that it may bear more fruit."

		9,[155] 11.[156] John 13:10b.[157] John 13:18b and c,[158] John 13:21.[159] The disciples ask "Who?" Jesus excuses Himself and weeps.
8:30		Introduction
9:31	⊕	8 months earlier. There is a Sanhedrin meeting. Nicodemus is there and runs into Shmuel.
11:28	⊕	Nicodemus is having dinner at his home while a Pharisee catches him up on the events of the past 8 months. He tells Nicodemus about the beheading of John the Baptist. They speak about Jesus and Nicodemus excuses himself.
14:31	⊕	Nicodemus and Mary Magdalene talk. He tells her that what she is doing is very dangerous. He asks, "Why is Jesus turning allies into enemies? Nicodemus quotes Matthew 23:27-28,[160] Isaiah 35:5-6a,[161] Isaiah 9:2,[162] and Micah 5:2.[163] Nicodemus says, "I needed Him to be a fraud." Mary Magdalene asks his why he has been absent. Mary Magdalene tells him that Jesus needs his help. She begs him for help. She thanks him for his

---

[155] John 15:4-9, "Abide in me, and I in you. As the branch cannot bear fruit by itself, unless it abides in the vine, neither can you, unless you abide in me. 5 I am the vine; you are the branches. Whoever abides in me and I in him, he it is that bears much fruit, for apart from me you can do nothing. 6 If anyone does not abide in me, he is thrown away like a branch and withers; and the branches are gathered, thrown into the fire, and burned. 7 If you abide in me, and my words abide in you, ask whatever you wish, and it will be done for you. 8 By this my Father is glorified, that you bear much fruit and so prove to be my disciples. 9 As the Father has loved me, so have I loved you. Abide in my love."

[156] John 15:11, "These things I have spoken to you, that my joy may be in you, and that your joy may be full."

[157] John 13:10, "Jesus said to him, "The one who has bathed does not need to wash, except for his feet, but is completely clean. And you are clean, but not every one of you."

[158] John 13:18, "I am not speaking of all of you; I know whom I have chosen. But the Scripture will be fulfilled, 'He who ate my bread has lifted his heel against me.'"

[159] John 13:21, "After saying these things, Jesus was troubled in His spirit, and testified, "Truly, truly, I say to you, one of you will betray me."

[160] Matthew 23:27-28, "Woe to you, scribes and Pharisees, hypocrites! For you are like whitewashed tombs, which outwardly appear beautiful, but within are full of dead people's bones and all uncleanness. 28 So you also outwardly appear righteous to others, but within you are full of hypocrisy and lawlessness."

[161] Isaiah 35:5-6a, "Then the eyes of the blind shall be opened, and the ears of the deaf unstopped; 6 then shall the lame man leap like a deer, and the tongue of the mute sing for joy."

[162] Isaiah 9:2, "The people who walked in darkness have seen a great light; those who dwelt in a land of deep darkness, on them has light shone."

[163] Micah 5:2, "But you, O Bethlehem Ephrathah, who are too little to be among the clans of Judah, from you shall come forth for me one who is to be ruler in Israel, whose coming forth is from of old, from ancient days."

		attempt to cast out her demons. Nicodemus promises to search the Scriptures to find out what is in store for Jesus. Mary Magdalene leaves.
22:30	➕	Zohara, Nicodemus' wife enters. They talk. She knows something has been bothering him for the past few months. On the wall behind them is a conspiracy theory-like system with dozens of papers attached to each other with strings.
23:55	➕	Judas is at Caiaphas' house. Judas tells him, "We are not the same." He also says that he believes that "Jesus is most likely the Messiah. They talk for a bit. Judas says, "All we have to agree on is a price." Caiaphas offers him 20 pieces of silver. They haggle. Caiaphas' final offer is 30 pieces of silver. He then threatens Judas with the temple guards. They agree on the conditions of Judas' betrayal. Caiaphas tells him, "This could be your best chance for your family name to be remembered." Judas leaves.
29:48	➕	Kafni is bound in a chair. Atticus enters. Kafni says, "I have a right to speak to my legal representative." Atticus unlocks Kafni's shackles and pours himself a drink from a flask. They discuss Jesus and His role in Ramah's death. Atticus threatens Kafni with "unlawful assembly, possession of illegal weapons, incitement to violence, conspiracy to commit murder, and possible insurrection." Kafni agrees to attempt to turn the crowd against Jesus.
37:06	👍	Mary Magdalene walks through Jerusalem at night. She recites Isaiah 9:2.[164] She then thanks God for the "light that has shined."
38:26	➕	Caiaphas' house. His servants clean the house to remove any signs of leaven. Pilate bursts in. They talk. Caiaphas says, "This city has a messianic fever and I need to bring the temperature down." Pilate tells Caiaphas that if Jesus is arrested, their alliance will be over. Pilate leaves.

---

[164] Isaiah 9:2, "The people who walked in darkness have seen a great light; those who dwelt in a land of deep darkness, on them has light shone."

42:20	➕	Atticus and the soldiers leave Kafni's house. Simon the Zealot follows them.
43:17	➕	Kafni and his friends are at his house. Kafni quotes Psalm 84:11.[165] One of the men quotes Psalm 34:17,[166] Another quotes Jeremiah 32:18.[167] They recite Job 42:2[168] together. Kafni's wife (Naomi) enters and questions their motives then leaves. Kafni follows her.
45:01	➕	Kafni and Naomi argue about Jesus. She is sad about what Kafni's hate and guilt have done to him. She speaks of leaving Kafni and returning home.
46:28	➕	Simon the Zealot approaches Atticus outside the prison. They discuss Jesus' safety. Atticus says that he is at the prison to question another zealot, Barabbas. Simon says that Barabbas saw many of Jesus' miracles and should have believed but didn't.[169] Atticus quotes Seneca, a Roman philosopher, "Luck happens when preparation meets opportunity." Atticus leaves two swords on the ground and enters the prison. Simon picks up the swords.
50:19	👍	Nicodemus studies the notes on his wall. He quotes Isaiah 61:1,[170] Luke 4:21,[171] John 10:30,[172] and Isaiah 53:3a.[173] Someone knocks on his door. He quotes Matthew 5:17.[174] Yussif (a Pharisee) barges in and tells Nicodemus that Caiaphas is making plans to arrest Jesus.

[165] Psalm 84:11, "For the LORD God is a sun and shield; the LORD bestows favor and honor. No good thing does He withhold from those who walk uprightly."

[166] Psalm 34:17, "When the righteous cry for help, the LORD hears and delivers them out of all their troubles."

[167] Jeremiah 32:18, "You show steadfast love to thousands, but you repay the guilt of fathers to their children after them, O great and mighty God, whose name is the LORD of hosts."

[168] Job 42:2, "I know that you can do all things, and that no purpose of yours can be thwarted."

[169] This is never indicated in Scripture.

[170] Isaiah 61:1, "The Spirit of the Lord GOD is upon me, because the LORD has anointed me to bring good news to the poor; He has sent me to bind up the brokenhearted, to proclaim liberty to the captives, and the opening of the prison to those who are bound."

[171] Luke 4:21, "And He began to say to them, 'Today this Scripture has been fulfilled in your hearing.'"

[172] John 10:30, "I and the Father are one."

[173] Isaiah 53:3, "He was despised and rejected by men, a man of sorrows and acquainted with grief; and as one from whom men hide their faces, He was despised, and we esteemed Him not."

[174] Matthew 5:17, "Do not think that I have come to abolish the Law or the Prophets; I have not come to abolish them but to fulfill them."

		They speak of a traitor amongst Jesus' followers. They discuss Jesus a little more.

Episode six contains a fair amount of Scripture being quoted by an assortment of characters. In the opening scene at the Last Supper, Jesus quotes from Luke, John, and 1 Corinthians. Nicodemus quotes a significant amount of Scriptures in several scenes. Even Kafni and his friends quote Scripture. For that, I applaud this episode.

That being said, there are many fictitious characters and conversations in this episode. While they are important for the plot of the show, they are not Biblical and can confuse new Christians as to what is from the Bible and what is not.

⌒⌒

Episode 7 – "The Upper Room, Part 1"

This episode has the disciples preparing for the Last Supper. They get the upper room, just as Jesus said they would, and travel there separately for safety reasons. Along the way, some of the disciples have flashbacks to their lives before Jesus.

5:7 Plot Summary		
0:00	👍 ➕	Upper room: Jesus enters with a young Mark and tells him to go eat the Seder meal with his parents. Jesus announces that after dinner, they will go to Gethsemane for prayer and reflection. (This scene loosely follows John 13:3-14.)[175] Jesus prepares to wash the disciples'

---

[175] John 13:3-14, "Jesus, knowing that the Father had given all things into His hands, and that He had come from God and was going back to God, 4 rose from supper. He laid aside his outer garments, and taking a towel, tied it around His waist. 5 Then He poured water into a basin and began to wash the disciples' feet and to wipe them with the towel that was wrapped around Him. 6 He came to Simon Peter, who said to Him, "Lord, do you wash my feet?" 7 Jesus answered him, "What I am doing you do not understand now, but afterward you will understand." 8 Peter said to Him, "You shall never wash my feet." Jesus answered him, "If I do not wash you, you have no share with me." 9 Simon Peter said to him, "Lord, not my feet only

		feet. The disciples object. Jesus tells them, "Tonight is our last meal together. Will you just please do what I say and not object for once?" James turns around to allow Jesus to wash his feet. Jesus washes his feet while quoting Isaiah 52:7.[176] Peter prepares to wash feet too.[177] Jesus washes Judas' feet. Peter offers to wash Jesus' feet. Peter quotes John 13:9[178] word for word. Jesus begins to wash Peter's feet. Jesus then quotes John 13:13-14[179] word for word. There is some non-biblical discussion. Jesus tells them that they should serve friends and enemies alike. He looks at Judas.
8:30		Introduction
9:45	✚	Mark sets up tables in the upper room. His father enters. Mark tells him about his dreams from Adonai. They leave.
11:36	✚	They go outside and find that their house has been vandalized with the phrase "Jesus is Messiah." Mark leaves to get water.
12:47	✚	In the market place, James sits alone, having a drink. He pays for his drink and leaves. One of Kafni's men follows him.,
13:55	✚	Peter is preaching. James attempts to get Peter to stop preaching and leave with him. Peter does so. They see Kafni's men speaking to Roman soldiers.

---

but also my hands and my head!" [10] Jesus said to him, "The one who has bathed does not need to wash, except for his feet, but is completely clean. And you are clean, but not every one of you." [11] For He knew who was to betray Him; that was why He said, "Not all of you are clean." [12] When He had washed their feet and put on His outer garments and resumed His place, He said to them, "Do you understand what I have done to you? [13] You call me Teacher and Lord, and you are right, for so I am. [14] If I then, your Lord and Teacher, have washed your feet, you also ought to wash one another's feet.

[176] Isaiah 52:7, "How beautiful upon the mountains are the feet of him who brings good news, who publishes peace, who brings good news of happiness, who publishes salvation, who says to Zion, 'Your God reigns.'"

[177] This is fictitious and conflicts with Scripture. According to John 13:6, Jesus came to Peter. Peter did not approach Jesus.

[178] John 13:9, "Simon Peter said to him, 'Lord, not my feet only but also my hands and my head!'"

[179] John 13:13-14, "You call me Teacher and Lord, and you are right, for so I am. [14] If I then, your Lord and Teacher, have washed your feet, you also ought to wash one another's feet."

14:53	👎	Inside Phoebe's house, the disciples are cleaning in preparation for the Seder feast. Peter, James, and John find Jesus in the courtyard. They tell Jesus that Passover is tonight. Jesus pretends to have forgotten, just to make a joke.[180] Jesus then quotes Luke 22:10-12.[181]
17:39	➕	The disciples clean Phoebe's house. James tells them about Kafni's men following him. He also tells the disciples that Kafni and his men are in league with the Roman soldiers. Peter, John, and Thaddeus have left to prepare a place for their celebration of the Seder meal. Thaddeus will report the location back to James so that the disciples can take separate routes to get there.
19:20	➕	Judas is walking (presumably on his way to Caiaphas' house. He runs into his sister, Devorah. She believes that Jesus is the Messiah. She said that she knows when Judas is hiding something. She tells him, "All of your life has led to this moment." "You were right. The name Iscariot won't be forgotten." They embrace and Judas leaves.
23:15	➕	Peter, John, and Thaddeus walk. They get to the well and see Mark drawing water. They follow him home. Thaddeus leaves to give the location to the other disciples. Peter quotes Luke 22:11.[182]
26:09	➕	Peter and John are in the upper room preparing for the feast. Mark tells them about his dreams. They discuss following Jesus and his current state of sadness.
29:54	➕	Simon the Zealot is in the market. He sees blood on the ground coming from a butcher shop. He has a flashback to his Zealot days. He comes back from his flashback and walks on.
33:02	➕	Nathaniel is walking through Jerusalem. He sees a woman selling stringed instruments. He flashes back to when he was an architecture student. In that flashback,

[180] This implies that Jesus was lying. This scene contradicts the very nature of God.
[181] Luke 22:10-12, "He said to them, "Behold, when you have entered the city, a man carrying a jar of water will meet you. Follow him into the house that he enters [11] and tell the master of the house, 'The Teacher says to you, Where is the guest room, where I may eat the Passover with my disciples?' [12] And he will show you a large upper room furnished; prepare it there."
[182] John 22:11, "and tell the master of the house, 'The Teacher says to you, Where is the guest room, where I may eat the Passover with my disciples?'"

		he hears a woman singing Psalm 130:1[183] and receives a letter of encouragement from Philip.
37:25	⊕	Andrew and Philip walk through the streets of Jerusalem. They see Roman soldiers carrying a carriage. They flash back to the days they followed John the Baptist. John quotes Luke 3:16b,[184] Matthew 3:10,[185] and John 1:7,[186] but then tells a soldier not to extort money from anyone. Andrew is hungry. Philip offers him candied locusts.
41:41	⊕	Thomas walks through the market. There is a flashback to his father being arrested for murder.
43:50	⊕	Matthew walks past a tax booth. He sees a Jewish man spit on the tax collector. This reminds him of his first day as a tax collector. He and Gaius talk, and Matthew tells Gaius that he thinks there is something wrong with him.[187]
49:10	⊕	Little James walks near a temple. He hears the temple choir singing. He flashes back to singing Psalm 28:7[188] with a choir in school. He finishes his training and desires to be assigned to the temple choir in Jerusalem. He is denied Jerusalem because of his limp. The choirmaster references Leviticus 21:16-19.[189] He leaves and falls asleep in the wilderness. Thaddeus comes across him. Jesus approaches Little James and talks to him.

---

[183] Psalm 130:1, "Out of the depths I cry to you, O LORD!"

[184] Luke 3:16, "John answered them all, saying, 'I baptize you with water, but He who is mightier than I is coming, the strap of whose sandals I am not worthy to untie. He will baptize you with the Holy Spirit and fire.'"

[185] Matthew 3:10, "Even now the axe is laid to the root of the trees. Every tree therefore that does not bear good fruit is cut down and thrown into the fire."

[186] John 1:7, "He came as a witness, to bear witness about the light, that all might believe through him."

[187] Matthew is alluding to being on the autism spectrum. The entire concept of Matthew having autism is fiction. There is no biblical evidence to support it.

[188] Psalm 28:7, "The LORD is my strength and my shield; in Him my heart trusts, and I am helped; my heart exults, and with my song I give thanks to Him."

[189] Leviticus 21:16-19, "And the LORD spoke to Moses, saying, [17] "Speak to Aaron, saying, None of your offspring throughout their generations who has a blemish may approach to offer the bread of his God. [18] For no one who has a blemish shall draw near, a man blind or lame, or one who has a mutilated face or a limb too long, [19] or a man who has an injured foot or an injured hand."

56:29	✚	The disciples are waiting for Jesus and Thaddeus in the upper room. Roman soldiers approach but then leave.

Episode 7 has some moments of Scripture, but sadly, the majority of the episode is fiction. The episode opens with Jesus washing the disciples' feet in the upper room. The scene generally follows John 13:3-14. The primary deviation from Scripture is that Peter wants to wash Jesus' feet. The character of Mark is introduced. Tradition maintains that the upper room was owned by Mark's parents. However, the show has Mark having prophetic dreams about Jesus, which is not found in the Bible.

The most troubling scene occurs at 14:53, where Jesus is talking to Peter, James, and John. Jesus jokingly pretends to have forgotten when the Passover is. The fact that Jesus would pretend something like that shows that He is willing to deceive, and that runs contrary to Scripture.[190] It is one thing to add non-biblical things to the story, as long as they don't conflict with the Bible, but it is a completely different thing to have the story contradict Scripture.

Episode 8 – "The Upper Room, Part 2"

This episode follows Jesus and the disciples from the upper room to the Garden of Gethsemane, culminating with Judas' kiss of betrayal.

5:8 Plot Summary		
0:00	✚	Thaddeus is walking through the market. He sees hammers for sale. He has a flashback to when he worked as a stonemason. Jesus was at the same project (a latrine), working as a carpenter, and was singing Psalm 39:4-6.[191]

---

[190] 2 Corinthians 5:21, "For our sake He made Him to be sin who knew no sin, so that in Him we might become the righteousness of God."

[191] Psalm 39:4-6, "O LORD, make me know my end and what is the measure of my days; let me know how fleeting I am! ⁵ Behold, you have made my days a few handbreadths, and my lifetime is as nothing before you. Surely all mankind stands as a mere breath! *Selah* ⁶ Surely a man goes about as a shadow! Surely for nothing they are in turmoil; man heaps up wealth and does not know who will gather!"

		As a joke, Jesus says that He has no idea what a stonemason does.[192] They eat lunch together. Jesus says that some of the wonders of Egypt will remain for thousands of years. Jesus tells Thaddeus that He will build a fortress stronger than stone and invites Thaddeus to join Him. Jesus tells him, "I am a rabbi, and I'm asking you to follow me." He describes the other disciples.
10:50	⊕	Thaddeus enters the upper room. The disciples wait for Jesus. When Jesus enters the room, they all stand.
12:40		Introduction
13:42	⊕	Mark is in bed. He hears the disciples singing Psalm 118:22-23[193] in the room above him. He hears Jesus say, "My friends, it is time." Then he hears footsteps. He gets out of bed.
14:45	⊕	The disciples prepare to leave. Peter grabs two swords. He gives one to James. John and Peter talk. John quotes John 13:18c.[194] They leave.
15:45	👍	The disciples and Jesus walk toward Gethsemane. Jesus tells the disciples to sit by the garden gate while He prays. (Matthew 26:36)[195] Jesus takes Peter, James, and John into the garden.
17:15	⊕	Pilate is at home. Atticus enters and they talk about Jesus and the peace of Jerusalem. Atticus leaves and Claudia, his wife, enters. They speak of her dreams, but she doesn't reveal any details. She leaves.
24:18	⊕	Caiaphas has called an emergency meeting of the Sanhedrin. They argue and Nicodemus bursts in.
25:42	⊕	Judas visits Caiaphas' house. He tells Malchus that he knows Jesus' location and can bring them to Him now.

[192] By saying that He doesn't know what a stonemason does, Jesus is showing that He is not omniscient (all knowing). This is the opposite of what Scripture says about Jesus. In an attempt to make light-hearted conversation, the writers have painted Jesus in a sinful light. He never sinned. He was perfect.

[193] Psalm 118:22-23, "The stone that the builders rejected has become the cornerstone. 23 This is the LORD's doing; it is marvelous in our eyes."

[194] John 13:18, "I am not speaking of all of you; I know whom I have chosen. But the Scripture will be fulfilled, 'He who ate my bread has lifted his heel against me.'"

[195] Matthew 26:36, "Then Jesus went with them to a place called Gethsemane, and He said to His disciples, "Sit here, while I go over there and pray.""

		Malchus and Judas step outside to the temple guards, who are waiting.
26:49	👎	(The Garden of Gethsemane scenes generally follow Matthew 26:36-46.)[196] Jesus and the disciples are at Gethsemane. Jesus breaks down and cries. Jesus quotes Matthew 26: 38.[197] Jesus then said, "The Great Physician Himself will minister to me."[198] Jesus prays a non-biblical prayer and sobs. He sees Abraham preparing to sacrifice Isaac. Jesus watches as Abraham loads the wood on Isaac's back. From there, the scene follows Genesis 22:7-8.[199] Jesus then quotes Matthew 26:39b.[200] There is some non-biblical prayers, and Jesus quotes Matthew 26:39c. He then prays the first four lines of the Lord's Prayer.[201]
36:42	👍	Jesus returns to Peter, James, and John, but they are asleep. See Matthew 26:40.[202]

---

[196] Matthew 26:36-46, "Then Jesus went with them to a place called Gethsemane, and He said to His disciples, "Sit here, while I go over there and pray." [37] And taking with Him Peter and the two sons of Zebedee, He began to be sorrowful and troubled. [38] Then He said to them, "My soul is very sorrowful, even to death; remain here and watch with me." [39] And going a little farther He fell on his face and prayed, saying, "My Father, if it be possible, let this cup pass from me; nevertheless, not as I will, but as You will." [40] And He came to the disciples and found them sleeping. And He said to Peter, "So, could you not watch with me one hour? [41] Watch and pray that you may not enter into temptation. The spirit indeed is willing, but the flesh is weak." [42] Again, for the second time, He went away and prayed, "My Father, if this cannot pass unless I drink it, your will be done." [43] And again He came and found them sleeping, for their eyes were heavy. [44] So, leaving them again, He went away and prayed for the third time, saying the same words again. [45] Then He came to the disciples and said to them, "Sleep and take your rest later on. See, the hour is at hand, and the Son of Man is betrayed into the hands of sinners. [46] Rise, let us be going; see, my betrayer is at hand."

[197] Matthew 26:18, "Then He said to them, "My soul is very sorrowful, even to death; remain here and watch with me."

[198] This is not something Jesus said, nor is it something He would have said. On the cross, he asked, "My God, my God, why have you forsaken me?" On the cross, God turned His back on His Son. The Great Physician did not minister to Jesus in those moments.

[199] Genesis 22:7-8, "And Isaac said to his father Abraham, "My father!" And he said, "Here I am, my son." He said, "Behold, the fire and the wood, but where is the lamb for a burnt offering?" [8] Abraham said, "God will provide for Himself the lamb for a burnt offering, my son." So, they went both of them together."

[200] Matthew 26:39, "And going a little farther He fell on his face and prayed, saying, "My Father, if it be possible, let this cup pass from me; nevertheless, not as I will, but as you will."

[201] Matthew 6:9-10, "Our Father in heaven, hallowed be your name. [10] Your kingdom come, your will be done, on earth as it is in heaven."

[202] Matthew 26:40, "And He came to the disciples and found them sleeping. And He said to Peter, "So, could you not watch with me one hour?"

38:28	👍	Jesus goes back to pray. Jesus quotes He quotes Matthew 26:42b.[203] Jesus cries. A fog rolls in. Jesus has a flashback to the valley of dry bones. He sees the prophet, Ezekiel. The rest of the scene with Ezekiel follows Ezekiel 37:1-3.[204] Jesus cries on Ezekiel's shoulder.
43:16	👎	Jesus returns to Peter, James, and John. They are asleep. This time though, they appear as boys. Jesus goes off to pray again. Jesus sweats blood.[205] Jesus' father Joseph comforts Him.[206] Joseph says to Jesus, "I'll be waiting for you." Jesus returns to Peter, James, and John. Jesus quotes Matthew 26:45-46.[207] They exit the garden through the gate and see the temple guard, Judas, Malchus, Pharisees, and Kafni and his men coming to arrest Jesus.
50:56	👍	The disciples prepare for a fight. Jesus tells them to stay back. Judas steps out from behind the guards. Judas kisses Jesus.

Jesus feigns ignorance as a joke twice in the last two episodes of the season. As was mentioned before, Jesus would never do that because it is deceptive, and Jesus was never deceptive. This is an attempt to paint Jesus in a human light, which fits in with Mormon theology that He was only a man.

The scenes with Jesus and the disciples in the Garden of Gethsemane were, for the most part, true to Matthew 26. Additionally, the scene beginning at 38:28 in which Jesus runs into Ezekiel in the valley of dry bones was very well done, sticking closely to Ezekiel 37:1-3. The scene at 43:16 got it wrong that an angel came and ministered to Jesus, not Joseph, His earthly father.

---

[203] Matthew 26:42, "Again, for the second time, He went away and prayed, "My Father, if this cannot pass unless I drink it, your will be done."

[204] Ezekiel 37:1, "The hand of the LORD was upon me, and He brought me out in the Spirit of the LORD and set me down in the middle of the valley; it was full of bones. ² And He led me around among them, and behold, there were very many on the surface of the valley, and behold, they were very dry. ³ And He said to me, 'Son of man, can these bones live?' And I answered, 'O Lord GOD, you know.'"

[205] Luke 22:44, "And being in agony He prayed more earnestly; and His sweat became like great drops of blood falling down to the ground."

[206] Joseph comforting Jesus contradicts Luke 22:43, "And there appeared to Him an angel from heaven, strengthening Him." Joseph was human, not an angel.

[207] Matthew 26:45-46, "Then He came to the disciples and said to them, "Sleep and take your rest later on. See, the hour is at hand, and the Son of Man is betrayed into the hands of sinners. ⁴⁶ Rise, let us be going; see, my betrayer is at hand."

Season 5 Assessment

While Season 5 contained some Biblical scenes, the vast majority of the scenes were fiction. One of the themes in Season 5 is especially troublesome. In episode 4, Jesus and Judas talk. Jesus tells Judas that "he has a choice as to whom to give his heart to." Jesus tells him, "I want it and I've had it before." This discounts the fact that Satan entered Judas' heart. [208] This would not have happened if Jesus had Judas' heart before. According to John 10:27-29,[209] no one, not even Satan can snatch someone from God's hand. That means that Jesus did not have Judas' heart before, which makes Jesus a liar in episode 4.

The opening of each episode with a portion of the Last Supper was a great way to break up the supper, and plenty of Scripture was quoted. Sadly, however, plenty of non-Scripture was also included. Unless one knows the Gospels extremely well, it is difficult to know when Jesus' words are Biblical or not.

---

[208] Luke 22:3, "Then Satan entered into Judas called Iscariot, who was of the number of the twelve."

[209] John 10:27-29, "My sheep hear my voice, and I know them, and they follow me. [28] I give them eternal life, and they will never perish, and no one will snatch them out of my hand. [29] My Father, who has given them to me, is greater than all, and no one is able to snatch them out of the Father's hand."

Appendix A – Jewish Daily Prayers

THROUGHOUT EACH SEASON OF *THE Chosen*, many of the characters offer prayers that begin with "Blessed art Thou, O Lord our God, King of the universe." These prayers are known as berakah, which is a Hebrew way of expressing thanks to God. These prayers are often used in the synagogue, during private prayer, and on other special occasions. There are multiple forms of this prayer with each form depending on the occasion for which it is prayed. Here are a few:

- When drinking wine, the prayer is, "Blessed art Thou, O Lord our God, King of the Universe, who hast created the fruit of the vine."
- When lighting candles, the prayer is, "Blessed are you, Lord our God, King of the Universe, who created the light of fire."
- Before eating a meal, the prayer will be, "Blessed are you, Lord our God, King of the Universe, who brings forth bread from the earth."
- When viewing nature, the individual would pray, "Blessed are you, Lord our God, King of the Universe, who made creation."
- Before major holidays, the prayer is, "Blessed are you, Lord our God, King of the Universe, who has kept us alive and preserved us and enabled us to reach this season."
- Before weddings, the prayer is, "Blessed are you, Lord our God, King of the Universe, who created joy and gladness, groom and bride, mirth, song, delight, dancing, love, harmony, peace and companionship."
-

Appendix B – The Book of Mormon

THE OPENING LINE OF THE to the *Book of Mormon* says that it is a holy scripture comparable to the Bible. Is it, though? The bottom line with all holy Scripture is whether or not we can trust it. Mormons will tell you that the *Book of Mormon* is the most recent revelation of God. Like Muslims, Mormons maintain that the Bible has been corrupted. Head bishops within the Mormon church will tell you that the *Book of Mormon* is more correct than the Bible.

We will compare the Bible and the *Book of Mormon* in ten different areas: history, geography, peoples and empires, cities, plants and animals, ancient writings and metallurgy, coins, warfare, temples, and historical figures. After comparing these ten areas, it should become evident which book is fiction and which is true.

History

The Old Testament contains two things in the Bible: the history of God's people from creation until 400 BC and prophecies concerning the coming of God's Son, Jesus Christ. The New Testament contains the fulfillment of Old Testament prophecies about Jesus Christ and the history of the young church.

According to the *Book of Mormon*, a group known as the Jaredites migrated to North America following the events surrounding the tower of Babel. This would have happened around 5000 years ago.[1] The Jaredites wiped themselves out in a bloody civil war, with over 2 million Jaredites dying in a single battle on the Hill Cumorah. After the Jaredites died out, an Israelite man, Lehi, and his family sailed for North America around 600 BC.

---

[1] It is important to remember that we have plenty of artifacts this old. For example, archaeologists found a 5,000-year-old drum, a clay ball, and a polished bone pin at a burial site in the English village of Burton Agnes. In December 2017, archaeologists discovered a collection of unique Egyptian artifacts unearthed in the ancient city of Jericho. Five mother-of-pearl shells were unearthed while exploring a house inhabited 5,000 years ago. In 2021, researchers discovered arrowheads, awls, and pottery that were 5,000 years old in a Northeast Baltimore park. There is no shortage of artifacts from 5,000 years ago. There are plenty, and they do exist. However, none exist from the Jaredite immigration.

His son was Nephi, and a nation of white-skinned (no longer Jewish) people grew from him called the Nephites. His other sons, Laman and Lemuel, fathered the Lamanite nation but were rebellious and cursed with dark (brown and black) skin. Following his death and resurrection in 34 AD, Jesus appeared in the Americas to the Nephites and the Lamanites. Jesus' visit brought centuries of peace between the two nations. However, this peace did not last, and the Hill Cumorah was again the site of a bloody battle. The Lamanites wiped out the Nephite nation except for one man – Moroni.

One thousand four hundred years later, Moroni appeared to Joseph Smith as an angel, telling him that there was a book written on gold plates that contained the history of the former inhabitants of this continent. Smith translated those plates into the *Book of Mormon*, published in 1830. From then on, Joseph Smith and every LDS prophet and apostle after him proclaimed it to be a true and accurate history of ancient America. For Mormons, the Bible is a historical account of the Old World, while the *Book of Mormon* is a historical account of the Americas.

Geography

One way to verify whether a historical document is true is to compare it to the location's geography. We need to ask, "Does the geography of each location match the account?"

For the history of the Bible, many of the locations mentioned in Scripture still exist today, *using the same names*. These include the Jordan River, the Sea of Galilee, Capernaum, and Jerusalem. We know precisely where these Biblical locations are today, and the geography matches exactly.

The Book of Mormon fails this test altogether. The locations described do not match anything in North America or anywhere else. When asked about this, LDS archaeologists state, "The LDS church does not officially take any position regarding the geography contained in the *Book of Mormon*." Yet they claim that it is a perfect book.

Peoples and Empires

Another test of truth in the Bible and the *Book of Mormon* is to examine the peoples and empires of that area. According to the Bible, the Jews were God's chosen people. The Jews still exist today, both in the land to which they were exiled and in Israel.

All Biblical nations surrounding Palestine have been verified through history and archaeology. Mormon archaeologist William Wilson, from NAU, says, "It's very evident that when you are talking about the Bible, that they are talking about very real places." We know that the Roman and Greek empires existed because of the vast amount of archaeological evidence – buildings, coins, pots, and more. The Bible also lists people groups that no longer exist today, such as the Canaanites and the Philistines. However, we know much about these people groups due to Egyptian history and archaeological sites.

The *Book of Mormon* states that the Jaredite nation was the most prominent nation on earth. And yet, this "most prominent nation" in the world left no trace of evidence of its existence. Additionally, according to the *Book of Mormon*, the Nephites were a large nation that built cities of rock, wood, and copper. There is no evidence whatsoever that the Nephites ever existed. The Nephites lived at the same time as the ancient Greeks, so there should be plenty of evidence for their existence. According to the *Book of Mormon*, at around 400 AD, the Lamanites became the ancestors of the Native Americans. However, the Native Americans existed much earlier than 400 AD. There is no evidence of a Jewish settlement in the Americas before 1500 AD. This begs the question, "Could these three massive nations – the Jaredites, the Lamanites, and the Nephites have existed and left no trace of themselves?" It is not likely.

Cities

The permanent settlement of almost all cities mentioned in the Bible is well documented and agreed upon by scholars today. Many are still in existence. These include Hazor, Jerusalem, Capernaum, Beersheba, Jericho, Nazareth, Ephesus, and Bethsaida. These cities have the same names as they did thousands of years ago because the inhabitants of those cities have passed them down from generation to generation. We can easily travel to any of these cities to see where the events described in the Bible took place.

The cities in the *Book of Mormon* have names such as Nephi, Jershoh, Sidom, Bountiful, and Zerahemla. All in all, thirty major cities are mentioned in the *Book of Mormon*. And yet, there is no evidence that any of these cities existed. Unlike Biblical towns, we cannot travel to any of these.

Plants and Animals

Plants and trees described in the Bible still exist today. These include figs, almonds, palm trees, wheat, barley, and olives. Animals depicted in the Bible are still in existence today, although they may not exist in Palestine anymore. The Bible mentions lions, horses, doves, quail, cows, bears, sheep, wolves, and fish.

We see the wrong plants at the wrong point in history in the Book of Mormon. According to the *Book of Mormon*, Nephi, Laman, and Lemuel planted corn, wheat, and barley seeds. We don't see the types of plants described in the Book of Mormon in the Americas at that time. As Nephi, Laman, and Lemuel explored the new world,[2] they stated that "the beasts of the forest were every kind: both the cow and the ox, and the ass and the horse, and the goat and the wild goat."[3] The issue here is that the Mayans did not have beasts of burden. There were no oxen or donkeys in the Americas at that time. The *Book of Mormon* speaks of plains abounding with horses and battles with horse-drawn chariots by the tens of thousands. However, horses were not brought to the Americas until the late 1600s. We don't see evidence of cows and oxen, donkeys, and horses from the times found in the *Book of Mormon*. In Ether 9:19,[4] Joseph Smith claims that elephants existed in the Americas. However, there is no evidence of elephants in the Americas between 2600 BC and 600 BC.[5]

Ancient Writings and Metallurgy
The Bible contains the most copied, well-preserved texts in human history. Over the years, thousands of fragments of Scripture have been found. Archaeologists have found portions of Numbers 6 dating back to the seventh century BC. Every book of the Old Testament, except Esther, is found in the Dead Sea Scrolls, dating between 200 and 100 BC. We have over 500 manuscripts that contain the entire New Testament, some from the second century AD.

What about the *Book of Mormon*? The *Book of Mormon* claims that the Nephites were a "people of writing." However, no trace of Nephite writing

---

[2] The New World refers to South, Central, and North America.
[3] 1 Nephi 18:25.
[4] Ether 9:19, "And they also had horses, and asses, and there were elephants and cureloms and cumoms; all of which were useful unto man, and more especially the elephants and cureloms and cumoms." According to Mormon lore, the cumom and the curelom are "useful" animals that may have existed in North or South America.
[5] The Book of Ether allegedly occurred between 2600 BC and 600 BC.

has been found, even more so that no metal plates exist. There is no physical evidence of a manuscript from the *Book of Mormon* before Joseph Smith wrote it in 1830. Since the events in the *Book of Mormon* ended in 400 AD, there is a 1400-year gap without any documental trace of the *Book of Mormon*. According to the *Book of Mormon*, the language used in early America was called "Reformed Egyptian." All linguists will tell you that they have never heard of reformed Egyptian. There is no evidence that ancient Americans wrote in reformed Egyptian or Hebrew. Where are the ancient documents? We have them with the Bible. Why do we not have them with the *Book of Mormon*? If the *Book of Mormon* were true, we should be able to dig up the gold plates from the Hill Cumorah and put them on display for everyone to read and interpret for themselves. This is what we have done with the Bible.

According to the *Book of Mormon*, Nephi's family processed gold, silver, and copper ore. However, those metals are never described as being processed with bellows and other tools, as mentioned in the *Book of Mormon*. The *Book of Mormon* specifically stated that there was steel in the New World. (Ether 7:9) No site has been found where steel was smelted. According to the *Book of Mormon*, the Jaredites and Nephites used metal armor in warfare, metal coins, and metal plates to write upon. No evidence of any of this has ever been found.

Coins

The Bible mentions many Roman coins being used in the days of Jesus. We have thousands of coins dating back to 100 BC. What does the *Book of Mormon* say about coins? In Alma 11, the *Book of Mormon* describes the money system. Two issues arise if we compare the *Book of Mormon* coins to those in the Ancient Middle East. No metallic coins were being used in the Ancient Near East 5000 years ago, and metallic coins only existed in America in the coming of the colonists. Where are all the Nephite coins used for thousands of years? No one knows.

Warfare

The Old Testament contains accounts of the Israelites' numerous battles and wars. Archaeologists have found spearheads and arrowheads, and evidence of warfare has been found throughout Palestine.

Footnotes in Mormon 8:2 place the destruction of the Nephites at Hill Cumorah around 400 AD. According to the *Book of Mormon,* the death count was 200,000 people. The Hill Cumorah has no skeletons, mass graves, weapons, animal skeletons, steel swords, chariot parts, or anything else. By contrast, Jewish historian Josephus speaks of Masada, which occurred some 300 years before the destruction of the Nephites. Masada has been excavated, and we have ruins and skeletons. No civilization can be wiped out to the point that nothing is left. Where are this ancient catastrophe's bodies, weapons, and homes? We don't find them because they do not exist. Why doesn't the LDS Church do excavations on Hill Cumorah? Since the Mormon church owns the land, they could excavate. But they don't because they know that nothing is there.

The Temple

The Bible, in Matthew 24:2,[6] refers to the temple in Jerusalem. In addition to the wailing wall, the piles of huge rocks where the temple once stood prove Jesus' statement that not one stone will stand on another.

According to the *Book of Mormon*,[7] Nephi's family built a temple like Solomon's. Jews, however, were not allowed to sacrifice at a temple other than the one on the temple mount in Jerusalem.[8] Additionally, according to 1 Nephi 5:14,[9] Lehi and his sons were descendants of Joseph, not Levi. The appointing of priests outside of the Levitical line was forbidden. Therefore, if Lehi were a Hebrew, he wouldn't have appointed his sons priests. And yet, the *Book of Mormon* claims to uphold all of the Old Testament laws.

Historical Figures

We have plenty of extra-Biblical evidence that validates the existence of people in the Bible. Let's examine some of them. Throughout Scripture, there are multiple references to the House of David,[10] which archaeological remains can verify. The Tel Dan Stele is a fragmentary pillar containing an Aramaic inscription that reads, "king of the House of David," dating back to the 9th

---

[6] Matthew 24:2, "But he answered them, "You see all these, do you not? Truly, I say to you, there will not be left here one stone upon another that will not be thrown down."

[7] 2 Nephi 5:16

[8] Deuteronomy 12:13-14, "Take care that you do not offer your burnt offerings at any place that you see, [14] but at the place that the LORD will choose in one of your tribes, there you shall offer your burnt offerings, and there you shall do all that I am commanding you."

[9] 1 Nephi 5:14, "And it came to pass that my father, Lehi, also found upon the plates of brass a genealogy of his fathers; wherefore he knew that he was a descendant of Joseph."

[10] Some of these references include 2 Samuel 7:8-17, Isaiah 9:6-7, Jeremiah 33:17, Genesis 49:10, Psalm 89:34-37, Isaiah 11:1, Jeremiah 23:5, and Amos 9:11-12.

century BC. Another example is Caiaphas, the high priest, who is mentioned repeatedly in the New Testament.[11] In the 1990s, a group tomb was found in which one of the labels on a bone box was, "Joseph, son of Caiaphas the high priest." We have physical evidence that David and Caiaphas, the high priest, existed. What about Jesus? What proof do we have that Jesus existed? Not only is he mentioned in Christian texts but also in non-Christian texts. The Jews talk about Him in their writings, albeit not favorably. Josephus speaks of Jesus – the Messiah, the teacher, crucified under Pilate, who was resurrected. Tacitus, a Roman historian and politician, mentions Jesus Christ in his writings. Multiple ancient documents have established the historicity of Jesus Christ. There is no doubt among secular archaeologists that Jesus existed.

The *Book of Mormon*, in its introduction, claims that it was written by many "ancient prophets." We have no evidence that these prophets ever existed, let alone that they wrote down these prophecies. While there is plenty of proof that Jesus lived in ancient Palestine, to say that He existed in the Americas is ludicrous. It is certainly not backed by evidence. The *Book of Mormon* maintains that there was a massive conversion to Christianity after Christ's appearance in 34 AD. There is no evidence to support this – no ancient historians, no archaeological evidence, and no oral traditions passed down by Native Americans. The Jesus presented in the *Book of Mormon* can only be the Jesus Christ of Joseph Smith's imagination.

The Bible is an important historical source, even for secular archaeologists. The Bible is so archaeologically sound that the Smithsonian has used it as a historical source. The Smithsonian has never used the *Book of Mormon* as an archaeological source. It simply has no authority or integrity. If it was just one thing wrong, we could overlook it. If it gets everything wrong, we must not ignore it. Joseph Smith fabricated this history and called it the word of God.

Proof for the Truth of the Book of Mormon

Moroni 10:4 says, "I would exhort you so that when you read these things that you would ask God if these things are not true; and if you shall ask with a sincere heart, he will reveal the truth of it unto you by the power of the holy ghost." Mormons use this verse to establish the truth of their Scriptures. Truth, then, is to be found by examining one's own heart. This goes completely

---

[11] A few of these references are Matthew 26:3, Matthew 26:57, Luke 3:2, John 11:49, John 18:12-14, and John 18:24.

184 Whats Wrong with The Chosen?

against the Bible. Jeremiah 17:9 tells us, "The heart is deceitful above all things and desperately sick; who can understand it?" The hearts of men are corrupt. Why would we examine them for truth? For the Mormons, truth is obtained by gaining an emotional sense that something is true. A feeling does not determine truth.

Do the Bible and the *Book of Mormon* Conflict?

At the April 2002 general conference, LDS President Gordon B. Hinckley said, "As a church, we have critics – many of them. They say that we do not believe in the traditional Christ of Christianity. There is some substance to what they say. Our faith, our knowledge is not based on ancient tradition. Our faith, our knowledge comes from the witness of a prophet." And that prophet is Joseph Smith. Hinckley does not believe in the Scriptural Jesus. He believes in Joseph Smith's Jesus.

Galatians 1:8-9 tells us, "But though we, or an angel from heaven, preach any other gospel unto you than that which we have preached unto you, let him be accursed. [9] As we said before, so say I now again, if any man preach any other gospel unto you than that ye have received, let him be accursed." Paul's command is valid. Those who teach the Book of Mormon are accursed. The Mormon Church purports themselves to be Christian. As such, converting people from evangelical churches is easy. However, Galatians 1:8-9 should keep converts clear from the Mormon church. What we have in the Bible is sufficient for salvation. We do not need another gospel. Since the *Book of Mormon* is false, Mormonism cannot be true.

PLEASE REVIEW

★ ★ ★ ★ ★

You have reached the awkward part of the book where I ask you to leave me a review on Amazon, Google, or Goodreads. Believe me, I hate this as much as you do. However, I am swallowing my pride and asking anyway. Please! Whether you loved or hated it, you have made it this far, so please leave a review. Here's the thing: reviews play a big role in determining whether or not someone will read my book. Leaving a review will help me out a lot. If you liked this study, please recommend it to others. Oh, and thanks for reading my book. It means the world to me.

I can't stand typos. If you are like me, you can't either. Typos are like gremlins. No matter how many times a book has been edited, they magically appear. So, if you see a typo I missed, please email me at timothyjmulder@gmail.com.

Thanks!

More by Timothy J. Mulder

Suffering in Silence: Ministering to Those With Mental Illness

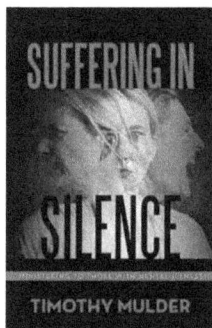

Mental illness affects millions of Americans. Often, those afflicted will develop substance abuse problems or will die from suicide. Surely, there must be something the church can do to help. The author considers questions such as: Why are those who suffer from mental illness so often misunderstood? What are common misconceptions about mental illness in the church? How are churches and other ministries well positioned to help people struggling with mental illness? How can you best minister to those with mental illness? Join the author as he explores how to better understand mental illness, so you may better minister to those who suffer from it.

Ruth: A Story of God's Redeeming Love

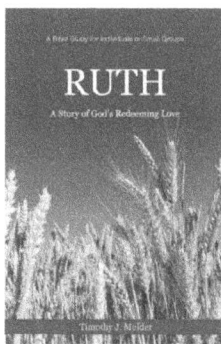

The Book of Ruth is one of the most famous short stories of all time. In just four chapters, the reader is exposed to faithlessness, death, unwavering integrity, and redemption. Ruth provides an intimate view into the back story of the lineage of King David. Set in the time of the Judges, when "everyone did what was right in their own eyes," the wholesomeness and honesty of Ruth are a welcome breath of fresh air. In this best-selling study, we cover such topics as God's loving-kindness, the foreshadowing of Christ, waiting on God's timing, the providence of God, and the redemption of Naomi. Join the author as he takes an in-depth, Reformed look into one of the greatest redemption stories of all time.

The Armchair Theologian's Guide to the Westminster Confession of Faith

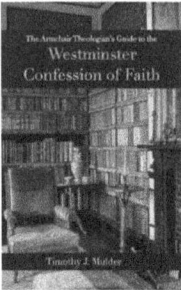

Do you ever feel as though you have read your Bible but wish you could better explain what you believe? Do you wonder how the Bible applies to our world today? Are you frustrated when confronted with viewpoints that are not Scriptural, but struggle to disprove them? The Westminster Confession of Faith is a topical arrangement of the Bible into doctrinal truths. It was written to organize the Bible into a unifying summary of what Christians believe and to combat heresy. The Westminster Confession of Faith is as relevant today as when it was written nearly 400 years ago. This book goes through the WCF in a user-friendly format, which includes the traditional and modern English versions of the WCF. It also highlights and counters unbiblical doctrine and creates talking points perfect for explaining Scripture to young believers or for cozy armchair discussions with friends.

The Despicable Dozen – Bad Guys of the Bible

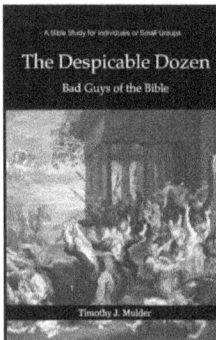

Browse any Christian bookseller, and you will see plenty of Bible studies on the heroes of the faith. What about the terrible, evil people in the Scriptures? God's inerrant Word includes these villains for a reason. Why are there no Bible studies about them? We know that God uses the "good guys" and the "bad guys" of the Bible to accomplish His perfect will. This study looks at the baddest of the bad: the despicable dozen.

The twelve villains in this study include those guilty of heinous sins, while others are included because of *whom* they sinned against. Our study will examine liars, adulterers, traitors, murderers, corrupt politicians, human traffickers, and despots guilty of murder and infanticide on an unfathomable scale. Upon finishing this study, you should better understand the sovereignty of God: His ability to use good and evil to accomplish His perfect, eternal plan.

Jonah: God's Holy Runaway

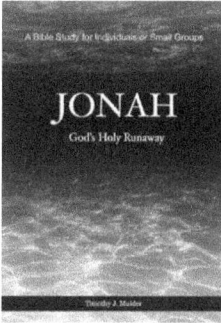

The Book of Jonah is far different than what we have been taught in Sunday School, acted out with a felt board whale, Jonah, and an evil Nineveh. It is not primarily about the fish. The Book of Jonah contains so much more: nationalism, hatred, unspeakable violence, and pagan omens. In it, the reader encounters a series of unexpected shocks. Jonah foolishly ran *from* God, while Gentile sailors ran *to* God. Jonah was thrown overboard and swallowed by a large fish. After Jonah delivered one of the worst calls to repentance, the entire city of Nineveh repented and turned toward God. This small book of 1368 words contains tales of storms and seas, winds blowing in the desert sands, a fish with a considerable gut, a fast-growing plant, Sheol, and penitent pagans. It challenges our preconceived notions about who the Gospel is for and hits at the heart of deeply held religious discrimination. Jonah is about second chances, bringing death to life, and how salvation belongs to the Lord.

www.ingramcontent.com/pod-product-compliance
Lightning Source LLC
LaVergne TN
LVHW091255080426
835510LV00007B/268